The

EVERYTHING®
Improve Your Credit Book

Dear Reader,

Your credit is one of the most important things in your life. It is your reputation, and often the only thing that business partners judge you on. Because of this, you may get uneasy just thinking about credit.

Let's change that right now. By demystifying the world of credit, you'll know what is good and bad for your credit, much like you know what's good and bad for your health: if you feel like indulging yourself, you can decide if it's worth it; if you need to shape up, you'll know how.

While having good credit can help you get lower loan rates, credit is increasingly used for other purposes as well. Employers screen job candidates for responsible credit use. Insurance companies offer their best rates and products to people who have great credit. Without a doubt, we will see credit pop up in more and more personal areas of our lives.

This book is intended to ensure that you have strong and healthy credit. If your credit needs to be fixed, we'll teach you how to do that. If you're fortunate enough to have good credit, we'll build a fortress around your credit so that you can keep it that way. I'm excited and honored to help you manage this part of your life. Now, let's get started.

Justin Pritchard, M.B.A.

The EVERYTHING® Series

Editorial

Publisher	Gary M. Krebs
Director of Product Development	Paula Munier
Managing Editor	Laura M. Daly
Associate Copy Chief	Sheila Zwiebel
Acquisitions Editor	Lisa Laing
Development Editor	Jessica LaPointe
Associate Production Editor	Casey Ebert

Production

Director of Manufacturing	Susan Beale
Associate Director of Production	Michelle Roy Kelly
Prepress	Erick DaCosta Matt LeBlanc
Design and Layout	Heather Barrett Brewster Brownville Colleen Cunningham Jennifer Oliveira
Series Cover Artist	Barry Littmann

Visit the entire Everything® Series at *www.everything.com*

THE
EVERYTHING®
IMPROVE YOUR CREDIT BOOK

Boost your score, lower your interest
rates, and save money

Justin Pritchard, M.B.A.

Adams Media
Avon, Massachusetts

Dedicated to the readers. Keep after it—you can do it!

This publication is designed to provide accurate and authoritative information with regard to the subject matter covered. It is sold with the understanding that the publisher is not engaged in rendering legal, accounting, or other professional advice. If legal advice or other expert assistance is required, the services of a competent professional person should be sought.

—From a *Declaration of Principles* jointly adopted by a Committee of the American Bar Association and a Committee of Publishers and Associations

Many of the designations used by manufacturers and sellers to distinguish their products are claimed as trademarks. Where those designations appear in this book and Adams Media was aware of a trademark claim, the designations have been printed with initial capital letters.

This book is available at quantity discounts for bulk purchases.
For information, please call 1-800-289-0963.

Contents

Acknowledgments

A very special thank you to all who gave me the support, nudging, and information to make this book a reality.

Top Ten Things to Know about Your Credit

1. Your credit reports may show that you're maxing out your credit cards, even if you pay your cards off in full each month.

2. You have more than one FICO score. Your scores will differ because they are calculated by different credit-reporting companies.

3. Most credit scores sold to consumers online are never used by lenders—the FICO credit score is most often used by lenders.

4. Closing inactive accounts does not help your credit, it lowers your score because it looks like you're using a greater percentage of your total available credit.

5. You may be denied auto insurance because of your credit.

6. Your credit tells companies how likely you are to leave for the competition.

7. You can get at least one free credit report a year from each consumer reporting company.

8. Some actions, like paying down balances and fixing errors, can dramatically improve your credit scores almost instantly.

9. Keep your balances at 35 percent or less of your available credit. Any more than that, and lenders will worry that you're about to default.

10. Your FICO credit score is designed to predict how likely you are to be more than ninety days late paying a creditor within the next two years.

Introduction

▶ PERSONAL CREDIT HAS BEEN important throughout history, and it continues to become more important. The world has become a much bigger place, and therefore your credit is used more often. Because lenders and other service providers cannot possibly know everything about you, they check your credit. Your credit is far more than a record of your borrowing habits—people also use your credit to judge your character. While many people understand that loan terms depend on their credit, many people do not understand the other ways that credit affects their lives. Depending on your credit, you may be more or less attractive as a job candidate or insurance-policy holder. If you already had some idea of how important your credit is, you're way ahead of the game. A large percentage of the population doesn't even know that a credit score is an indication of your risk as a borrower.

Credit is misused and misunderstood by many. Some people find the topic too confusing or too intimidating to understand. Others believe that they are powerless, that their credit controls them, and not vice versa. Nothing could be further from the truth. You can understand how credit works, and you can make it work for you. Credit is a powerful tool that you can use in your financial life. However, if you do not understand the world of credit you are, in fact, powerless. You'll simply have to take whatever offers you can get, and those offers probably won't be the best ones.

This book is designed to demystify the world of credit and credit scores. Knowing how this world works will empower you to manage your credit to your own advantage. You can start to think of your credit as your friend, not a skeleton in your closet. Your credit can get you things that you want, and it can help you save money. You'll have a clear idea of what your credit is, and how credit scores function in your life.

Your credit will be with you for a lifetime, so you should know how to manage it from start to finish. Things do not always work out the way we would like, so this book also prepares you for some of life's more challenging events. You can protect your credit from the unknown, and pick up the pieces when disaster strikes. If all goes well, you can continue to build on your successes. You'll discover secrets to developing great credit, and you'll learn about the traps that trip most people up. When it comes to credit, ignorance is not bliss. You can make your life easier by knowing how the system works and how to work within it.

The world of credit is actually quite fascinating. The world as we know it has evolved over years and years of borrowing, defaulting, repaying, and more. Consumers, lenders, and regulators have all done their part to bring about the current state of affairs. This book should fascinate you and educate you about the world of credit. Those completely unfamiliar with the world of credit will learn the basics, and they'll know what to do to make their credit a little better. Seasoned borrowers can also benefit from some of the more advanced information in this book. No matter what your level of expertise, you'll find information you can use to make your credit work better for you.

Chapter 1

Understanding Credit

Is credit a mystery to you? It shouldn't be. Instead of being intimidated by your credit and how the world of credit works, you should think of credit as your friend. In this section, you will get to know your friend a little bit better. You can find out where it came from, what it does, and where it is going. You will also understand what credit reports and credit scores are.

Your Financial Reputation

Your credit is simply your financial reputation. It gives lenders, and others, a tool to help decide whether or not they will do business with you. If you want to use their services, they want to manage their risk. The last thing a lender wants to do is give out money, only to have the borrower default on the debt. When this happens, the lender loses money. Of course, lenders are not charities—they are in business to earn money from interest payments, not to lose it.

The system of using credit in the United States serves a variety of purposes. First, this is a big country with a lot of people. It is difficult for any business to know everything about everybody. When the world was a much smaller place, a lender might make a lending decision based on an individual's reputation. In small communities, this would be easy. However, these days most loans come from large national, or international, organizations. They don't know your personal reputation, so they have to check your credit. In this way, credit serves as a way for lenders to share information so that they can make good decisions.

The fact that everybody can share information about you is extremely significant. Knowing that your creditors will spread the word about you gives you an incentive to pay your debts as agreed. If you knew you could borrow money and get away with defaulting on the debt, you might be tempted to do so quite often. After all, free money is enticing. Alas, there is no such thing. You might get away with it once or twice, but you will build up a bad reputation. Creditors depend on the fact that you want to have a good reputation so that you can borrow from others in the future.

Where Credit Information Comes From

Where does your credit come from? Are you born with it? No—if you don't use credit, you don't have credit; your credit is a result of your behavior in the world. Some of the most important information comes from your dealings with creditors. Of course, it is your credit, so the most relevant information comes from your use of credit.

Information Sources

The information that makes up your credit comes from numerous sources. Other sections of this book describe the sources in greater detail. For now, suffice it to say that there are a lot of organizations talking about you:

- Lenders
- Prospective lenders that you never worked with
- Government and court systems
- Collection agencies
- Credit-reporting companies

Depending on how you define your credit, information can come from a number of additional sources. Insurance companies report information on their customers to specialized databases. Landlords who rent properties share and use information about tenants. Finally, banks and retailers may share information about your check-writing habits.

Credit Scores

When you think about credit, you may think of the concept of a credit score. What exactly is a credit score? The credit score is a number that attempts to rank you on some level of creditworthiness. The credit score might tell potential lenders how likely you are to make late payments.

Your credit score does not determine whether or not you get a loan. The credit score is simply a number that ranks you with the rest of the population. Your lender may have a policy on granting loans based on credit scores, but the scoring programs do not know that. They just generate a score.

Imagine how difficult it must be to predict whether or not a customer is likely to pay late. Imagine yourself as a loan officer in a bank sitting across the desk from a potential borrower. What criteria do you use to judge this person's creditworthiness? You may pull credit reports from the major credit-reporting companies—if you have ever seen these reports, you know that they are full of information and can be several pages long. Then, you might read through their reports to get an understanding of how your potential borrower has behaved in the past. Finally, assume that you have three more potential borrowers waiting to see you, and you have not had lunch yet.

This scenario helps to highlight why credit scores may be useful. People have to make lending decisions with several goals in mind. They may want to grant the loan so that their organization earns interest income. They may also be motivated to grant loans in an effort to help serve the community, for example, making mortgage loans available to low-income households. On the other hand, the person making the lending decision has to try to minimize losses. The organization won't be able to help anybody if it loses all of its money.

Automate It

To make lending decisions easier, lenders often use credit scores. A computer program does a lot of the work, leaving just a few items for the person responsible for making a decision to fill in. In some cases, the computer program does all of the work, and human eyes never see the potential borrower's credit information. The credit-scoring model looks for good things and bad things in the borrower's history. It looks for late payments, bankruptcies, and maxed-out credit cards, among other things. These are the same items that a human would look for. Of course, the computer can do it in a split-second.

A 2005 study released by the Consumer Federation of America and Providian put a number on how much you can save with a better credit score. For consumers with an average credit score, a thirty-point increase would result in $76 of annual savings on finance charges. Of course, more significant positive changes in your score would yield more significant savings.

In addition to speeding up the process, credit scoring can level the playing field. Lenders might have biases that influence their decisions when considering an applicant's creditworthiness. From a fairness standpoint, creditworthiness should be the only factor considered. However, people responsible for making lending decisions might be swayed in one direction or the other for irrelevant reasons: if the applicant is good or bad looking; if the applicant has a health issue with negative stigma attached; or if the applicant seems friendly or unfriendly. In some cases, lenders may discriminate because of an applicant's sex, race, or creed. Credit-scoring models can eliminate these biases from the equation, because they look strictly at the credit history data. If the applicant has a good credit history, the score is high regardless of any personal traits.

Who to Lend To

Credit scoring makes it possible to make a large number of small loans. Lenders get flooded with applications for credit. How do they determine which ones to process? If they are strapped for resources (time and personnel), they might decide to limit themselves to the loans that are more profitable. In this case, they might focus on the larger loans only because smaller loans require the same amount of processing but pay less interest. Credit scoring makes it efficient to look at loans of all sizes, which makes it easier for consumers to get loans.

Where Scores Come From

Where exactly do these credit scores come from? There are a variety of companies that create credit scores. These companies are described in greater detail later in this book. For now, you should understand that the credit score may or may not come from your lender. In many cases, it does not. External companies create the computer programs used to generate scores.

The computer programs are just empty programs that take in information and process it. They're designed to work with different systems. For example, the FICO credit score is designed to work with the data held at the major credit-reporting companies (TransUnion, Equifax, and Experian). The credit-reporting companies load the software, and then load the credit history for the individual who they are going to score. The software spits out a score, and it is forwarded to whoever asked for the report.

Mass Confusion

The world is full of confusion about credit scores. In part, this is because credit scores were unavailable to consumers for many years. In addition, the entire world of credit and credit histories can be intimidating. Unfortunately, ignorance is not bliss when it comes to your credit. The majority of consumers, 69 percent of them, have not checked their credit within the last year.

In 2005, a study released by the Consumer Federation of America, Providian, and myFICO.com explained the state of affairs. They found that about half of the American population does not understand the basic concept of a credit score. Indeed, only 51 percent of respondents in the study knew that a credit score represents credit risk. The other 49 percent thought a credit score described credit availability, credit IQ, or levels of debt. In addition, 45 percent of respondents thought that getting a substantial pay increase would result in a higher credit score. While it is possible that there might be an indirect link between your pay level in your credit score, many highly paid people borrow too much (the more you earn the more you spend) and can end up with a very low credit score.

Not All Scores Are the Same

Many people are under the impression that they only have one credit score. In fact, if you have one credit score, then you likely have many more credit-based scores. For the most part, when a lender refers to your credit score they are talking about your FICO credit score. This is a score based on the Fair Isaac Corporation's credit-scoring model. At the present time, it is the most commonly used score.

When you take on the goal of improving your credit, it is essential that you get a little bit more specific. You need to know which credit score you need to improve. That will depend on your current goal, whether it's buying a house, getting insurance, or landing a job.

Variations on the Theme

While the FICO score is the current gold standard, you most likely have several FICO scores. Each of the three major credit-reporting companies can calculate a FICO score for you, but they also sell their own proprietary scores which are not based on the FICO model, so be careful what you buy. Because the major credit-reporting companies all have different data on you, your FICO credit score will most likely be different at each company. Most experts suggest that you use the middle credit score (not the highest or lowest one) as a gauge of your creditworthiness. Your lenders, on the other hand, might use a different method. They might give you the benefit of the doubt and use your highest score, or they might just buy a single score from one of the credit-reporting companies that they have a relationship with. If you are not sure which score they will use, just ask.

ALERT!

A lot of organizations will offer to sell you a credit score. Before you fork over your hard-earned money, find out what you're getting. Scores from different sources can look deceptively similar, but you need to use the same score that your lender is using if you want to know where you stand.

Other Scores

There are other scores in addition to your multiple FICO credit scores, and any company that you do business with may have its own internal model. The most common internal model might be an application-based model. These models judge your creditworthiness using information you provide on your credit application. For example, your lender may ask how long you have lived at your current address, how much money you make, or how long you have worked at your current job. Of course, lenders won't make a lending decision based solely on your answers to the application.

Instead, they use that information as a supplement to the information found in your credit history.

VantageScore

VantageScore is a relatively new scoring model developed by the three major credit-reporting companies: Equifax, TransUnion, and Experian. They suggest that the FICO credit-scoring system is too confusing for consumers. FICO scores range from 300 to 850. A pretty good score is 750, but you might not know that by looking at it. VantageScore uses a scoring system much like your high school teachers', with scores running from 500 to 990. If you remember the good old school days, a 99 percent was an A, anything from 80 percent to 90 percent was a B, and so on. The credit-reporting companies are hoping that this simplicity will help them win market share.

Behavior Scores

The scores described so far are used for a specific purpose, like deciding whether or not to grant you a loan, and at what terms. However, your credit information is used for a variety of other purposes. These stores might use the same credit-file data as your classic FICO credit score, but they analyze the data in a different way. In addition, they might incorporate information from other sources. The goal of these scores is to understand other parts of your behavior.

Profitability Scores

One of these scoring models is designed to determine how receptive you might be to new offers from your credit card company. If you are more likely to accept a given offer, the company is more willing to splurge and mail you an advertisement. Somehow, the way you use products and accounts can reveal how likely you would be to say yes.

Other scoring models help your creditors predict how profitable you will be as a customer. They get an idea of how much revenue you will generate, and they can predict how likely you are to switch brands. Presumably, they make attractive offers to customers who are less likely to switch, and they might create incentives (or penalties) to retain customers who are likely to switch.

Bankruptcy Scores

Creditors can even score you on the likelihood that you will declare bankruptcy. Not surprisingly, your credit history is a main ingredient to the score. A bankruptcy score is slightly different than your FICO credit score. The FICO score attempts to rank you based on the likelihood that you'll be ninety days late on any bill with any creditor. The bankruptcy score goes even further: it tries to determine whether or not you will declare bankruptcy and default on all of your debts.

Expanding the Reach

The FICO scoring model can only generate a credit score for you if you have a sufficient credit history. If you have not used credit accounts enough (perhaps because you are young or a new arrival to the country), there will not be enough data in your credit history to generate a score. In the past, individuals without a score had a hard time getting credit. However, Fair Isaac has remedied this situation in recent years. They created a score they call the Expansion credit score. This score judges your creditworthiness based on information from alternative sources. They examine your past for evidence of bounced checks, delinquencies with service providers, and other behaviors that might describe your creditworthiness.

The best thing you can do for yourself is be a responsible consumer. Pay your bills on time, and don't bounce checks. If you get in over your head, your credit scores will follow. A lot of different organizations check into your credit, so just do a good job and make it easy on yourself.

If your credit history is not sufficient to generate a FICO credit score, then you may be able to get credit because of the Expansion credit score. Once you get your foot in the door with lenders, you are building up your credit history. Over time, there will be enough information about you in the major credit-reporting company databases. As a result, they will be able to generate a FICO credit score on you eventually.

Insurance Scores

Insurers look at your FICO credit score to determine whether or not you are an attractive customer. In addition, there are specially designed insurance scores that help them further evaluate you. Based on your ranking, insurers may decide that they do not want you as a customer, or they might offer you coverage at higher-than-normal rates. The reverse is also true: if you score well, insurers may offer you a discount.

What's Not Part of Your Credit

The body of information called your credit is quite extensive. It contains data on all of the following:

- Every credit card you've ever used
- Every loan you've applied for
- Every loan you've actually used
- Any public records relevant to your credit
- Your residence and employment history
- And more

While some of these items may not appear in a given credit report, they are still part of your credit. However, your credit does not tell the complete story about you. There are a variety of things that are not part of your credit.

Irrelevant to Credit

A number of characteristics that might describe you are irrelevant to your credit because they have nothing to do with your creditworthiness. For example, certain characteristics are excluded by laws designed to limit discrimination. Of course, some of the common ones are race, color, religion, national origin, and sex. In addition, lenders may not discriminate against you based on the likelihood that you will have children or get married.

Despite these regulations, some of this information may be used by a potential lender. Although a credit-scoring model will ignore these characteristics, a human who looks at your credit report may be able to make some educated guesses. They may be able to guess your race or national origin based on your last name. Likewise, an applicant named Robert is most likely a male, while one named Susan is probably a female.

FACT

In the 1700s, borrowers could end up in prison if they did not pay their debts. Debtor's prisons punished defaulted borrowers, a stark contrast to today's practices. Ultimately, lawmakers found that debtor's prisons did not create enough of a deterrent to keep people from defaulting, and they are no longer used.

Your Personality

Your personality is also irrelevant to your credit. You may be the nicest person in the world, but you won't get a loan unless you have good credit. As the saying goes, actions speak much louder than words. Creditors will base their lending decisions on their knowledge of your previous actions. In some cases, you have the opportunity to sit face to face with a lender and explain that you have no intention of defaulting on your debt. For the most part, that's not an option. You have to work within the system and build good credit.

Your Burdens

Whether you love it or hate it, your credit just reports how you have paid your debts in the past. You might have missed some payments, or defaulted entirely, for a variety of reasons. Perhaps it was because you took on more debt than you should have. On the other hand, a freak accident or sickness could have overwhelmed you with medical bills. Whatever the case, your credit does not care. Credit scores don't explain why you missed payments or declared bankruptcy. They just slice and dice your account history and spit out a number.

Your Paycheck

Some people think that your salary is an important factor in your credit. It certainly is important for some scoring models, and those that ask for your salary on the credit application are obviously going to use that information. However, salary may be less important than you think. It is not a part of the FICO credit score. Therefore, you can have a high credit score even with a modest income. All you have to do is use credit wisely.

QUESTION?

Who should I contact with a complaint?
If you feel that you have been discriminated against, or you have any other credit-related complaints, start with the Federal Trade Commission (FTC). Their Web site (*www.ftc.gov/credit*) has a wealth of information on your rights. From there, you can find out exactly who to contact.

The opposite is also true: you can have a terrible credit score even with a million-dollar income. Creditors don't care how much money you have, or how much you make, they just want you to pay according to the terms of your agreement with them. If you can't do that, they get nervous and would prefer not to deal with you.

Net Worth

Creditors don't care whether you are rich or poor. Again, they just care how you manage your credit. You can have bad credit even if you have a lot of money in the bank and another million or two in the stock market. Granted, you could pay off your debts without batting an eye. However, your creditors do not want to spend extra time, money, and energy collecting debts from you.

A Brief History of Credit History

How did we get to this point? Credit is a part of our everyday lives, and good or bad credit can make you or break you. Because of credit, you can buy a home for your family without hundreds of thousands of dollars in the bank. You can spread out the payments on a large item like a new automobile. If you need a loan, your prospective lender can make a decision extremely quickly.

Old-Fashioned Credit

People have been borrowing since ancient times. How did somebody with resources know who to lend to? They made a decision based on that person's character. The grocer might allow a regular customer to pay later based on past experience. Since the customer always paid for her purchases, she would likely pay again in the future.

In cities and towns, a variety of merchants might offer credit. They would allow customers to walk out without paying for food, clothing, furniture, and more. As populations grew, it became harder to know every customer personally. Therefore, merchants began to share information on their customers. They formed associations that are the roots of today's gigantic credit-reporting companies. Chambers of commerce were also responsible for forming early credit-reporting associations. For the most part, these associations were within a limited geographical area, like a single city.

FACT

The National Association of Retail Credit Agencies, the first national credit-reporting association, changed its name to the Associated Credit Bureaus, Inc. Currently, it is known as the Consumer Data Industry Association (located on the web at *www.cdiaonline.org*), and membership consists of about 500 American credit-reporting companies.

As the population and the economy grew, it became necessary for associations to gain a wider geographic reach. A consumer might move to a town, but have a credit history in another town. To meet this need, a trade association was formed in 1906. The National Association of Retail Credit Agencies allowed associations to pool their knowledge and increase the number of consumers that they could report on.

Evolution of Credit

Through the years, smaller associations have merged or been bought by larger organizations. Bigger and bigger companies emerge with a single focus on consumer credit reporting. They developed sophisticated computer systems, and they amassed more and more information on consumers. Today, the market is dominated by three of the largest consumer reporting companies: Equifax, TransUnion, and Experian.

When consumer credit-reporting companies first started to operate in the United States, they mostly helped merchants. People did not use credit cards or finance companies in their everyday lives. Instead, the merchant would extend credit. For example, a clothing store might allow customers to pay for their purchases over time. If a customer failed to pay, the clothing store owner would lose money. These days, things are different. If you buy clothes with a credit card and then go bankrupt, the credit card company loses money, not the clothing store.

In the early 1900s, most debt was held directly with a retailer. Today, most debt is on the balance sheet of a finance company. Retailers benefit because they do not have to take the risk that somebody will not repay. They're in business to sell products, not manage loans. Finance companies also benefit because they earn interest. Part of the reason for this shift is the fact that finance companies were prohibited from charging interest rates high enough to make a profit on small loans. Because usury laws have changed, banks and finance companies can now make a profit on these loans.

Consumer Rights

Around the 1960s, consumers and regulators began to see just how important credit could be. It was a way for people to buy a home in pursuit of the

American dream. However, there was almost no transparency in the credit-reporting industry. The credit-reporting companies were mysterious organizations behind impenetrable walls. They had friends in high places, and they worked to protect their interests.

Consumers were powerless against the credit-reporting companies. Nobody knew who was checking up on them, and individuals were concerned about their privacy. Furthermore, a lender might deny credit to somebody based on information held in the credit bureaus. The lender did not have to explain why, so consumers were left in the dark. Often, there were errors in a consumer's credit history. Unfortunately, those errors persisted, because nobody could check their credit for errors.

Gaining Ground

Once consumers were granted the right to check their credit, they gained some ground. However, they were still largely powerless. Credit-reporting companies recklessly made errors and allowed them to persist. They made a point of digging up dirt on consumers, and were reluctant to fix errors. The history of credit reporting is marred with some truly sad stories about individuals who unfairly suffered from problems with their credit reports.

Regulators and consumer advocates agree: education is your most powerful tool. By knowing what your credit is and how it works, you make great strides toward protecting yourself. You need to know who is involved, what they do, and why they do it. Then, it is your responsibility to be vigilant and proactive.

Consumer protection continues to evolve. Over time, consumers have begun the process of understanding and managing their credit. Regulators have held the credit-reporting companies more accountable for errors and abuses. Consumers slowly earned more and more rights: the right to request a credit score; the right to a free annual credit report from any consumer-reporting company; and the right to have errors fixed in a timely fashion. Regulations continue to evolve as the times change. Identity theft and its effects on your credit is just one of the latest hot topics in credit-reporting regulation.

Collections

Debt collection is an area related to consumer credit rights. When a lender cannot collect a debt from a customer, they have to take extra steps to try and get the money back. Sometimes they outsource collection activities to a dedicated debt-collection agency, and sometimes they do it in-house. Whatever the case, collectors have certain rules they must follow. In the past, some of the worst agencies made life miserable for delinquent borrowers. Regulators have to walk a fine line between conflicting goals. They want to protect the consumer, while allowing lenders to collect the money that is owed them.

A Look into the Crystal Ball

As Yogi Berra explained, it's hard to make predictions, especially about the future. Nevertheless, you can try to look ahead to see what might lie beyond the horizon. What does the future hold for your credit? How will credit be used? And what should you do about it?

Global Credit

Credit scoring and reporting is well entrenched in several developed countries. However, other countries have not come as far. This makes it difficult for individuals who travel between countries. They might have to build credit under a new system, even though they have been a responsible borrower under another system for many years. Standard global scoring models can help with this. According to the Fair Isaac Corporation, the world is asking for it.

Credit scoring will also be refined so that it is used in more and more places. As businesses and regulators look at how to use these systems fairly, you'll see more and more scores. Hospitals and utilities might be pioneers in this area. Who knows? You might see suburban neighborhoods that limit who can live there based on models similar to your credit score.

Laying the Groundwork

The credit reporting and credit-scoring industries have shown how data can be used. Whether you love it or hate it, organizations that buy credit scores believe in them. Banks and insurers may not understand exactly how the models work, but nevertheless, they're happy with the results they get from using credit scores. More and more nonfinancial organizations may jump on the bandwagon. They will likely tap into the knowledge and processes that lenders have been using, and modify them for their own purposes.

Law-enforcement agencies have already begun to do this. The California Penal system has contacted the Fair Isaac Corporation to build models in the past. The proposed models would help predict whether or not released inmates were likely to commit another crime. ChoicePoint, a large consumer-data repository, works with small and large government agencies to fight crime and terrorism.

Chapter 2

Why Improve Your Credit?

Your credit is a complex beast. It affects many different parts of your life, and you might not even know it. In the background, your credit is telling other people what to think about you. Based on what it says, things can cost you more or less. In addition, doors in your life can open or close depending on whether you have good credit or bad credit. Overall, life is much easier and more rewarding if you have good credit.

Loan Rates

The number one reason to improve your credit is to have better loan rates. Simply put, the better your credit is, the less expensive it is to borrow. There are certainly other important areas of your life where having good credit is helpful, but lenders look at your credit as a major factor when making lending decisions. Your previous credit history is most relevant to lending decisions; the way you've handled loans in the past can be a hint as to how you will behave in the future.

QUESTION?

How does my credit affect my loan rate?
Many lenders set their loan rates based on a borrower's credit score. They set up various tiers, and assign a different interest rate to each tier. Those with the best credit fall into the best tier, and they pay the lowest interest rates on their loans.

Most people don't even know that a credit score is a number that tells lenders how risky you might be as a borrower. In fact, that is exactly the purpose it serves. As you'll see elsewhere, your FICO credit score attempts to predict how likely you are to be at least ninety days late on a payment within the next two years. That is the one magic answer that the credit score gives: relative to the rest of the population, how likely are you to fall behind? Of course, your credit score is created from the information in your credit reports. You will learn more about that process later in the book. For now, just be aware that your credit affects the quality of loans that you are able to get.

Risk and Return

You may be familiar with the risk and return tradeoffs. In general, something that involves higher risk should be expected to pay a higher return. Take the stock market for example. Stocks can be fairly risky investments. Some stocks (such as brand new start-up companies) are riskier than others (such as well-established profitable companies). Which one should you make more money on? If you could expect equal returns from each type of company, you would always buy the well-established profitable one. Why would you take the risk on the new one? However, the markets tend to be fair. Riskier stocks have historically returned more than less-risky stocks. Of course, don't forget that riskier stocks have also lost all of their value more often than less-risky stocks.

Lenders look at borrowers in a similar fashion. Borrowers with a long history of on-time payments are presumably less risky than borrowers with no documented past. If the customer has constantly paid his mortgage, car payment, and credit card on time for the past twenty years, it is a fairly safe bet that he will repay the future loan as agreed. As a result, you might lend money to this individual at a lower interest rate. You need to be competitive to get his business.

FACT

Lending money is risky business, even with sophisticated credit scoring models. Lenders know that they will occasionally lose money. They often budget for a small percentage of loans to be written off the books. Nevertheless, they like to minimize defaults. After all, they have to make up for these losses somehow.

Contrast the borrower with a perfect credit history with somebody who has a less-than-perfect credit history. This borrower may have only started using credit within the last three years. What's more, he recently paid his credit card bill three months late. If this person asks you for a loan, you should consider it a risky loan. But that doesn't mean that you should not lend the money. Instead, you might demand a higher return to compensate you for the higher risk you are taking.

This is exactly what your lenders do. They take a look at you and your credit history, and they determine how risky you might be as a borrower. Often, the question isn't whether or not to lend you any money, they just need to decide how much they want to earn for taking a risk on you. If they feel that they're not taking much risk, they might be happy with a lower return.

Eighth Wonder of the World

You can see how the interest rate is important to lenders. The higher the rate, the more they make on each dollar they loan you. How does the interest rate affect you then? Well, you are paying it, so it is important that you know. Higher rates can cost you a ton of money. You may not notice it month after month, but the effects are dramatic over the years. Your loan balances can increase substantially, and the opportunity costs mean you have to live on less for many years.

Compound interest, sometimes referred to as the eighth wonder of the world, is responsible for the dramatic effects just described. Compound interest refers to the concept of paying interest on top of interest. If you borrow money and pay it off slowly, chances are that compound interest is working against you. The reason is that your lenders charge interest, which increases your loan balance. Then, they charge you interest again on that increased loan balance. Therefore, you are paying interest on interest they recently charged you. Consider an example:

1. You borrow $100 at a 10 percent interest rate
2. At the end of one year, you are charged $10 in interest (10 percent of $100)
3. Now, your total balance is $110
4. At the end of next year, you will be charged $11 in interest (10 percent of $110)
5. Then, your total balance will be $121
6. And so on . . .

This example ignores any payments you might make on the debt. However, you can see how interest is charged on top of previous interest charges. Any payments you make will mitigate the effect, but many people do not make sufficient payments. For example, the minimum payment on your credit card barely covers the cost of interest. Try searching the Internet for a minimum-payment calculator, where you can see how this works for yourself.

Loan Products

Having good credit will ensure that the entire universe of loan products is available to you. With the best credit history (and therefore credit scores) you have more options. Lenders can make the best offers in the marketplace available to you. With bad credit, you will be somewhat restricted. Granted, you can almost always get a loan, even with very poor credit. However, you may not have all of the options available to you, so you may not be able to enjoy all of the flexibility that some products offer. Likewise, you may be restricted to a smaller universe of lenders. Typically, lenders who specialize in "bad credit" loans should not be your first, much less only, choice.

To be attractive to lenders, you should have a healthy mix of well-aged accounts. Shoot for three to five open and active revolving-debt accounts (such as credit cards), and another one or two open and active installment accounts (such as an auto loan or mortgage). Keep your balances low, and always pay on time.

Having good credit, and therefore getting the best loans and products, is about more than just avoiding mistakes. Beyond a doubt, you will damage your credit if you make late payments or default on your debts. However, lenders won't necessarily look favorably on you just because you have a spotless record. They also want to see that you have a healthy and robust credit history. For some lending products, the lender has a minimum number of open and active credit accounts that they want to see in your credit history. If you don't meet the minimum requirement, you may have to work with a different, and possibly less competitive, lender.

Landing a Job

Your credit can also affect the type of job you get—or don't get. Employers have made a common practice of checking potential employees' credit during the hiring and promotion process. The belief is that good credit is a sign of a good employee. This practice is gradually losing steam. Employers have other ways to systematically evaluate job candidates, such as background checks and personality profiles. According to Craig Watts of the Fair Isaac Corporation, credit scores are probably not the best predictor anyway. The link between a FICO credit score and employee performance is still somewhat unclear, and Fair Isaac does not encourage credit scoring for every single job applicant.

Employers Check Your Credit

Despite uncertainty as to its effectiveness, credit scoring is often used by employers. They may not fully understand how it works, but they like the results they get. All other things being equal, your chances of getting that job or promotion are much better if you have good credit. To some extent, this makes sense. A person with good credit has paid bills as agreed, and managed his finances responsibly. In addition, you could argue that he's had a little bit of good luck on his side (no major illnesses or accidents that threw him off track).

ALERT!

Having a serious error on your credit report can cost you a job. It will give potential employers the wrong idea about you, and they may think that you have failed to fulfill responsibilities that you have in fact met. For this reason, it is essential that you monitor your credit reports and fix any errors.

In some instances, it makes perfect sense to check a job candidate's credit, particularly when employees will have access to cash, valuables, or valuable information. If somebody is in dire financial straits, she may be tempted to use that cash for her own purposes. Bank tellers and armored-car drivers come to mind in this situation. Many employees at financial institutions such as banks and credit unions go through a credit check.

Top Secret

Individuals applying for sensitive government jobs often submit to a credit check. In the interests of national security, the government wants to make sure that people with access to sensitive information have good credit. Consider someone who knows the details of an ongoing overseas surveillance operation. If he spoke to the wrong person, other people could end up in grave danger.

Among other things, people who work with classified information are susceptible to bribe offers. If you have a financial hardship, you might be more willing to sell information to a high bidder. Obtaining government clearance requires that you go through a rigorous background check and interview process. Nevertheless, the stakes are extremely high, and foreign governments and others can come up with some pretty big bribes if they need to. If you have any ambition to work with sensitive information, it is extremely important that you manage your credit well.

The Marketplace

The world is full of companies that offer pre-employment and ongoing credit-check services. To get an idea of what your employer may be looking for, visit the Web sites of these companies. They claim that it is essential to screen any job applicant who may handle merchandise or money. They mention that pre-employment credit checks are a good way to find out if the candidate is likely to fulfill her obligations.

In addition to trying to predict your behavior, employers can verify your past. Employment-screening companies are selling the idea that your potential employer can view your previous addresses and previous employers. This gives them the ability to cross-reference information on your resume. In recent years, there have been several high-profile cases where an individual lied about his employment history. Some of these cases might have been avoided if the employee had a better understanding of credit histories.

Employers also benefit from viewing your employment history, because they can make a judgment on whether or not you change jobs too frequently. Your credit files may not have every single job you've held, but they might have several. If you change jobs frequently, this may be a tip-off that you will not be around for long. Employers typically want to hire individuals who will stick around for many years to come.

Always Get a Copy

When a potential employer is going to check your credit, or use some other type of background check, they must get your consent first. You may see a check box you can mark to get a copy of the report. You should always mark this box, so that you can see what others are saying about you, and you're entitled to a free report. In an ideal world, everything will be completely accurate. However, an employer could potentially use this information against you without telling you. They are required to inform you if they take adverse action against you based on this information, but they might just claim that they had a better applicant for the job. In such a case, you would never know what your report said about you.

Seven Years of Bad Luck

As a general rule, negative information stays on your credit reports for seven years. Late payments, chargeoffs, and paid-off tax liens will appear to anybody who pulls your credit. After seven years, the credit-reporting companies are supposed to stop reporting those negative events. However, they do not delete the records entirely. In fact, those items can be reported in some situations. One of them happens to be a credit check for employment that is expected to pay $75,000 a year or more. If you are applying for such a job, those old delinquencies may show up on your credit report.

You should take advantage of every opportunity you get to view your consumer reports. Whenever you apply for a loan, job, or insurance, see if there is a way to get a copy of the same report that the company looks at. Give it a quick glance to see if there are any errors or items that need attention.

Buying Insurance

By now you are starting to see that your credit can affect your life in a variety of ways. Not only does it affect the loans you get, it can make or break an employer's decision about you. The same thing goes for insurers: they may deny you or charge you extremely high rates depending on your credit.

What's Credit Got to Do with It?

You might wonder if your credit has anything to do with your insurance. Is it fair for an insurance company to set your rates (or deny you altogether) because of information in your credit history? That issue has been hotly debated for several years now. Different states have approached regulating and limiting insurance scoring in different ways.

Several studies have shown that there are interesting links between credit information and insurance claims. As you probably know, insurance companies use complex statistical models to predict the likelihood of various events. Recently, they have added statistical analysis of credit information to the mix. When they look at the data, they see that there is in fact a relationship between the customer's profitability and that customer's credit data. In particular, they try to predict the likelihood that a customer will submit a sizable claim within the next two years.

A Variety of Sources

Your insurance company may use a variety of different sources when evaluating you as a customer. For starters, they may dig into your credit history. To do this, they use information housed at the major credit-reporting companies like Equifax, TransUnion, and Experian. Based on the information in your credit history, they can come up with an insurance score. Of course, they could simply look through your credit reports and have a person make subjective judgments about you, but it is much more efficient and effective to use an automated scoring system.

Insurers have a lot of choices when it comes to purchasing insurance scores. The Fair Isaac Corporation has its own insurance-scoring model to supplement the FICO credit score. Their view is that the FICO credit score is irrelevant to insurance-related decisions. While there may be some overlap—

for example, making late payments is bad no matter what—there are subtle differences that insurers find useful. The credit-reporting companies also offer insurance-related scores. Finally, some insurance companies have their own internal models that they use.

FACT

Some insurance companies use shared databases to track claims history. They keep records of how often you make claims, and they might track a house to see how many claims have been made on it over the years (even with different owners). Like other consumer files, you are entitled to view these reports for free each year.

Scoring models might look at characteristics other than the information at the credit-reporting companies. They might take information that you provide on an application, and they may even dig deeper. Insurers also use specialized services that track your interactions with other insurance companies. These are similar to your credit reports at the credit-reporting companies, except that the subject is insurance instead of credit. You will learn all of the juicy details about these services in Chapter 5.

Figures Lie and Liars Figure

Insurers rely on numbers to help them make decisions. They gather vast amounts of data, and employ armies of mathematical experts to crunch the numbers. These experts can predict how likely an event is given a set of circumstances. For example, they might say that you are more or less likely to be in an auto accident given your credit history. In a large population, they do quite well; their models provide useful information that seems to correspond with reality. However, you are not a large population. You are one individual who will be judged as if you are part of a large population. If your credit is bad and you are an excellent driver, it simply doesn't matter. The fact that you share a characteristic, bad credit, with other bad drivers means that you'll have to pay more for insurance.

The Big Picture

Insurance companies use your credit history for the same reasons that lenders do. They're trying to predict the future, and determine whether or not you will be a profitable customer. If they sense too much risk, they will either deny you coverage or ask for more money in return for that risk. They believe that somebody who has handled his finances responsibly is likely to take good care of his home, drive carefully, and otherwise make less expensive claims.

Your auto insurance, homeowner's insurance, and other types of insurance can be affected by the information in your credit reports. Insurance-scoring experts are not even certain why credit information can successfully be used to predict your costs to an insurance company. Nevertheless, they have found that it works, so you should expect them to continue using credit-based insurance scores.

Renting a Place

If you are ever going to rent an apartment, you need good credit. Perhaps you are at a place in your life where you will no longer rent. If you are already established and settled down, you might have to use the topics previously discussed as motivation to improve your credit. Nevertheless, you never know what will happen—you might find a need to temporarily rent a place. Alternatively, you may have children who have not yet settled down. It is important to let them know that bad credit will limit their choices if they want to rent.

Landlords often pull credit reports on potential tenants. They want to see if you have paid your obligations in the past. Of course, they're kind of extending credit to you by letting you live on their property. In some areas, the rental market is extremely competitive. Having bad credit can mean that a landlord chooses somebody else, and you have to keep hunting for a home.

Peace of Mind

By now, you can see the variety of ways in which your credit affects your life. Some of them are more obvious and observable than others. The bottom line is that your life is easier if you have good credit. You have more options, they all cost less, and things happen more quickly. As a result, you can enjoy peace of mind if you have good credit.

Peace of mind should be your main motivation for improving your credit. If you have less-than-perfect credit, you constantly have to worry, and wonder when it will affect you.

With poor credit, you will find yourself in a risky situation every time your auto insurance is up for renewal. You will not be happy knowing that it costs you more to borrow a dollar than it costs somebody else. The only reason you pay more for the same things is the fact that you have bad credit.

The person with good credit lives a more carefree life. If you need to borrow money for something you really want, you can do so. If you run into hard times, it's easier to borrow and get yourself through. Emergencies, sicknesses, and other surprises do not push you down the slippery slope to financial ruin. As a result of your good credit, many things in life are less expensive. Instead of paying for bad credit, you can save those extra dollars or spend them on the finer things.

Chapter 3

The Major Players

When you watch a good movie, often a portion of the film will follow the main characters through a "daily life" scene. You get to see how one character does her job or how another interacts with his family. The purpose of these scenes is to help you understand the characters' actions later in the film. In pursuit of the same goal, you should get to know the major players in the credit system, what their goals are, and what they do.

The Gossips

Your credit is a story about how you use credit. It is told by others, not you. Who are these people who insist on sharing every bit of information about you? You can think of them as information providers. Information providers provide the ingredients that show up in your credit.

Your Lenders

Your lenders are perhaps the most important information providers in this story. When they talk, others listen. Your lenders have already done business with you, so they know how you really work. You can say all you want about how reliable you are as a borrower, but your lenders can show some previous actions that speak a lot louder than any words from your mouth.

Lenders constantly report on you. They let others know how you handle your accounts. Among other things, they report the following:

- How much you are borrowing
- When you started borrowing
- The type of loan you have (mortgage, revolving, etc.)
- If you make payments on time
- If you have outstanding unpaid debts
- Your maximum borrowing limit

Why do they provide all of this information? Because they want you to handle your accounts responsibly. They figure that the threat of having bad reports will give you an incentive to pay as agreed. Indeed, if you mess things up with one lender, it is difficult to go to another lender and get a good deal. The new lender will be suspicious of you, and offer more restrictive terms, if they offer you a loan at all.

Keeping Secrets

Note that some of your lenders decide not to provide information about you and your accounts. The reason for keeping quiet about you is to keep the competition out. If you have a clean record, the other creditors may try to win more business from you. They might see that you have a lot of debt, but you always pay on time. Therefore, you might be a profitable customer that they'd like to do more work with.

This is especially an issue in predatory-lending environments. Creditors who charge high interest rates to folks without much credit are fiercely competitive. They are earning above-market interest from you, and they want to keep it that way. Therefore, they try to keep you a secret so that you don't take your business anywhere else. While this helps them, it does not help you at all. You need to get your good credit-behavior reported so that everybody knows how responsible you are. If that doesn't happen, you can't build credit and you can't get more credit.

ALERT!

If a creditor does not report your maximum available balance, the credit-scoring models often take the high balance to replace the maximum available balance. High balance is the most you've ever borrowed, which might be much less than your maximum. This makes it appear as if you are more stretched than you really are, and hurts your scores.

Note that predatory lenders are not the only ones who withhold information. A number of large reputable banks occasionally decide not to report your credit limits (the maximum amount of available credit) to the credit-reporting companies. In their mind, telling everybody that you have a high credit limit is just a way of saying, "We trust this borrower, so we let her have lots of credit." The only reason they would trust you so much, of course, is because you have been a responsible borrower. As with the predatory lenders, this might be an invitation to steal business.

Collection Agencies

Another important information provider is the collection agency. These agencies are hired to collect debts that your original lender was not able to collect from you. Alternatively, they might buy defaulted accounts from lenders and try to collect what they can. These agencies typically operate as a one-way street: they report information to the credit-reporting companies, but they do not have much use for that information. A collection agency may not care how good your credit is, unless good credit is a sign that you are likely able to pay your debt. Instead, they have leverage as an information provider: they can report your delinquency to the world at large if nobody else has yet.

Nosy Folks

The world is full of all kinds of juicy information about you. Who cares? Who is it that actually wants to see that information? The organizations that care about your history vary, but most likely they are:

- Potential lenders
- Potential employers
- Current lenders and employers who want an update
- Potential landlords
- Insurance companies

Asking Around

These organizations want to know a little bit more about you. If you live in a town with more than 100 people, there is probably no way for the lenders to know everything about everybody. Furthermore, many lenders are not based where you live; for instance, you might borrow from a bank in another state. Therefore, it is impossible for the lenders to judge you as a borrower without asking around.

The way they ask around is to check your history. For lenders, the most important thing is your credit history. For employers, it may be an employment history and credit history. Likewise, landlords might want to know your credit history along with other public information about you. Finally, insurance companies check your claims history and credit-based scores that tell them if you will be profitable. These organizations rely on others to help them figure out who you are and if they want to do any business with you.

Give and Take

Some information users are also information providers. Your lenders, for example, are both. They ask around to find out if you are going to be a good customer. At the same time, they report an inquiry to let others know that you are applying for credit. After you open an account and start using their money, they continually report on the account and monitor your credit use elsewhere by making periodic inquiries.

Some information users are only users. Employers and landlords, for example, do not typically report information on you to the credit-reporting companies. Even some utility companies and cell phone providers do not report your payment history to anybody as long as you pay as agreed. However, if you make late payments or skip town without settling up, they will be sure to spread the word, either to the credit-reporting companies or through a collection agency.

Information Warehouses

All of this information sharing could not take place unless somebody organized the whole thing. Information providers need to know who to tell. Information users need to know who to ask. It seems that they have figured this out pretty well.

Credit-Reporting Companies

The main stores of information are the credit-reporting companies. The three major ones, Equifax, TransUnion, and Experian, are practically household names. Sometimes these companies are referred to as credit agencies or credit bureaus. These three companies have established themselves as the major players in the credit-reporting industry. If you want to find out about somebody, chances are that your prospective customer has a file at one or more of the major companies.

Which Company Is Best?

These days, there is not much difference between the three major credit-reporting companies. There was a time when one might have had an advantage over another. For example, one credit-reporting company might have had more complete information for consumers in a certain geographical region.

Some of the information on your credit report comes from public records. These might be court records that somebody thinks are important to a lending (or other) decision. This information is gathered from publicly available sources. You could go to the county courthouse, or perhaps their Web site, and find the exact same information.

The main differences come from who reports to the companies. Many creditors will report to all three of the major companies. However, not all do, so some companies have different information than other companies. Likewise, some lenders decide to buy credit information from just one of the reporting companies. The decision is usually not based on the quality of their data. The credit-reporting companies know that they are dependent on creditors for their information. Instead, information users buy credit information based on standard business decisions: service from the company, price, relationships, and ancillary products.

Other Sources

The credit-reporting companies are the most important sources of information regarding your credit. However, there are other organizations that keep information that can be used for lending decisions, insurance underwriting, and employment screening. Companies that track your bounced checks, public records aggregators, and employment- or rental-history firms all exist. These may be large firms like ChoicePoint and ChexSystems, or small specialty companies that only track niche items. These other sources of information can have a direct or indirect effect on the products and services that are available to you.

Number Crunchers

All of that information stored on you is useless unless you can make sense of it. If your potential lender asked for a report on you, they might get thousands of pages of information. They would see printouts full of numbers and dates, and they would need weeks, at least, to decipher all of the information. As a result, several number-crunching firms do the work for them.

Fair Isaac Corporation

Perhaps the best-known number cruncher out there is the Fair Isaac Corporation (FICO). FICO is obviously the creator of the FICO Score, the most popular credit score used today. FICO refers to itself as an applied mathematics company, which does not keep any information on hand. It uses consumer information when it builds its mathematical models, but it is not a warehouse for information like the credit-reporting companies.

FICO works more like a consultant. The company works with service providers like lenders, insurance companies, and others to try and predict how people will behave. In the lending industry, for example, FICO helps lenders determine how likely a borrower is to become ninety days late with at least one creditor in the next twenty-four months. Working with lenders, FICO determined that this knowledge would be helpful. To do this, they use a proprietary algorithm (a secret math formula) to find patterns. Once they figure out the formula, FICO sells its analytical software to others. The credit-reporting companies use the software, and they load data into it to create scores.

The FICO Score has changed the way lending works. As a result of automated scoring, lending decisions are faster than ever. Lenders no longer have to read through credit reports and look for hints that suggest a prospective borrower is a good or bad risk. Personal judgment, prejudice, and human error are all but eliminated from the equation. Sometimes a lending decision will be made without any human input; if the model says your score's too low then you can't get a loan. As you can see, automated scoring has its advantages and disadvantages.

FICO has established a strong lead in the credit-scoring business. Most lenders look at your FICO score when they are deciding what kind of terms to offer. There are a lot of other credit scores out there, but the most relevant one is probably the FICO Score. In 2006, the major credit-reporting companies announced that they created a new scoring system called VantageScore. This system, a competitor to the FICO Score, would offer an alternative to consumers and financial institutions. However, as of this writing there was concern about the viability of the score: lenders already use the FICO Score and understand it, and learning something new might not be worth it. Furthermore, if lenders want to resell a mortgage in the secondary market, the mortgage is usually evaluated by the borrower's FICO Score.

FACT

The Fair Isaac Corporation's analytical skills can go far beyond lending and insurance decisions. The California Penal System reportedly asked the company to build a model that helped predict whether or not convicts would commit additional crimes after being released from prison. The project was never brought to completion, but you can see how these techniques get used elsewhere.

ChoicePoint

ChoicePoint is another major number cruncher. The company, as previously noted, also keeps a store of data, so it plays several roles. ChoicePoint does not really create credit scores that are used for lending. However, they create scores that may use information from your credit reports. ChoicePoint is known for insurance scores and an insurance-claims history database. The company might not have much to do with your loans, but they are likely involved in your insurance offerings.

Like FICO, ChoicePoint uses mathematical models to try and predict outcomes. The company helps insurers figure out who might be a profitable customer. In addition, ChoicePoint uses its expertise in a variety of other ways. For example, they work with law-enforcement agencies, and have won some large government contracts. The same concepts apply: they look for cause-and-effect relationships in huge volumes of data, then the model spits out an easy-to-understand answer.

Other Scorers

There are plenty of other number crunchers out there. The credit-reporting companies do some scoring, and specialty firms provide scores specific to whatever need comes up. If a product or service provider wants a score, somebody out there will build one. In general, scoring models follow a common set of steps.

1. **Identify the Need.** First, the scorer must determine what the score is intended to accomplish. For credit scores, they want to show if somebody is a good borrower. More specifically, you might ask: How likely is it that this borrower will become ninety days late with at least one creditor in the next twenty-four months?

2. **Get the Information.** Next, they get all of the information that might be interesting to the question at hand. For credit scores, you might want to collect data on previous credit accounts: how many there are, how much gets borrowed, whether payments are on time, and so on. You might decide to go even deeper: are public records important? Is a person's favorite color important?

3. **Crunch the Numbers.** Once you have an objective and all the data you need, you can start to look for relationships. Many software programs do this for you. The real challenge is in gathering the right data, categorizing it appropriately, and asking the right questions. Most tools use regression analysis to find relationships and make them understandable.

4. **Test the Output.** After you have a formula or a model, you need to test it to see if it really works. You can look back at the past, or you can test it going forward. With backtesting, you can use historical data on past customers over many years to see what would have happened if you had used that formula or model.

Of course, no scoring system is foolproof, all they can do is use your past credit history to try to predict your future behavior. This is why it's so important to be a responsible borrower—your credit history will indicate that you are a good credit risk.

The Regulators

Somebody has to keep all of this under control. Some businesses attempt to abuse the system. They might limit who gets access to money based on unreasonable criteria. For example, does one's race or sex determine whether or not they will be a good borrower? In the past, these factors have been used to discriminate, so the regulators stepped in to limit discrimination.

In addition, inaccuracies have hurt consumers over the years. If you have inaccurate information in your credit reports, it can make a huge difference in your standard of living. You might not be able to buy a home or a car. In the past, consumers were absolutely powerless. Newer regulations attempt to level the playing field so that information is kept accurate. The Federal Trade Commission (FTC) is the main watchdog when it comes to managing and improving your credit.

Fair Credit Reporting Act

The Fair Credit Reporting Act (FCRA) gives you rights related to the information that is kept by consumer-reporting companies. While the major credit-reporting companies might come to mind first, the Act also applies to companies that track check-writing history, medical records, employment history, and tenancy records. The gist of the law is that you have the right to know what your records say, and to correct inaccuracies.

You can find a lot of information regarding your rights on the Internet. The FTC's consumer credit site (*www.ftc.gov/credit*) is especially helpful. There, you'll find links to summaries of the laws discussed here, and explanations of your rights as a consumer. You can also file a complaint if any company has violated your rights.

The FCRA made credit reporting and scoring more transparent. Previously, you might have had a hard time finding out what your credit reports said. If there were errors, you could complain about them until you were blue in the face, but they probably wouldn't get fixed. The provisions for "fairness" in the FCRA make it easier for you to ensure the accuracy of your credit reports.

In addition to accuracy, privacy is an important part of the FCRA. The Act lays out specific circumstances that enable somebody to ask for your credit report. In general, these relate to applications for credit, underwriting for some insurance policies, and situations where you give somebody permission to view your report. In the past, people could violate your privacy more easily. These days, you sometimes hear about a person accessing an ex-spouse's credit reports. If there is no permissible purpose, you get in big trouble for this.

An especially important part of the FCRA is your right to a free credit report each year. Previously, there were a limited number of reasons that qualified you for a free report. For example, you had to have adverse action taken against you or suffer some other inconvenience. Now consumers nationwide can get a free report. Chapter 5 details how you can get your free credit reports.

The only place you can get your free annual credit reports under the FCRA is *www.annualcreditreport.com*. Since the law passed, numerous Web sites have targeted consumers hunting for their reports. These sites often give a free "teaser" report, but then charge you a fee in the future. The FTC continues to investigate and go after these sites.

Other Regulations

There are a number of other regulations related to your credit. While many of these do not have much to do with improving your credit, they are important to eliminating discrimination and abuse in the marketplace. The most important rules relating to your credit are probably those related to identity theft. They make it easier to recover from, and repair your credit after, a documented case of identity theft.

You Are the Star!

The most important actor in the story of your credit is you. Lenders, employers, and insurers are watching your every move. They want to know more about you. They want to send you letters and offer you credit cards, and they want to make sure that things in your life are not getting out of hand.

Where do you fit in with the other major players? You interact with them all of the time. In some cases you are an information provider. When asked for information on an application, you provide information that may go into a database or a model. For example, you are often asked for your income or how long you have lived at a given residence. These answers get turned into data for a variety of models.

Now that you know whom you are dealing with, it should be easier to understand their actions and motivations. You should also have a better idea of how these actors might view your actions. Your job as a consumer is to present yourself in the most favorable light possible. Remember that credit is a tool that you can use and control, not an obscure thing that all of these companies control for you. By working within the system, you'll do better for yourself. If anybody should make the mistake of mistreating you, you also know your rights and can get things fixed.

Chapter 4

Anatomy of a Credit Report

Your credit report contains the main ingredients in the feast called your credit. It is a repository where various lenders send information so that they can share experiences. These ingredients get measured, mixed, and baked, and the final product is your credit score. While there are other factors that are important to your credit, your credit report has the most important information. This section makes it easy to understand exactly what your reports contain.

4

Who Are You?

Your credit report has a section that contains personal information about you. Don't worry, it's not *that* personal. It is simply identifying information, so that creditors can report on you and find out more about you later. This section contains details such as:

- Your name
- Your date of birth
- Your Social Security Number
- Your current and previous employers
- Your current and previous residence addresses

There might be a few other pieces of information in there, such as phone numbers and information about your spouse.

You might be surprised at what you learn about yourself as you read through this section. Perhaps there are Social Security Numbers that you didn't know existed, or misspellings of your name. You should try and get everything corrected, but you might not have much luck. Even an erroneous Social Security Number often sticks. The reason? The credit-reporting companies do not want to fix something that they think is not broken. If they start using the correct SSN, they will lose all of that good information from your old SSN. Therefore, you should first try to get it fixed with whatever creditor is reporting with the wrong number.

All of the information in this section came from somewhere. Most of it came from information you gave your lenders when you applied for a loan. When they ask "Who do you work for?" you tell them who your employer is. Next thing you know, it shows up on your credit reports. The same thing goes for your residence history.

The first section might also contain a Consumer Statement. This is a statement that you add to your credit reports, typically to explain the less-flattering items within your report. You might mention that you had a bankruptcy because of a medical emergency, and you can hope that lenders will take this information into account. Truth be told, these statements probably do not add much value. First, automated credit-scoring models do not consider the statement because they can't understand the words, they just crunch numbers. Second, if you are going to have a human lender read your credit reports anyway, you will probably have the chance to explain any blemishes to that person, because you'll be sitting across the desk from them.

Your personal information in this section is what gets used when data is merged from a variety of sources. In other words, your Social Security Number might be the common link among various creditors, and between credit-reporting companies. Since different organizations have different borrowing information, it's important that they are able to merge everything correctly.

Executive Summary

The next section in your credit report is likely a summary of all of your accounts. This is a kind of scorecard that compiles all of the different items in your report so that you and your potential lenders can review them with a quick glance. This section is particularly helpful when you are trying to determine the differences between the major credit-reporting companies. If you view your credit report online, you can usually click on portions of the summary to drill down to the data underneath. The summary will typically show you the following items:

- **Total Accounts.** A count of all accounts that have ever shown up on that credit report. The accounts may currently be open or closed.
- **Type of Account.** The categories you might see are Mortgage, Revolving, Installment, Auto Loan, or Other.
- **Open and Closed Accounts.** A count of how many accounts are open or closed. While the Total Accounts section does not distinguish whether or not you've closed the accounts, this section breaks it down. Keep in mind, the accounts must be reported as closed by the creditor.

- **Accounts in Good Standing.** This section shows how many of the total accounts, both open and closed, are in good standing. To be in good standing, you must have paid, or be paying, everything as agreed.
- **Delinquencies.** Also known as Past Due, this section shows a count of how many accounts you are currently behind on.
- **Derogatory Items.** Sometimes referred to as Negative Account History. These are accounts that are reporting negative information about you and damaging your credit score. These might be accounts that you were previously delinquent on, or these could be accounts that were charged off or settled.
- **Total Balances.** The total balances section shows how much debt you currently have. In addition, this section might be broken down by account type: mortgage, revolving, and so on.
- **Total Payments.** If the information is available, this section contains the total of all of your monthly payments.
- **Good Standing.** A count of all of your accounts that are in good standing: your total accounts minus delinquent and derogatory accounts.
- **Public Records.** The lower the better. It is simply a count of how many public records are in your file. Public records are explained in greater detail below.
- **Inquiries.** The Inquiries section shows a count of inquiries in the last twelve or twenty-four months. Again, you want a low number here. Only hard inquiries, inquiries made when you apply for a new loan, are counted here.

Account History

Your account history is the meat and potatoes of your credit report. This is the detail section that is used for much of the summary information described above. It shows you, and your potential lenders, more of the raw information that your creditors report about you.

This section can be really easy or really difficult to read, depending on where you get your credit report. The credit-reporting companies have taken steps to improve readability, but there is still a ways to go. Some credit reports have the account history nicely formatted, with bold account names, and colorful payment history sections. Others are pretty much just text.

As with your summary information, the account details might be broken up into sections. You might find individual accounts grouped by type: mortgage, revolving, auto loan, and so on. However, not all credit reports do this. The ones that have gone to the effort to format things nicely are more likely to categorize for you as well. If your accounts are not broken into sections, you'll just see them listed one after another.

QUESTION?

What is a trade line?

A trade line is an account that appears on your credit report. You probably just call them accounts or loans, but your lenders may refer to them as trade lines. This is just another way of talking about a loan's attributes, like your balance, status, credit limit, and so on.

Your account history section shows you a few important details about all of your accounts. They tell other lenders and credit-scoring computer programs all about the loan in question. You should see the following bits of information:

- **Account Name.** Also known as Creditor Name, this field tells you where the account is located. It might say the name of the bank or credit card company that issued you a loan. If an entry has an error, this is the organization that you need to contact.
- **Account Number.** You might have several accounts with the same lender, so it is important to know which account is being reported in case of errors or disputes.
- **Account Type.** You already know this from the summary section. It tells you whether or not this is a mortgage, auto, revolving, or other type of loan.
- **Date Opened.** How long ago did you open the account? As you may know, it's good to have some old ones lying around. Check here to make sure your account age is accurate.

- **Balance.** How much the credit reporting company thinks you owe. This information comes from the lender, but it is not updated in real time. Therefore, recent payments and purchases may not be reflected.

- **Account Status.** Also known as Pay Status, this field notes whether or not you are paying as agreed. If not, it may have additional details about your delinquency. See that these are updated if you have recently made amends with a creditor.

- **Remark.** Sometimes a Comment field, this is where you will often see a remark that your account was "closed by consumer" if you have requested that they close the account.

- **Date Updated.** This is the last time the creditor reported information about you to the credit-reporting company. This can help you figure out why any recent activity is missing.

- **Responsibility.** This section states what your responsibility is to the account. You might be the only user on the account, or you could share it with others.

- **Terms.** Here you see the terms of your agreement. If it's an installment loan, how many payments, and how frequent are the payments? If it is a revolving loan, this section may be blank. Sometimes you'll see a minimum payment here.

- **Past Due.** This displays the dollar amount that you are behind on. Ideally you want to see a "0" here.

- **Credit Limit.** The maximum amount you are allowed to borrow for that account. This is most important on revolving accounts. This number is used to determine how much of your available credit you are using. In addition, high credit limits on your report can show that some lenders trust you.

- **High Balance.** This is like a high-water mark for revolving loans— it notes the highest balance you've ever had on the account. For installment loans like mortgages and student loans, this number is the original loan amount.

- **Scheduled Payment.** This shows your minimum payment due.

- **Actual Payment.** The last payment that you actually sent in before your account details were sent to the credit-reporting company.

Your account history makes up the bulk of information that the credit-scoring models use to determine your credit score. You need to make sure all of this is accurate in order to ensure a reasonable score.

Public Records

Your credit report shows any public records related to your finances. In general, you want this part of your credit report to be empty. You can expect that almost anything that happens in a courtroom will appear in the public records section. However, nonfinancial matters will not show up. The types of public records most likely to appear on a credit report are:

- Bankruptcies
- Tax liens
- Civil judgments against you
- Foreclosures
- Wage garnishments

As you can probably tell, if these items show up on your credit report, it will hurt your credit. These items will stay for seven years, and then drop off. However, if you owe a tax debt, it will never go away—you have to pay it and then wait seven years for it to disappear. Tax liens can come from the federal government, as well as state and local agencies.

A Chapter 7 bankruptcy will stay in your reports for ten years. Chapter 13 bankruptcy, like most other negative items, will drop off your reports after seven years.

Inquiring Minds

Your credit reports show a history of all inquiries made into your credit. This section shows who has been asking about you, and you may be surprised to see how many people care about you. Inquiries will remain on your credit report for up to two years.

Hard Inquiries

Hard inquiries are the most important as far as your credit scores go. Hard inquiries are inquiries that happen anytime you apply for new credit. The potential lender checks you out by pulling your credit, and a history of this activity stays in your credit files. Why would this be important? If you run all over town asking for credit, it could be a sign of trouble. Lenders want to know if you are opening up a bunch of new accounts at once. In fact, each hard inquiry costs your FICO credit score a few points (less than five).

Hard inquiries will be shown on your credit reports with the following details:

- Name of the inquiring company
- Contact information for the company
- Date of inquiry

If you use a merged, or 3-in-1, credit report, you will also see which credit-reporting company reported the inquiry.

See if you can figure out exactly when your lenders report to the credit-reporting companies. If they report at the end of the month, send payments in before that date. That way, your balances look lower, and you can boost your credit score. Even if you pay in full each month, your credit reports might always show a balance.

Soft Inquiries

Soft inquiries are inquiries that do not affect your credit score. In fact, you might be the only person that can view these inquiries. Your prospective lenders do not see them, and they are not included in the inquiry count in your credit report's summary.

After you open a credit account with a lender, they periodically check in on you to see how you are doing. No, they don't call you up to ask how you are. Instead, they pull your credit. They want to see if you are taking on too much debt, or if anything else of interest has happened. Note that these inquiries are the ones that can get you in trouble with a variety of lenders. If you have universal default clauses on your credit cards, these inquiries will let them know if you've defaulted or paid late anywhere else.

Watch your inquiries for signs of identity theft. If you see a bunch of new inquiries and you cannot figure out where they came from, you should make sure it's not an identity thief. Inquiries will be the smoke before the fire, and you can limit the damage by alerting the credit-reporting companies early.

Promotional Inquiries

You will also see a slew of soft inquiries that are promotional inquiries. These inquirers do not get to see your entire credit report, but they learn something about you. When you get a preapproved offer, chances are it is a result of a promotional inquiry—you met their criteria for the marketing campaign. Note that you can opt out of those offers by telling the credit-reporting companies to stop selling your information. Alternatively, you can call 888-5-OPTOUT to opt out for two years.

Who Gave You the Right?

Your credit report contains sensitive information. A credit inquiry can give somebody a wealth of information about your finances, and it might not be any of their business. In addition, hard inquiries can ding your score up, and having too many will make your loans more expensive or unobtainable.

For the reasons listed above, there are limitations on who may request your credit report. An inquirer must have permissible purpose when requesting your credit. If they don't have permissible purpose, they can't get the report without your permission. Credit-reporting companies may provide your credit reports in these situations:

- As required by a valid court order
- With your written permission
- For a credit transaction
- For employment decisions
- For underwriting insurance
- In the application process for some licenses
- Ongoing checkups of existing customers
- Some procedures related to child-support awards

As you review your credit reports, see who is asking about you. If they do not appear to have a permissible purpose, they may be violating some serious laws. You can stop them from requesting your credit reports.

What's Not in a Credit Report

Credit reports have a lot of information in them. If they tried to add any more, it probably would not even fit. Fortunately, there are plenty of things that are not, and cannot, be in your credit reports. Since the definition of credit report is somewhat fuzzy, this section only refers to credit reports issued by the three major credit reporting companies: Equifax, Experian, and TransUnion.

Hot Potatoes

There are several bits of information that cannot appear in your credit report. These are items that could potentially cause a lender to discriminate against you. Of course, you wouldn't want to work with lenders who discriminate anyway, but there are regulations that help to reduce discrimination.

Some of the items that are kept out of your credit report are the usual "hot potatoes" that can get lenders in trouble. These include:

- Your ethnicity
- Your religious beliefs and affiliations
- Your political beliefs and affiliations
- Your sex

Out with the Old

Credit reports are important because they let everybody know if you have been a responsible borrower in the past. If you have made mistakes in the past, it's reasonable to expect that you might make mistakes again. However, everybody makes mistakes, and ideally you learn from your mistakes. Therefore, old items need to be deleted from your credit reports so that you can get a fresh start now and again. After seven years, almost all negative items fall off your credit reports. These include:

- Charge offs and settlements
- Collections
- Chapter 13 bankruptcy (Chapter 7 stays for 10 years)
- Late payments

Once these items fall off your credit reports, it is easier to get loans and improve the terms on loans that you already have. You might not see dramatic changes, because the most recent items on your credit reports carry the most weight. However, you will see improvement.

As with most rules, there are always exceptions. The FCRA allows information older than seven years to appear in some situations. Presumably, these are situations where somebody is taking a great amount of risk on you, and they should be allowed to know more about you. These situations include:

- Credit transactions for amounts greater than $150,000
- Underwriting life insurance for more than $150,000
- Employment for a job paying more than $75,000 annually

Other Business

The major consumer credit-reporting companies only create reports that deal with consumer credit. Other factors may be relevant to your credit-worthiness; however they are not necessarily shown in your credit reports. If a lender, landlord, or insurer is going to use additional information, they have to get it somewhere else. They might ask you for the information on your application, or they might use a variety of other consumer reporting organizations to get the information they need.

Does everything fall off a credit report after seven to ten years?
No. If you have tax liens, they are not going anywhere until you actually pay the taxes you owe. Back taxes due to the IRS, for example, will not go away until seven years *after* you have paid the money due.

Rubber Checks

Consumer credit does not include your check-writing behavior. While writing rubber checks is probably a bad sign for lenders, it is technically not a credit account. However, don't get any wild ideas: there are consumer-reporting companies that track check-writing behavior.

ChexSystems, as well as a number of smaller companies, keeps files on consumers who have a history of mishandling their accounts. Note that ChexSystems operates differently from the major consumer credit-reporting companies. The credit-reporting companies track any information they receive, both good and bad. If you always pay as agreed, there is a record of it. On the other hand, ChexSystems only keeps a file on you if you have been reported for writing bad checks. In other words, it's good to have a credit file, but it's bad to have a ChexSystems file. Institutions that use Chex-Systems report bad-check writers, and check on new account applicants to see if they've had trouble in the past.

ALERT!

For people with no credit history at all, your check-writing behavior is very important. The FICO Expansion Score, a newer score for the previously "unscorable," uses a variety of information other than your credit reports to determine your creditworthiness. One of the things they look at is how you have used checking accounts.

Medical Information

You will not find information about your medical history in a credit report issued by the major credit-reporting companies. As discussed elsewhere, that data is kept by the Medical Information Bureau, among others. However, confusion arises because medical bills can appear on your reports. Because accidents and sicknesses tend to be quite expensive, patients and their families often can't pay the whole bill at once. These bills sometimes show up as collection items.

In the past, one could make a pretty good guess at what happened based on your credit report. For example, there might have been an entry for The Broke-Your-Ankle Recovery Clinic or the Chronic Depression Treatment Center. In an effort to reduce discrimination, recent regulations require that these entries do not identify the type of organization where you originally received care. When a potential lender sees your credit report, the entry is identified only as a medical entry. However, when you look at your report, the entry is more detailed. This allows you to contact the information provider if you need to dispute the entry.

Not Applicable

You could list thousands of things that are just not relevant to your credit report. Your favorite color, night owl vs. early riser, and so on. While these examples might be obvious, there is no shortage of confusion about which consumer records and public records pop up in a credit report. In general, the only records that appear are those which would reasonably be related to your handling of personal financial matters.

Because a business loan is not a personal financial matter, business loans are not included in your credit report. However, keep in mind that if you signed on as taking personal responsibility for the loan, it will appear on your credit.

For many new businesses, a business loan is simply a personal loan, but the bank calls them business loans to make you feel important. One way to tell if it is a personal loan: did they ask for your Social Security Number? If yes, you are probably personally on the hook for any unpaid debts.

In addition, your criminal and driving records are not on your standard credit reports. If this makes you breathe easier, don't forget that other organizations do collect and sell that data. For lending decisions, you might not be affected by a few run-ins with the law. However, if you are seeking employment or licensing in a sensitive area, your prospective employer will surely purchase a background check and ask about any blemishes.

Consumer Resources

The bottom of your credit report has resources and information that help you manage your credit reports. Most of this information should not be news to you; it is placed at the bottom of credit reports for people who do not know how to improve their credit. Even though after reading this book you will have a head start, you should still read over the disclosures so that you are fully informed about your legal rights.

You will find a summary of your rights under the FCRA, complete with contact information if you need help from the regulators. If you enjoy the legalese, you might want to read the entire Fair Credit Reporting Act (or at least skim through it). The Act shows you what the regulators are trying to accomplish, and why.

In addition to the summary of the FCRA, you will find details on how to dispute or correct information contained within your credit report. You should see complete contact information, and instructions on how to submit corrections. Finally, your credit report might have additional state law resources and information.

Chapter 5
Watching Your Credit

It's essential that you keep an eye on your credit. Nobody knows your credit better than you do, so if there are errors, you'll know it. Is somebody stealing your identity? You'll know that, too. You'll be able to gauge whether your credit is looking good, getting better, or getting worse. With this knowledge, you can manage your credit and make it better. This section focuses on the variety of ways you can monitor your credit and enlist others to do it with you.

ir Free Credit Reports

The Fair Credit Reporting Act (FCRA) is a good deal. Under the FCRA, all U.S. consumers are entitled to a free credit report each year. This allows you to get a free credit report from each of the three major credit reporting companies annually. Before paying for a credit report, take advantage of this benefit.

When you go through the process of viewing your reports, you get a credit-file disclosure. This disclosure has all of the information that the credit-reporting company might send to a potential lender, employer, or other party that asks for your report. It also has information meant for your eyes only, such as soft inquiries and more detailed information about any medical accounts. These additional details help you keep tabs on who is doing what with your credit.

Instant Access to Your Reports

The quickest and easiest way to get your free credit reports is online. The three major credit reporting companies—Equifax, TransUnion, and Experian—joined forces to create a Web site for this purpose, *www.annual creditreport.com*. When you visit the site, you can view your report immediately, provided that you prove your identity. To do this, you'll need to provide the following:

- Full name, including middle initial and suffix (Jr., Sr., etc.)
- Current address (and any recent previous addresses)
- Social Security Number
- Date of birth

You'll then have a choice of which credit report you want to view, Equifax, TransUnion, or Experian. In addition to the personal information above, you'll have to provide additional details to each credit-reporting company for final verification. You'll be asked a question that only you should know the answer to. For example, you might be asked for an account number, payment amount, loan provider, or loan balance.

When you successfully prove your identity, you'll be able to see your credit file online. In addition to your reports, the credit-reporting agencies will offer to sell you a credit score and other services at this time.

Other Ways to Order Reports

As part of the FCRA's free credit-report program, you can order your credit-file disclosures in a variety of ways. If you can't or don't want to view your reports online, you can order them via phone or mail. To order your credit reports over the phone, call 877-322-8228. You'll go through a verification process similar to the one described above. Your reports will be mailed to you within fifteen days.

ALERT!

Watch out for imposters and online scammers! You might think you're at a reputable Web site, but in fact you're giving out information that will be used for identity theft (you may have misspelled the Web site's address or followed a deceptive link). Always double check before you submit your personal details.

If you'd like to request your reports via the mail, you have to send in a request. You can download a request form at *www.annualcreditreport.com*. If you can't use the Internet, simply write a request with the information in the bulleted list on page 58, and instruct them to send you a report from one, two, or all three of the credit-reporting companies. Mail your request to: Annual Credit Report Request Service, P.O. Box 105281, Atlanta, GA 30348-5281.

Don't Get Them All at Once

You don't have to order all of your free credit reports at once. The program keeps track of which credit-reporting company you have ordered from each year. If you want to get all three at the same time that's fine, and it's a good way to compare the differences among reports. You'll probably find that one company has more complete or accurate information. A one-time snapshot helps you see the different information credit-reporting companies have on you.

If you want to stagger the dates, you can get periodic reports throughout the year. For example, you might get a credit report from a different reporting company every four months. This would help you monitor your credit over time. You won't have to wait a full year to discover if somebody is reporting that you make late payments. Also, you can see if there are any new unauthorized accounts in your name, which might indicate identity theft.

Other Ways to Get Free Information

The free credit reports that you can get are a great resource. You should take advantage of the program as a first step toward watching your credit. However, there are other ways to get free access to credit scores and the information in your credit reports.

Free Credit Report Triggers

The laws described above entitle you to view your credit reports annually no matter what. In addition to those rights, federal laws entitle you to free credit reports in specific situations. If you are denied credit, insurance, or employment based on information in the reports, you should receive a notice explaining what happened. Simply ask the credit-reporting company named in the notice for a free report within sixty days.

When somebody pulls your credit, they are required to inform you if they've used the information against you. Any adverse action like a denial of credit, employment, or insurance triggers the disclosure. They must also give you contact information for the credit-reporting company that they used to make the decision.

There are a few other triggers as well. If you're unemployed and you intend to apply for a job within the next sixty days, you can ask for a free credit report. People on public-assistance programs can ask for free reports. Finally, placing fraud alerts in your credit files entitles you to a free credit report to check for signs of fraud.

Inquiring Minds Can Tell You

Since your lenders keep tabs on your credit, they can help you do so, too. Lenders periodically check your reports to make sure that you have not become a greater risk to them over time. They may offer you some of this information as a value-added service. For example, some credit card companies will show you your FICO score, as well as a charted history of your FICO score values, free of charge. By keeping an eye on that number, you'll know if anything major is happening to your credit.

Every time you get your credit checked, for a mortgage, loan, employment, or phone service for example, you can ask the inquirer what your credit reports say. They may or may not have details, but they can probably at least tell you whether it's excellent or not. Make a habit of asking anytime you authorize somebody to check your credit. In some cases, you might be able to request a copy of the reports when you authorize the credit check.

Purchasing Credit Information

There are a variety of ways to get free information from others. However, you have to qualify, and you might not qualify. Annual credit reports from each credit-reporting company are extremely helpful, but a lot can happen at one of these companies in a year. Therefore, you might consider purchasing credit information so that you're even more informed.

3-in-1 Reports

Some people pay for credit reports because they like 3-in-1 reports. These reports consolidate the information from all three major credit-reporting companies. This saves you the trouble of getting the three reports yourself and then matching up all of your accounts.

Because 3-in-1 reports are fairly inexpensive, if you're really curious about your credit they might be worth it. One reason to pay for them is that you get a better idea of what lenders see when they look at your credit. Lenders often use 3-in-1 reports because not every account shows up at every credit-reporting company. Data from the different sources is merged to put everything onto one sheet. You might be surprised at how the merging works, or doesn't work.

FICO Scores

Along with your different credit reports, you can purchase your FICO score from each of the major credit-reporting companies. Because each company has different information, they'll end up spitting out a different FICO score. You never know if a lender is only going to use one or two FICO scores in the lending decision, so you'll want to make sure they're all good. You can easily have a difference of fifty points among credit-reporting companies. By knowing the score, you can see if anything is really hurting or helping one of your FICO scores.

Paying for Protection

There's a right time and a wrong time to pay for your credit information. If you've got an ordinary life and you're careful about your personal information, you might not need to pay a cent. However, plenty of situations arise when you'll need to watch your credit like a hawk.

If you've had problems with identity theft or fraud, one or two credit report reviews each year is not enough. You'll want to consider a credit-monitoring service, and manually review your credit reports periodically. If you haven't had any problems with fraud but you're really worried about it, go ahead and pay for a service—the peace of mind is worth it.

These days, your Social Security Number is everywhere. It is considered to be one of the most sensitive pieces of data, but is not treated that way by most organizations. You might find your Social Security Number on your paycheck, as your student ID (in college), on contracts that you sign, on a variety of employment documents, and, of course, on credit applications. Think of all of the people who can get access to your Social Security Number. If there are a few too many of them, you might benefit from paying for help.

Pay for Peace of Mind

Another time to pay for credit information is when you're considering a large purchase. Mortgage loans in particular tend to be large loans, so it's worth it to make sure your credit is as clean as possible. A slightly higher rate on a mortgage can cost you thousands over the years, so a few dollars to review your credit information is money well spent. Make sure you get your credit information well in advance of the day you apply for the mortgage—it can take a few months to find, fix, and follow-up on errors.

As you shop for an information provider, make sure you are buying your FICO credit score. Because of the FICO's dominance and history in the marketplace, lenders typically use that score. For a purchase as important as your home, you want to look at the same score your lenders will look at. There are a variety of places that offer to sell FICO credit scores, including the consumer site of the Fair Isaac Corporation, *www.myfico.com*.

Credit-Monitoring Services

To keep tabs on your credit, it's best to enlist the help of others. Checking your free credit reports and purchasing additional reports throughout the year is great, but you can take an even more proactive approach. Credit-monitoring services can keep you up-to-date with the most important information.

What They Do

Credit monitoring services "push" information to you so you don't have to "pull" your credit. They periodically check your credit reports and inform you of any changes. You might receive an e-mail every time an inquiry is made or a new account is opened in your name. In addition, they typically offer unlimited viewing of one or more of your credit reports and credit scores. Sometimes you can view your FICO score, sometimes it's just a proprietary credit score. Note that your scores and reports may not be updated daily; rather, they might only update weekly or monthly.

Finding a Credit-Monitoring Service

Credit-monitoring services are not hard to find. In fact, it's really hard to check your credit report or credit score without getting an offer to use a service. If you need to go looking, you can start with the major credit-reporting companies—Equifax, Experian, and TransUnion. Next, you might visit myFICO.com (run by the Fair Isaac Corporation) for services offered there. Finally, see if your bank or credit card company can get you a deal.

Credit-Monitoring Service Benefits

Before you fork over the money to use a credit-monitoring service, make sure you're using all of the free resources available to you. The most extensive services are quite expensive, and you might not need them unless you're really worried or you're having a hard time getting your credit reports fixed. If you are going to use a service, make sure you get everything you need.

Credit-monitoring services are best for people who need and want a lot of information. Victims of identity theft and people who want constant access to their credit information and scores will benefit most. If you won't take the time to order and review your free credit reports, you might also benefit from using a service.

When shopping for a credit-monitoring service, make sure you get what you need. This section highlights some of the features you will find most useful.

Frequent Monitoring and Notification

You want a service that checks early and often. Find out how often they access your credit files to check for changes. Likewise, find out how often they notify you of any changes. Ideally, you want them to do it daily.

Who do They Monitor?

Some monitoring services only monitor one credit-reporting company. Others monitor all three of the big ones, and they track other databases that you might be interested in. You'll benefit from more information, not less.

Error-Resolution Services

Some services help you fix errors and recover from identity theft. They typically say they'll do most of the work once you alert them to a problem. This will cost more, but you might want it. Make sure you read the fine print and understand what you do, and don't, get from this.

Identity-Theft Insurance

Some services offer to reimburse you for your time and expenses related to recovering from identity theft. The ID theft must occur while you're using the service. Again, this costs money and you will want to view the insurance contract so you know what to expect.

Pitfalls of Credit Monitoring

You can get a lot of valuable information from a credit-monitoring service. In addition, you save time and automate a process that you might not enjoy. Nevertheless, there are a few pitfalls associated with using these services.

Not Enough Information

In the past, most credit-monitoring services were offered by the main three credit reporting companies. These services only included information held in your credit files at that company. If you've ever checked your three credit reports at the same time, you know that information and errors can differ among credit reports. Increasingly, you'll find 3-in-1 credit-monitoring services. However, the lower-cost services still exist, and they don't give you enough information.

Why don't credit-reporting companies have the same information?
Credit-reporting companies only hold data that their clients report. Lenders are the most common clients of credit-reporting companies, and different lenders choose to work with different companies. They might only report to one or two companies.

In addition, credit-monitoring services won't give you information on every aspect of your credit, including the factors that lenders, insurers, and employers might look at. They typically don't track information related to insurance claims, medical records, or employment history. While some of the most extensive services can keep you updated, most do not.

Slow Reporting

When you purchase a credit-monitoring service, you may find that you can log in every single day and view your reports. How often does the report get updated? It's important that your reports are monitored and updated frequently. Some services only update your report weekly, monthly, or quarterly. If you need up-to-date information, don't buy a service with quarterly updates.

Keep in mind that data providers like credit card companies, finance companies, and courts may also be slow in reporting information. If you pay down a credit card balance or change your address, the credit-reporting companies might not hear about it for several weeks. You just need to know that there can be a long lag between when something happens and when you are notified.

A False Sense of Security

Using a credit-monitoring service can help quite a bit. You enlist the credit-reporting companies and others to keep you informed. Computers search for problems while you sleep or go about your daily life. However, is this enough to keep your credit clean?

You really need to take an active role in monitoring your credit. While computers can do a lot, nobody knows your credit better than you do. A service can do most of the heavy lifting, but you shouldn't assume that everything is on autopilot. Check your reports manually from time to time—you'll be glad you did.

Your Not-So-Credit Reports

Your credit is about more than just credit use. Lenders want to know about your employment, assets, and income when they make a decision. Employers want to know about your credit use and any public records. Insurers want to know how you use credit and how often you've made insurance claims in the past. You need to make sure all of the different puzzle pieces are arranged to present the most attractive picture. To do this, it's important that you know what people are saying about you.

ChoicePoint

A company that may say a lot about you is ChoicePoint. ChoicePoint compiles information from a variety of sources to create a consolidated snapshot of who you are. Information comes from credit-reporting companies, insurance agencies, government databases, and more. Most of this information is available for you to view direct from the sources; however, ChoicePoint merges the data so you can see it all in one place.

Your homeowner's and auto insurance claims are shared among insurers. The practice started in order to detect and reduce fraud. For example, it would answer the question, "How many times has this client had his home burn down?" Nowadays, the information is used for additional purposes. If insurance companies find that you make a lot of claims, they don't want to insure you. Likewise, if the home you just bought has had a history of problems, they don't want to insure the home.

In addition to monitoring claims history, ChoicePoint issues insurance scores. These scores are based on information in your credit reports. Auto and homeowner's insurance companies will use the score to decide whether or not to insure you. Somehow, they've found a way to link your credit behavior to your claims behavior. If you've got a bad credit history or certain public records on your reports, you're likely to cost them more.

ALERT!

Think twice before calling your insurance company to inquire about a claim. Simply asking questions about coverage can add a record to your insurance files which may be used against you. Some states are trying to limit this practice, but it just goes to show that you have to be very careful.

Under the Fair Credit Reporting Act, you can request free annual reports on some of the information ChoicePoint keeps. However, you'll have to pay if you want to get all of your scores and files, and they have a lot of scores and files available. To get your reports, visit ChoicePoint's ChoiceTrust site (*www .choicetrust.com*). There are other companies out there that do reporting similar to ChoicePoint's, but they are not as user-friendly at the present time.

Medical Information Bureau

If your credit report contains information on your credit past, your medical reports will contain history on your medical past. The main place for centralized medical reporting is the Medical Information Bureau (MIB). Many people don't even have a MIB file. You will only have information there if you have applied for individual insurance coverage.

The MIB gets information from insurers and health care providers. When you apply for insurance, you typically disclose any conditions that you've had in the past. In addition, you'll often consent to have the insurance company investigate your past with your health care providers. The information that your health care providers report can end up in the MIB files.

As with your auto and homeowner's insurance, you need to make sure that your MIB files are accurate. Any errors can be costly. For example, when you buy health, life, or long-term care insurance, your MIB history can put you into a much more expensive risk category. The insurer might even reject you altogether. Like many consumer-reporting companies, the MIB will provide you a free report annually, or if anybody has taken adverse action against you based on information held at the MIB.

Be Your Own Consumer Advocate

This chapter just scratches the surface on some of the consumer-reporting companies out there, and what they do. By now, you should understand that organizations are constantly inquiring about you, reporting on you, and double checking your files. Based on what they find, services could cost you thousands of unnecessary dollars every year! Keeping an eye on your credit is essential. If you are unaware of negative information, it can be devastating. Yes, employers, insurers, and lenders (and who knows who else) should notify you if they take adverse action based on information in your consumer files. However, it might be too late. Imagine being left without homeowner's insurance or auto insurance while you correct errors. Perhaps you won't be uncovered, but you might have to spend a lot more in premiums while you fix your reports.

Businesses are watching you, and they make periodic checkups to see what you are up to. Watch them back, and do your own checkups. You don't have to make this your life, just make it a point to find out what other consumer advocates think is a big deal.

Lenders and others have a right to know something about you. Otherwise, how could they decide whether or not to lend to you? The appropriate extent of their knowledge and how they use it is what's up for debate. However, most consumers benefit by having some information-sharing take place. If everybody had to pay equal rates, the more-responsible borrowers (like you) would have to pay extra to cover the costs of the less-responsible borrowers.

Just like they have a right to know something about you, you have the right to know what they're saying about you. Exercise your rights. It's not always easy or pleasant, but pulling your reports and fixing errors are the only way you can make sure you get what you deserve. You have to be your own consumer advocate, because nobody knows the truth about you better than you. Keep your ears open: new consumer-reporting companies will undoubtedly appear and use information for new purposes.

Chapter 6

A Closer Look at Credit Scores

A credit score is often the only thing that will get you a loan, or prevent you from getting a loan. Unfortunately, most people don't even know their credit scores, much less understand how they work. Because of their significance in your life, you should become intimately familiar with credit scores. When you know how things work, it is a lot easier to work on them. This section will demystify the world of credit scores so that you can start improving yours.

How to Get a Credit Score

If you have not already done so, you will need to get your hands on a credit score. This is the magic number that lenders and others judge you by. Once you know the number, you take a big step toward managing your credit. As you go looking for credit scores, you'll be inundated with offers. Go to any search engine and type in the words "credit score." Every one of the listed results will have your phrase prominently displayed and bolded.

Any time you get a loan, ask your lender for your credit score. Since they just pulled your credit reports, they will have an up-to-date credit score for you. If you don't like what you see, dig deeper. Order your credit reports and see what may be affecting your scores.

You need to be careful out there because you're working with some very sensitive information. If you give your sensitive personal information to the wrong party, you risk becoming a victim of identity theft. Stick with the big names, or ask your lender which credit score they use when evaluating a borrower.

Your FICO credit score

The granddaddy of all credit scores is the FICO score. The Fair Isaac Corporation pioneered credit scoring, and is deeply entrenched as a market leader. For most mortgage loans, lenders will look at your FICO credit score. This is because selling mortgages in the secondary market has traditionally been easier if the borrower had a good credit score. The use of the FICO score for automated underwriting is beginning to shift, but the FICO credit score is still by far the dominant scoring model.

Because of its dominance, you might consider buying your credit score directly from the Fair Isaac Corporation. That way, you will be sure to get a FICO credit score, not an imitation. You can purchase your FICO credit scores directly from Fair Isaac at their consumer web site, *www.myfico.com*. If you only need one credit score (because you know which credit-reporting company your lender will use) then you can buy a single score from a single bureau. If you want a FICO credit score from all three of the credit-reporting companies, you can buy those as part of a complete package.

FACT

While the FICO credit score is a strong market leader, the VantageScore may catch up. VantageScore is the scoring model created by the three major credit-reporting companies: TransUnion, Equifax, and Experian. To purchase your VantageScore, you can visit one of the credit-reporting companies' Web sites, or you can do so at *www.vantagescore.com*.

Buying Other Scores

You can buy other scores, but you may not want to. There are a million different vendors out there selling credit scores of questionable value. There is so much confusion about credit and credit scores that these companies get away with selling consumers a score that a lender will never use. The major credit-reporting companies are guilty of this. However, they also sell FICO credit scores, so you have to be careful when buying from them. You might get a proprietary score, or you might get the genuine article. Read the fine print to make sure you get what you want. Other scores typically score you a little higher than your FICO credit score would be, giving you a false sense of security.

Monitoring Services

You can also buy credit scores in conjunction with credit-monitoring services. Typically, these services might hold themselves out to be identity-theft protection services. As an added bonus, they say that they will throw in a credit score. Unfortunately, these credit scores are rarely FICO credit scores. They might move up and down similar to the way the FICO credit score will move, but they're not exactly the same.

Managing Your Credit Score

If you're going to look at your credit score, it is reasonable to assume that you will try to increase your credit score. You want your credit score to be as high as possible. If you develop the right habits and behaviors, your credit score will follow. In other words, you don't necessarily need to focus on your credit score; focusing on the right activities will do the trick.

If you focus on your credit score, you will focus on behaviors that are intended only to improve your credit score. This may not be the most effective way to manage your credit. You may be able to force your score higher because of a few strategic actions. However, do you really have good credit?

QUESTION?

How can I improve my credit score?
There are several ways to improve your credit scores. The basic, simple way (the method of choice) is to simply improve your credit. If you do that, your credit scores will follow. How do you improve your credit? Just use credit wisely and responsibly. Follow the tips found elsewhere in this book.

Your credit should have a wide and strong foundation, and you can't build this foundation by trying to fiddle with your credit score. You build a foundation by using credit wisely and responsibly over a long period of time. You only take on debt when you need it, you make your payments on time and as agreed, and you use different types of loans for different types of things.

Of course, you might benefit in the short term by fiddling with your credit score. For example, suppose that you are buying a house. This is a huge loan, and saving a little bit on your interest rate can go a long way. If you have a quick and easy way to raise your credit score, you should do it. For example, you might pay down some debts so that you are using a lower percentage of your total available credit. This will give you an important short-term boost in your credit scores, but you need to address the issue of why you were previously using so much credit.

Credit Score Versus Credit Report

It is essential that you can distinguish between a credit score and a credit report. There is a major difference. Credit reports are just reports that have information on your credit use. They show accounts that you have used in the past, and those that you use today. They show whether or not you paid on time, and how much you have borrowed.

Credit List

You will learn all of the details of your credit reports later in this book. For now, it might be wise just to think of your credit report as a credit list. Your credit report is like a big sheet of paper with a listing of your past behaviors. It also has personal information on you, such as your name, address, and Social Security Number. It is full of information, and looking through this list will take several minutes or more.

A Three-Digit Number

A credit score, on the other hand, is a three-digit number. The higher the number, the better (for most lending-oriented scores). Doesn't that sound simple? Credit scores exist to simplify the lending process. Instead of spending several minutes looking for a long list of data, a person or computer can just look at a three-digit number. This makes the process go faster, which means more people can get more loans at better rates. This is a win-win for consumers and lenders: when lenders switch from using credit reports to credit scores, they end up granting loans to an additional 20 percent to 30 percent of applicants (FICO statement to the Senate Committee On Banking, Housing, and Urban Affairs, 2003).

Just a Number

Just like your credit report, your credit score doesn't tell lenders whether or not to grant a loan. Your credit reports (or credit lists) are simply testimonials from other lenders. A new prospective lender may look through your credit reports and decide whether or not they wish to loan money to you. The report itself does not make the decision. Likewise, credit scores are just another piece of information that lenders use. A score below a certain number does not mean that you won't get a loan. It simply means that you may be more likely to fall behind on a payment.

Always remember the distinctions between FICO scores, other scores, and credit reports. Credit reports are raw data, typically from the credit-reporting companies. Credit-scoring models analyze the data. The most popular score for lending decisions is the FICO score. Other scores may be based on the same information as the FICO score, or they may incorporate additional information.

Nobody is 100 percent likely to make all of their payments on time. People may pay on time all the time, but no model in existence can claim that anything is 100 percent certain. Because of this, credit scores cannot rule you out as a borrower. Instead, lenders make decisions on how much risk they want to take. If they are unwilling to take much risk, they have to limit their lending. They can only accept customers who are least likely to fall behind on a payment. They accomplish this by setting an internal policy. Different lenders will set their limits at different credit scores, so it is the lender who ultimately makes a lending decision.

The Secret Mathematical Formula

Credit scores are based on mathematical formulas. A computer program looks at all of the information in your credit report, categorizes it, and spits out that three-digit number. You don't necessarily need to know the details of how the math works. If you wanted to know, it would be very difficult to find out; the mathematical models are "trade secrets," or proprietary intellectual property. The Fair Isaac Corporation does not publish its mathematical formula anywhere.

Multivariate analysis is a method that statisticians use to see how numerous inputs affect a single output. In the case of your credit, we can use the FICO credit score as an example. The FICO credit score is designed to predict how likely you are to be more than ninety days late on a payment with any creditor within the next two years. The input data include a variety of different factors, including:

- The number of credit accounts you have open
- The average age of your credit accounts
- The number of late payments in your credit history
- If you're behind on your payments, how much you owe
- If you're behind on your payments, how long you have been behind
- What percentage of your total available credit you are currently using
- Number of revolving accounts (such as credit cards) you have
- Whether you have a mortgage account

In all, your credit score might take twenty to thirty different factors into account. Depending on how you mix and match all of these moving parts, you wind up with a good or bad credit score. To complicate matters, the FICO scoring-model groups consumers into various categories for scorecards while crunching the numbers. If your eyes are beginning to glaze over at this point, remember the three-word secret to improving your score: use debt responsibly.

FICO Score Simulator

You might not be able to see exactly how your credit score is compiled, but there are some useful tools that can help you understand how your behavior will affect your credit score. At *www.myfico.com* you can use the Fair Isaac Corporation's Personalized FICO Simulator. You have to pay and sign up for this service, but it may be worth the cost if you need to perform major surgery on your credit score.

With the Personalized FICO Simulator, your actual credit history is used to run some what-if scenarios. The Simulator will show your balances, loans, and delinquencies. You can see what would happen if you take a variety of different actions. For example, you can find out what would happen if you were late on one of your bills. At the click of a button you can see what your current score is, and what your score would likely be after this action.

Does Credit Scoring Work?

Credit-scoring models are extremely complex. Even if you had the time, desire, and mathematical genius to validate the scores, you would not be allowed to. Credit-scoring models are top-secret. This may lead you to wonder if they are fair and accurate. In fact, this question has been raised frequently throughout the history of credit scoring.

Are They Discriminatory?

One of the major criticisms of credit scoring is that nobody except the scorer understands how they work. Because of this, consumer advocates worry that the scores could be discriminatory, or just plain useless. According to Craig Watts at the Fair Isaac Corporation, government regulators have taken a look under the hood of the FICO credit score. They have seen how the model works, and which factors pushed the score up or down. Regulators did not find that the models were discriminatory.

FACT

It is difficult to determine exactly how credit-scoring models do what they are supposed to do. Nevertheless, market forces have shown that credit scoring does something right. Lenders and insurers, even though they may not understand the exact process, are willing to pay for credit scores and base decisions on them.

While the models themselves may not be discriminatory, this subject continually sparks heated debate. It seems that some minorities may appear less favorable under certain scoring models. Is this because the model is discriminatory, or because historical discrimination still affects society? There are a number of studies on each side of the debate, all of which claim to provide a definitive answer. Because credit data is used in more and more places (like insurance scoring, for example), this debate is sure to continue.

Are They Accurate?

While regulators may say the models are not discriminatory, another question remains: does a credit score accurately predict whether or not a borrower is likely to fall behind on payments? To answer this, you may expect that lenders would want to look under the hood just like regulators have. They might want to see how the various inputs affect the output.

The models are top-secret, and lenders are not allowed to look at the nuts and bolts. However, they continually use credit scores as a major part in their lending decisions. Why would this be? According to the Fair Isaac Corporation, lenders use the FICO credit score because it works. They have tested and retested this score against their own internal decision-making process. They found that the score seems to work, and that's all that matters to them.

The Main Ingredients

The specifics of your FICO credit score are a closely guarded secret. Try as you might, you will not find out that a given action raises or lowers your score by a specific number of points. However, the Fair Isaac Corporation has offered some guidance for consumers. For starters, be aware that your credit score is based on five key factors (listed in order of importance):

- Payment history
- Amounts owed
- Length of credit history
- New credit
- Types of credit used

Payment History

Your payment history accounts for 35 percent of your FICO credit score. It is the most important category. It looks at how you have paid your bills in the past. If you always pay at least the minimum required payment, and you get your payments in on time, then you are doing well in this category. When you think about it, this is the most important thing to lenders. All they want you to do is pay on your accounts as agreed.

If you need to improve your credit score, you can do so by attacking this category. Make sure that you are current with all of your creditors. If you're behind on payments, write a check to get caught up. If you can't get caught up, call them up and see if you can agree on some type of payment plan.

When evaluating your payment history, the scoring models dig into the details. If you're behind on a debt, the model checks to see how long you've been delinquent. The longer it has been, the more it affects your score. If you continually pay your bills on time, any late payments will become less and less significant.

Amounts Owed

The amount of your debt accounts for 30 percent of your FICO credit score. The scoring models look to see if you are using debt, how much, and what type. In general, you want to avoid the appearance of being maxed out. Therefore, you should only use a small portion of the total available to you. Ideally, keep your credit card balances at 35 percent or less of the maximum borrowing limit.

For installment loans such as mortgages and auto loans this is not as important. The scoring models calculate the maximum borrowing limits as your original loan amount, so you will be using a high percentage of that amount in the early years of your installment loan. As time wears on and you have paid off the majority of your installment loan, you will have demonstrated that you are a responsible borrower. This can only help your score.

If you need to improve your credit score, the best thing you can do is pay down your debts. If you're using $8,000 of credit on a card with a $10,000 limit, you are using 80 percent of your available credit—that is too high. If you write a check to that credit card company and bring your balance under $3,500, your credit score should increase almost immediately.

Length of Credit History

The length of your credit history accounts for 15 percent of your FICO credit score. The scoring models look to see how long you have been using credit. If you are a seasoned credit-using veteran, you are presumably more responsible (if you're not, it will be obvious in the payment history category). You can optimize your credit by keeping old accounts open.

New Credit

New credit accounts for 10 percent of your FICO credit score. The scoring models check to see if you are opening too many new accounts. You should avoid opening several new credit card accounts within a short period of time. This type of activity makes it look like you're desperate for cash, and lenders are hesitant to lend to people in desperate situations.

You should have a healthy mix of credit types. You might shoot for two to six revolving accounts, and a few installment loans. Some lenders require a minimum number of accounts to offer a loan, and these numbers will keep you in the ballpark. Don't do anything drastic to get there, you should open and close credit accounts slowly and carefully.

The scoring models also look at recent inquiries into your credit. Only hard inquiries are used in the score—inquiries as a result of your request for credit. Again, if you have too many inquiries within a short amount of time, you appear desperate for money. Therefore, you should limit the number of lenders that pull your credit. If you are shopping for a home or auto loan, the models will not penalize you as long as you keep all of your inquiries within a few weeks of each other.

Types of Credit Used

The types of credit you use account for 10 percent of your FICO credit score. The scoring models are looking to see if you use different types of loans. You should have a mixture of revolving debt, mortgage debt, and installment loans. While it may not hurt you if you don't have a mortgage on your credit report, having one will most likely help your score.

Your FICO credit score only uses information that is found in your credit reports. In fact, there is information on your reports that is ignored by the FICO scoring models. Your lenders may use some information in addition to your credit score. That information—such as your income or number of years at your job—might help you or hurt you.

"Thin" Files

If you have a "thin" credit history, it means that there is not much information about you on file at the major credit-reporting companies. This may be because you have not used credit much in the past—perhaps you are young, recently divorced from a spouse who used credit, or new to the United States. When you have a thin file, every move you make has more impact on your credit scores. Upward and downward swings will be more dramatic.

Average Credit Statistics

With all of this talk about credit scores, you're probably eager to look at some numbers. What is the average credit score? What does the average person's credit report look like? With this information, you can see where you fit in with other consumers.

What's the Score?

The Fair Isaac Corporation publishes information on the national distribution of FICO credit scores. In the United States, here is where consumers fall:

FICO Scores of U.S. Consumers	
FICO Score	**Percent of Population**
800+	13 percent
750–799	27 percent
700–749	18 percent
650–699	15 percent
600–649	12 percent
550–599	8 percent
500–549	5 percent
499 or less	2 percent

As you can see, 58 percent of the U.S. population has a FICO score above 700. This shows that a healthy portion of the population has a pretty good credit score. An additional 15 percent have a score above 650. Therefore, roughly three out of four consumers qualify for a standard loan rate or better.

FACT

In 2006, the median FICO credit score in the United States was 723. This means that half of the people had scores below that number, and half of the people had scores above that number. This number is considered a pretty good FICO score, so most people are doing a good job with their credit.

As you make improvements on your credit, it is important that you understand how you stack up. According to the Fair Isaac Corporation, credit scores rank you relative to other consumers. In other words, a relatively high score means that you are less likely to fall behind than somebody with a relatively low score. How did they decide what to measure? Why did they try to determine how likely you are to be ninety days late within the next two years? They researched what lenders wanted.

Chapter 7
Costs of Bad Credit

Along with the pride of having good credit, there are some valuable financial rewards as well. Any time you get a loan, your lender will look at your credit to determine what type of risk you are. If you are a low-risk borrower, you'll get a better loan. What exactly does it mean to get a better loan? It means that you'll pay a lower interest rate, which means that you'll save a lot of money you can use elsewhere.

Risk-Based Lending

Lenders often use risk-based lending when making lending decisions. Risk-based lending is a policy that helps institutions determine the borrower's interest rate. If a borrower is seen as a higher risk, then the bank will charge a higher interest rate on the loan. Of course, if the borrower is a low-risk borrower, then she can enjoy one of the best interest rates available. Often, lenders assign a letter grade to each borrower. As in school, an A is best, and D is often the worst.

How do you get the best grade? By having a good credit score, of course. Those with higher credit scores are the A borrowers, and those with lower credit scores are the D borrowers. Keep in mind, as your credit improves, your grade will also improve.

About the System

Risk-based lending gives institutions the ability to serve a wider population. In the past, lenders might have avoided customers with any blemishes in their credit history, and they might only have had one interest rate for each type of loan. If an applicant with bad credit tried to get a loan, the lender would probably respond, "Sorry, we can't offer you a loan." The result was that these customers had to resort to finding loans in other places; typically they fell victim to predatory-lending practices. Finance companies, title loan programs, and rent-to-own stores were some of the only alternatives available to this population.

Nowadays, these folks can get a loan at a more reputable institution. Of course, the institution is entitled to be compensated for taking more risk with a borrower who has bad credit. How do they get compensated for this? They earn a higher interest rate on the money they're lending.

In addition to helping people who don't have good credit, risk-based lending helps people who do have good credit. Borrowers with a clean history enjoy low rates. They don't have to pay more to cover the losses on bad borrowers. The system gives borrowers the rate they deserve.

These programs are especially helpful for people who need to build credit, and for people who need to rebuild credit—they either have no credit history, or they have a bad credit history. For them, it is really difficult to get a loan. Risk-based lending may be the only option for them to find financing.

More Than the Score

Ultimately, getting a loan is about more than just your credit score. Lenders who use risk-based lending place a lot of weight on your score. However, they look at other factors, too. For example, they want to make sure that your income is sufficient to cover any debt payments that you're about to take on. Likewise, they will consider whether or not the debt is secured (such as an auto that can be repossessed, or a home that can be foreclosed on). Finally, they want to make sure that you can put some money down. If you don't make any down payment, or if the loan-to-value ratio is too high, they will be more reluctant to make a loan

If you want to calculate payments and fiddle with the numbers, you can use a spreadsheet program like Microsoft Excel. By using the PMT function, you can see how an installment-loan payment will change as you change the ingredients. Try increasing the interest rate to see how a hypothetical loan would change.

How Payments Are Calculated

Do you know how your monthly payment is calculated? There are only a few ingredients. To solve for monthly payment, you need to know the interest rate, the time period, and the loan amount. You can mix and match these ingredients to change how much the monthly payment will be. For example, if you increase the amount of the loan, it's pretty obvious that, all other things being equal, the monthly payment will go up, too. Likewise, if you stretch out the number of months over which you'll make payments on the loan, the monthly payment should decrease.

Do you know what happens if the interest rate goes up? That's right, the monthly payment increases. What do you get for this higher monthly payment? Not much. The lender earns extra income to compensate them for taking a risk on you. However, you don't get anything extra. You're buying the exact same auto, home, or other product, you just have to pay extra for it.

Buying a Car

When you're buying a car, your credit history can determine what you drive. What is the most important factor for a car buyer? Often, it's the monthly payment. While there are a lot of ways to fiddle with the payment, at some point you run out of tricks. If a car payment is just too high, then you have to find something else.

Running the Numbers

To see how your credit affects your finances, consider a sample auto loan. You'll see that modest differences in a credit score can save you a bundle. Assume you're buying a new car and you want to borrow $25,000 over 5 years. Next, assume your FICO credit score is 650. Whether you get a standard loan or a sub-prime loan depends on which side of 650 your score is on (give or take a few percent, depending on who you ask).

MyFICO.com has a useful calculator that will help you figure out how this loan would look. Based on national averages in the summer of 2006, you'd get the following loan:

- Your loan's APR would be 11.12 percent
- Your monthly payment would be $545
- The total interest you would pay over the life of the loan is $7,703

Now, consider an improvement of 100 points in your credit score. While a 100 point change is significant, it's not that difficult to have that point change. An account sent to collection could easily cost you 100 points. You can easily have medical bills that end up in collection because there is confusion about your insurance coverage, for example. Most importantly, an error on your credit report could cost you 100 points.

If you can get your credit score to 750, your loan would look like this:

- Your loan's APR would be 7.045 percent
- Your monthly payment would be $496
- The total interest you would pay over the life of the loan is $4,734

This is a significant difference. You save about $50 a month, and you save $3,000 over the life of your loan—that's $600 per year. Consider all of the things you could do with that money. Keep this figure in the back of your mind as you look at the other results in this chapter. For a used car, the difference is even greater, by about $10.

The Human Factor

While your credit scores are extremely important, you may have a human helping you get an auto loan. Perhaps a loan officer at your bank or credit union is working with you to finance a vehicle. If you don't have an excellent credit score, then other aspects of your credit may be important. Sitting face to face with the lender, you can plead your case, but you'll need to have something to back it up. Hopefully, you can show that you've got a good work history, a disciplined monthly savings habit, or some other reason that you're a better risk than your credit score indicates.

ALERT!

If your credit score is too low, you might not be able to get the car loan. Some lenders have a cutoff point (599 for example) below which they won't make any loan. They're not interested in charging you a higher interest rate, they're just too scared that you'll default on the loan.

Buying a Home

Buying a home is a major milestone in most peoples' lives. You finally get to paint the rooms a color you can live with, and you can benefit if the home increases in value. Whether you live comfortably or in cramped quarters depends on your credit. As with an auto loan, your lenders can figure out the maximum they'll give you based on your credit.

Imagine that you are making the biggest purchase of your life. You're talking with a mortgage lender, who is working on getting you the best rate possible. After going through your credit, it turns out that you have a credit score of 650. Next, imagine that you are hoping to borrow $250,000 for your new home, and you want to use a 30-year fixed mortgage. Based on these numbers, the mortgage lender would come back to you with the following loan:

- Your mortgage's APR would be 8.376 percent
- Your monthly mortgage payment would be $1,900
- The total interest you would pay over the life of the loan is $434,129

Once again, consider a 100-point improvement in your credit score. Your dream home will get even better! If you have a score of 750, your loan improves:

- Your mortgage's APR would be 6.564 percent
- Your monthly mortgage payment would be $1,591
- The total interest you would pay over the life of the loan is $322,655

Now you're getting into some serious numbers. An extra $400 per month could come in handy. On a similar 15-year mortgage, you would save about $100 per month. Again, this is money you could put to better use elsewhere.

If your credit score is too low, you might not have the full range of loan options available to you. Below 620 or so, lenders might decide that they are unwilling to give you certain types of loans, 15-year fixed-rate mortgages and 7/1 ARMs, for example.

You'll also find that having good credit gives you more options. For example, your ratios might not have allowed you to get into a loan with a $1,900 monthly payment. Depending on your income and your other monthly payments, the lender might determine that you're taking on too much debt. In that case, your credit would have priced you out of the market. You would have to settle for a smaller loan, which means you may not get the house you really want. You can also look at this from the opposite direction: if you can afford the $1,900 payment with a credit score of 650, then you can afford an even bigger loan with a credit score of 750. Having good credit means you have more flexibility.

Costly Credit Cards

Having good credit makes any type of borrowing less expensive. Credit cards are no exception. You'll get better offers and pay lower rates with a stronger credit history.

Fixed credit card rates may be 10 percent or 20 percent or more, depending on your score. It doesn't take a mathematician to see that your rates may double if you've got bad credit. Assume you've got a credit card balance of $10,000. Of course, you need to pay this off. It will be a lot easier if you've got that 10-percent rate. For this example, assume that you want to pay the debt off within two years. At the 10-percent interest rate, you would have to pay $461 per month to eliminate that debt. In that case, you would pay total interest costs of $1,075.93. What if you have that 20-percent interest rate? It would take $509 per month and you would pay $2,214.83 in total interest.

ALERT!

Compound interest is your friend when you're saving, but it's your foe when you borrow. Your revolving loans probably add interest due to your loan balance. Then, they charge you more interest on the interest they just charged you. A higher interest rate will make it harder to pay off those balances.

In the example above, you're paying an extra $40 per month. Can you think of anything you'd rather spend $40 on each month? If that number sounds small, consider that you would pay an extra $1,100 or so to pay off the exact same loan. That's $550 each year that you could have put to better use.

When you have bad credit, you don't even get the best offers out there. If you have a debt that you are looking to pay off, sometimes it makes sense to transfer the balance in order to save a few dollars on interest. With a good credit history, your mailbox is constantly full of credit offers. Typically, they offer teaser rates, like 0-percent interest rate for the next year. If you put your $10,000 debt on a 0-percent credit card, you can save a lot on interest payments. However, if your credit has some blemishes, you won't get these same offers. Don't worry, the creditors will not ignore you. Instead, they'll fill your mailbox with offers that are not as attractive.

Insurance Rates

As you may know, your credit is used for purposes other than setting up loans. Bad credit can really cost you a bundle when it comes to insurance. Insurers use your credit information to set your rates. Typically, they use an insurance score developed by ChoicePoint, Fair Isaac, or in-house developers.

Different insurers use your credit in different ways. Some of them don't even use credit information when they look at your policy. However, those that do want to see a good credit history. If you've got good credit, you can expect to get attractive discounts from these companies. A Michigan study in 2002 found that an average discount for consumers with the best insurance scores was about 35 percent. Would you like to save 35 percent on your auto insurance and homeowner's insurance premiums?

Remember that your insurance score is different from your credit score. They are based on information in your credit reports, and they may have a few pieces of additional information. The factors that make up good credit (paying on time, avoiding bankruptcy, etc.) will also lead to a good insurance score, so you should just strive to have good credit.

Other studies, and anecdotal evidence, show that bad credit can yield even more dramatic results. In recent years, news reports have told disturbing stories about consumers who suffered due to their bad credit. In some cases, premiums increased tenfold for a simple automobile policy. In other cases, an individual was unable to renew their insurance at all. Imagine going without auto insurance, even if it was only temporary. You might be unable to commute to work, which would create additional financial hardships. If you did drive to work, you'd be taking a huge financial risk: an accident could cost tens or hundreds of thousands of dollars.

In 2003, the Texas Department of Insurance issued a report that showed, among other things, how credit information affects rates in the area. They found that consumers with the worst credit history pay anywhere from 19 percent to 113 percent more than consumers with the best credit history. Individual credit scores were not part of the report, but you can see how good credit in general will help you save money. A few missed payments can do the damage that will change your insurance rates.

Opportunity Costs

By now, you've seen several examples of how bad credit can cost you money. Likewise, it's obvious that good credit will save you money. However, there's more to the story. A higher mortgage payment does not exist in a vacuum. It will affect your entire financial situation. Therefore, you are paying opportunity costs in addition to the more obvious costs.

The Golden Years

First off, consider how higher monthly expenses might affect your ability to save. If you remember previous examples (the car payment and mortgage examples), you know that it's easy to spend an extra $450 per month because of bad credit. Those extra dollars don't really buy you anything. Instead, they're paying for interest that you don't need to pay. What if you saved that money for your retirement instead?

Consider this simplified example. If you saved $450 per month and earned a 9-percent rate of return, you might have saved about $276,000 after twenty years. That's not money you kissed goodbye and gave to your lender, it's money that you can use for whatever you want. You can use it as part of your retirement paycheck, or you can use it to buy yourself something nice.

Keeping or building good credit should be a part of your overall financial plan. Having bad credit will take dollars away from important goals that cost money. Don't think of your credit as separate from everything else—it's an important piece of the puzzle.

So many people don't save anything for retirement, simply because they don't have any money left over at the end of the month to save. This problem can be avoided, in part, by building and keeping good credit. Once your credit goes downhill, it can be hard to do other important things.

A Vicious Cycle

Having less-than-perfect credit can build on itself in a variety of ways. Consider how potential employers look at your credit. They might not want to hire you unless you have great credit. Why might you have less-than-perfect credit? It could be because you need more money. If you could get a better job, then you might have more money. However, it's hard to get that better job with blemishes in your credit reports. Getting yourself out of the hole can be hard work.

Less Leverage

In general, having good credit makes it easier to borrow. You can borrow more, or you can borrow at a more attractive rate. One of the most important things that people borrow for is their home. They use a great deal of leverage to purchase a house. While leverage is extremely risky in some areas (like speculating in the stock market or on investment properties), almost anybody will tell you that it's okay to borrow 80 percent or more for your primary home purchase.

Part of the reason that homes build wealth for people is the leverage involved. You can start with just a little bit of money and end up with a lot of equity over the years. Of course, you need to be able to get that big loan. If you have questionable credit, you have less opportunity. You might be forced to buy a less-expensive home, perhaps in an area that won't appreciate as much as other areas. Even though you might have the same down payment as a buyer with good credit, you can't get into the same house.

Less Coverage

Another negative of having bad credit is that it's harder to get the insurance coverage you need. You leave yourself with too much risk. Consider the risks of having your home uninsured, even for a brief period of time. This could happen if your insurance company decided not to renew your policy, or if the rates were so high that you had to find something else. You could be risking thousands of dollars or more during this time.

Less Fun

Finally, having bad credit could take a toll on your mental health. You won't have as much money in your budget for the finer things in life—vacations, entertainment, and life's little luxuries. If nothing else will motivate you, imagine a serene scene on a pristine beach. It is easier to get there if you have a few extra dollars each month. Not only will you be able to splurge now and then, you'll also avoid unpleasant situations. You won't have to spend as much time hunting for decent loans and insurance products, and you won't have to work a second or third job to make ends meet.

Crunch Your Own

Understanding the costs of bad credit can be a great incentive to manage your credit wisely. When you see the numbers in dollars and cents, your credit becomes more concrete. You can look at a change in your credit score next to your monthly budget, and see just how important good credit is.

To help you crunch the numbers, the Fair Isaac Corporation has a Loan Savings Calculator on their consumer Web site (*www.myfico.com*). The Loan Savings Calculator allows you to see what various loans would look like depending on your credit score. The samples used in this chapter may not be the exact same loans that you might use. You might use larger or smaller loans, and you can get a more specific idea of how much bad credit might cost you if you run the calculator using your own numbers.

In addition to using more personalized numbers, you can use the Loan Savings Calculator to see how your loan payments might change in your particular state. The examples used in this chapter were based on national averages, and the calculator makes some assumptions that you may want to look at. Especially at the lower end of the FICO score range, your monthly payment can vary depending on the state you live in. Finally, you can use this calculator as a decision-making tool. If you are familiar with your credit score, you can run some what-if scenarios with different loan types. Based on your credit, your budget, and your goals, you can take the loan type that will work best for you.

Chapter 8

There's Nothing Wrong with Borrowing

There is some wisdom to Shakespeare's admonition, "neither a borrower nor a lender be." Even today, some people believe that you should not borrow money for anything. However, many of the finer things, and plenty of necessities, cost a lot of money. To achieve some goals, you have to borrow, but you might as well do it wisely. This section highlights some of the times when it might be appropriate to borrow, and ways to protect your credit while you do so.

A Home of One's Own

One of the best reasons to borrow money is to purchase a home. Houses are extremely expensive, but the benefits of owning a home are great. In the first quarter of 2006, the median sales price for a single family home was $217,900 (National Association of REALTORS, Metropolitan areas). Do you have $217,900 sitting around for a home purchase? Depending on where you live, $217,900 might buy a castle, or it might get you a small condo.

Help from Uncle Sam

Homeownership is a national priority because of the benefits to society. In addition to helping individuals build equity that they can use later on, communities grow and improve thanks to homeownership. If you own a house, you have a vested interest in keeping it nice, and you'll be more engaged in the surrounding community. You'll want it to be a safe community with commerce and culture. This helps the economy and your neighbors (who are also helping you), and you stand to make a few dollars over the years.

QUESTION?

How does a tax deduction help me save money?
A tax deduction allows you to reduce the amount of income that you have to pay taxes on. If you get a tax deduction, you subtract the deduction from the income you report to the IRS. You take your tax deductions when you file your taxes each year.

To make it possible for more people to own their own homes, the United States government has a few programs. The Department of Housing and Urban Development (HUD) is just one resource that helps increase homeownership. In addition, government agencies like Freddie Mac and Fannie Mae help add liquidity, and some studies suggest that these agencies result in lower borrowing costs for homeowners. Next, you get a tax break for owning a home. The interest you pay on your mortgage, as well as on some home-equity loans, may be tax deductible. In essence, the government helps to subsidize your interest costs, especially in the early years of a loan.

Bridging the Gap

In order to enjoy the benefits listed above, you pretty much have to borrow. Unless you are born with a huge trust fund that provides for all of your needs, a mortgage may be the only way you'll ever own a home. If it makes you feel any better, mortgages are actually considered good debt. They are a type of installment loan, so they are viewed favorably by lenders. While you should have a mix of different loan types for optimal credit, installment loans, and especially mortgage loans, are good to have. Because they require so much structure (a minimum dollar amount must be paid every period), they show lenders that you are responsible and dependable.

Why do some people *not* own homes? HUD published a study in 2002 called "Barriers to Minority Homeownership." The study found that (among other things beyond the scope of this book), people did not own homes because:

1. They had not built credit, or they had bad credit
2. If they had bad credit, they were rejected or offered very expensive loans

If you have to borrow, at least do a good job of it. Elsewhere in this book you can read about special topics for first-time homebuyers. In this section, you'll find some very basic information that you'll need when you go shopping for a mortgage loan.

Getting a Good Loan

Most experts suggest that you get preapproved before you go househunting. By getting preapproved, you are in a position to pull the trigger and actually buy a place if you find the one you want. How do you get preapproved? Ask a lender. They will gladly review your background and find an amount. Keep in mind that you should not borrow too much—when you get preapproved you might see some big numbers. You do not need to borrow every penny that they will lend you. Think of their numbers as a maximum.

How do lenders decide how much money to offer you? They use a variety of methods, but one important factor is your debt-to-income ratio. The debt-to-income ratio looks at how much income you have per month, and how much your monthly debt payments are. Lenders want to make sure that your income will support the payments you are signing up for. To do this, they might require a 28/36 ratio. The first number, 28 percent, means that they want no more than 28 percent of your gross income per month to go toward your housing payments. Housing costs are typically defined as principal, interest, taxes, and insurance (PITI). The second number, 36 percent, tells you that they only allow up to 36 percent of your gross income to go toward all debt payments—PITI, as well as your other debt payments like credit cards and car payments.

Adjustable or Fixed?

When you borrow money, you have many choices to make. One of them is whether to use a fixed-rate mortgage or an adjustable-rate mortgage. The choice you make can save or cost you thousands.

A fixed-rate mortgage has a fixed percentage rate throughout the life of the loan. An adjustable rate has a rate that changes. Which is better? It depends on a variety of factors. With a fixed-rate mortgage, you know what your payment will be every month and you can budget for it, and you know that your payment will never change. You can keep making the same payment for fifteen years, thirty years, or until you sell the house.

There are only a few factors that determine how much house you can buy. The interest rate, the length of the loan (in years), and the monthly payment are enough to figure a loan amount. Once lenders figure out the maximum payment, they can determine a maximum loan amount. The interest rate is influenced by your credit.

However, it might be a bad thing that your mortgage payment never changes. If you got into your mortgage when interest rates were relatively high, you'll be paying more interest over the life of your loan. In addition, your monthly payments may be greater than they would be if you had a lower interest rate. With an adjustable-rate mortgage, your interest rate changes with interest rates in general. When they go up, the mortgage's rate goes up. When they go down, the rate follows.

What about Points?

A final consideration on wise borrowing for your home relates to points. Should you pay points? As with most things in life, the answer is frustrating: it depends. Points (discount points, to be specific) are payments you make in order to lower the interest rate on your mortgage loan.

By paying a little bit more up-front, you can lower the rate and your monthly payments. A lower rate means that you'll spend less on total interest over time. So, having a good idea of how long you'll keep the house is essential to determining whether or not to pay points. In general, the longer you'll be in the house, the more likely it is that you should pay points. Yes, it might hurt a little more up-front, but it can save money over long periods of time. To figure out exactly how long, ask your lender. If you're mathematically inclined, you can even calculate the break-even point yourself.

Home Equity and Investments

Once you own a home for a while, you build more and more equity. Of course, this means that more and more of the home's total value is yours to keep—it does not belong to the bank anymore. One of the ways you can borrow throughout your lifetime is to use your home's equity as collateral. As with all loans, this can be a wise move, or a surefire way to damage your credit.

Big Loans, Little Rates

Home-equity loans are often used for large loans. Why? Your home is likely one of the most valuable assets you own. Furthermore, you may have much of your net worth tied up in your home's equity. After years of making mortgage payments, and enjoying some price appreciation if you are lucky, you may end up with a huge resource.

Because you have good equity in your home, you can take big loans off it. To sweeten the deal, your interest rate is likely to be lower than other interest rates you might find in the marketplace. For example, if you have the choice of borrowing on a home-equity loan versus a credit card, the home-equity loan should have a lower rate. Lenders offer you a slightly better rate because the loan is secured by your house. If you don't pay it back, you might lose your house. Lenders figure that you will make repayment on a home-equity loan a priority above other unsecured loans if you fall on hard times.

Banks do not like foreclosure—when they take your house—any more than you do. They're in the business of lending money, not selling houses. It costs them money and resources to do a foreclosure. Therefore, you can often work something out with them if you are proactive and sincere about saving your home.

Smart Home-Equity Loans

You can use a home-equity loan for a lot of different things, but if you want to improve and protect your personal financial situation, you should probably limit yourself to a few areas. In general, a home-equity loan might be a good idea if you will use the loan proceeds for some kind of investment.

One example of an investment you might make is an investment in your home. If you want to spruce the place up and make some improvements, a home-equity loan seems reasonable. You borrow money from the house, but you increase the value of the house with the loan proceeds. If done right, you can more than repay the loan when you sell. Common examples of home improvements might be:

- Adding or updating a bathroom
- Remodeling the kitchen
- Adding rooms or levels to the home
- Purchasing a second home or investment property

Another use for your home-equity loan might be an investment in your child's education. Borrowing for education is discussed later in this chapter.

Investment in the Future

When you are building up home equity, you are giving yourself more options in the future. You will have a large pool of resources that you can draw upon if the need ever arises. As you grow older, you may find that you want to just take that money back out and live off it. This is possible with the use of a reverse mortgage. Instead of making payments that build equity, you receive payments that reduce equity. You are borrowing back your own money.

Reverse mortgages are complex, and you should spend a lot of time researching how they work before you even think of pulling the trigger. However, they are worth the research for many. They offer a way to get income if there are no other options, and they have some built-in features that allow for flexibility and limit your family's risk. A reverse mortgage will never be a possibility if you don't take the steps to own a home and build equity.

Home-Equity Tax Breaks

When you borrow against your home, you may be able to take a tax deduction on the interest you pay for the loan. This lowers the effective cost of the loan: you pay interest, but you get a break on your taxes later. Keep in mind that there are limits to how the tax deduction is applied. You might want to have your tax advisor calculate the deduction, or you can view the details in IRS Publication 936.

ALERT!

You can lower your total costs of borrowing by deducting the interest you pay on a home-equity loan. However, the deduction is not unlimited, and there are restrictions that apply to the source of equity and the use of funds. Before you claim a deduction, be sure you are entitled to it.

Home-Equity Loan Pitfalls

Home-equity loans can be very tempting: big loan, small rate, and potential for a tax break. Nevertheless, you need to proceed with extreme caution. The main risk is that you put your home on the line. If you cannot repay the loan as agreed, your home is the collateral that banks will seize. Before taking that risk, decide whether it is worth it to you.

Plenty of people use home-equity loans for debt consolidation. While this certainly works, they sometimes put themselves in a worse situation. Home-equity loans should only be used for debt consolidation when you have a formal plan for debt reduction, and the ability to execute it.

Finally, be on the lookout for scam artists. Home-equity loans have been a notorious area of abuse in the past. When you have a large-ticket loan, unscrupulous people get tempted to take advantage of a situation. In fact, predatory lenders target people with bad credit because they figure that people with bad credit are less sophisticated. In general, they tend to fleece people into agreements they don't understand, they charge high fees or unnecessary fees, and they find ways to repeat the charges over and over. If you have any doubts about a lender, ask your friends, family, and acquaintances you trust.

Emergencies Happen!

Sometimes life throws you an expensive curveball. When it happens, you end up reacting to the circumstances, and you do the best you can. When emergencies pop up, you may need to borrow some money. Here are a few ways that you can improve your chances of coming out of the emergency with decent credit.

The word *emergency* here is relative. It could be that your home was damaged in a storm, it could be an automobile accident, or perhaps you have to travel to the funeral of a loved one. In any case, it will take some money to get through the emergency.

An Ounce of Prevention

The only thing you can be certain of is the fact that you'll be surprised someday. With that in mind, it pays to be prepared for emergencies. Keep an emergency fund of three to nine months' expenses saved in a safe place that pays some interest. When emergencies happen, you'll know why you made an emergency fund. Granted, successive emergencies—or one really big one—will wipe out your fund and then some, but a savings buffer can lessen the blow of most emergencies.

Unforeseen emergencies are probably the biggest threat to your credit. Borrowing to pay for them is fine, but be vigilant. Because you're reading this book, you are probably motivated to manage your spending. However, health issues and accidents are major causes of bankruptcy. Be sure you have adequate insurance coverage to help manage the risks of everyday life.

Another way to keep the cost of emergencies at a minimum is to shift the risk. As discussed elsewhere in this book, you can insure a lot of different things: your house, your life (or your family), your income, and more. Some emergencies can be insured against. It does not make them any easier emotionally, but you'll get some financial help when you need it most. Check over your coverage to see what you are, and what you are not, covered for. One of the best things you can do is to know and understand your coverage and all of the risks out there. Then, you can decide the extent to which you cover the risks.

Communicate

Emergencies can be overwhelming. You may be upset about things, have large expenses, and be unsure how things work. If you find yourself in such a situation, talk with any lenders and let them know what's going on. People in the financial world are actually human beings, and they may be able to work with you, by allowing missed payments, offering higher credit limits, and so on. It is always better to communicate with your lenders than to surprise them.

Business Built on Borrowing

Borrowing makes the most sense when you are making a good investment. Often, an investment can only be judged as good or bad with hindsight. Nevertheless, you can find ways to choose your risks and improve your chances. When borrowing for your business, you will know better than anybody how much risk you are taking.

Business or Pleasure?

Business loans help small-business owners get things done. You can buy materials, pay employees, and much more. Without a loan, you often can't get your product or service out to paying customers. If you need a business loan, what do you do? The first idea is typically to ask a bank for a loan. While it makes sense intuitively, you should also consider the bank's perspective. For them, you could be a brand new business with no (or very little) operating history, no employees, and no clients.

There are a variety of funding sources for small-business owners. You should start by looking at the Small Business Administration (*www.sba .gov*). There, you can find out what options are available and how to improve your chances of winning a loan. They also have special programs that might help you get a loan.

Most banks are very conservative. They have an extreme fear of losing money. If your business is too small, it might be too risky. A solution, in the bank's opinion, might be to make you personally liable for the loan. Because the business may not have assets to pledge, history, or revenue, the bank can't expect much from the business. You, as an individual, might be more likely to pay. Therefore, don't be surprised if the bank asks you to be personally liable for the loan.

Many small-business owners (and potential small-business owners) find themselves asked to lay their personal credit on the line. Once you become personally liable for a loan, everything changes. The lenders know they can come after you for repayment, even if your business goes belly-up. They have insight into your past payment behavior through your credit history. Furthermore, they know that the threat of messing up your credit will encourage you to repay the loan no matter how your business does.

Signing on personally might be your only option. If you have exhausted every resource available, you might have to decide between a loan or no loan. If you must sign on personally, consider the risks you take for yourself and your family. Granted, running a business is always risky to some extent, but your credit score does not distinguish between money you squandered and money from a business venture that didn't work out. You have to pay it back if you are personally on the loan.

A Credit Card and a Dream

Some businesses take off and are wildly successful. Occasionally, you hear of somebody who started out by maxing out credit cards and not really knowing what they were doing. While this is possible, it is risky. If you are up for the risk, that's fine, but there are less risky ways to raise money.

One way to get money is to sell a portion of your business. This is technically not borrowing, since the buyer gets an ownership interest, but it does place the risk in the buyer's hands. If the business goes under, you don't have to pay the money back.

This type of arrangement has its pluses and minuses. The main drawback is that you give up some ownership if the thing takes off, and you might even have to follow some rules set by the buyer. To find this type of arrangement, look for angel investors or venture capitalists. They might look at a business that the banks won't touch, but they want something in return. Note that it is quite difficult to find this kind of funding. You'll need to do a lot of legwork, preparation, documentation, and you'll need to sell your concept.

Another way to manage risk as a small-business owner is to use a franchise. If you don't have your heart set on starting things from scratch, you could find a franchise that you're interested in. The reason franchises reduce risk is that the selling company has already taken a lot of the risk. They figure out how to do things, how to market, which markets are good, and more. Success rates for franchises are somewhere above 80 percent. Contrast that with non-franchise businesses, where the failure rate is closer to 80 percent.

Most people think of food and restaurants when they hear about franchises. While there are plenty of big-name restaurants that use a franchise model, you can get into other lines of business as well. All you are doing is buying a business model from somebody. That model can be for hamburgers, handyman services, sandwiches, or staffing.

Education Ain't Cheap

College offers a lot, and costs a lot. When people go to college, they typically have new experiences that help them grow. They also learn about themselves, the topics they study, and the ways of the world. Furthermore, college graduates tend to earn more than those without a degree. All things considered, college can be an investment worth borrowing for.

What's It Worth?

If you want to talk numbers, there is no doubt that a college degree is worth the cost. According to the United States Census Bureau, those with college degrees have earnings that almost double those of non-degreed people. A 2005 press release stated that college-educated citizens over the age of eighteen earned an average of $51,206 per year. Meanwhile, those with a high school diploma earned an average of $27,915. Over a lifetime, college can really pay off.

There are also benefits that don't come in your paycheck. Alisa Cunningham, Director of Research for the Institute for Higher Education Policy in Washington, D.C., authored an informative paper on some of the softer benefits of higher education. Complete with charts and citations to the data, she shows how college graduates impact the world around them. They are more likely to:

- Have better health
- Vote in elections
- Volunteer in the community
- Read to their children at an early age
- Use critical thinking skills

Certainly, there are plenty of individuals without a college degree in society who have the same attributes listed above. Furthermore, you can probably think of more than one college graduate who does not display any of those qualities. However, when looking at large numbers you will see unmistakable trends.

How to Pay

So, if college is a priority, how can you pay for it? Prices for a college education are going up faster than general costs in the United States. That means the younger a future scholar is, the more it'll cost. The ideal solution is to have somebody pay the costs for you. It may be hard to get grants and scholarships that will offer a full ride, but you can do it, even if your child isn't the best student in their class or the best athlete in the world. Boutique college-planning practices are increasingly helping people find ways to get assistance from colleges, foundations, and the government (in the form of tax incentives). There are a lot of shady operators out there, but a good college planner is worth her weight in gold.

If you can't get somebody else to pay, you might have to borrow the money. There are many loan choices out there, so get some help from an advisor. Your financial aid office will have resources to help you understand what is available to you. In general, you should start by looking at government loan programs. These programs might allow you to borrow without accumulating any interest while you are in school. Of course, you will have to pay them back later, but you can get favorable terms on your student loans. In addition, these are installment loans, which will affect your credit (and your pocketbook) more favorably than if you used credit cards to fund your education.

Investing to Invest

If you have enough time before the bills are due, you could consider investing some money to help cover your investment in education. Because college costs go up so fast, it's a good idea to get started as soon as possible, like when you have a newborn child. There are a variety of options out there for college savings, including an ordinary savings account. The newest option is the 529 College Savings Plan, which is more flexible than most other education savings vehicles. To learn more about paying for college, you might try the College Board's Web site (*www.collegeboard.com*).

FACT

The majority of financial aid comes in the form of loans. This means that you can expect to have loans if you or somebody in your family is going to college. Use them wisely, because they can affect your credit later in life, and they might be with you for a very long time.

Good Credit Makes It Better

There are times in life when you need to borrow. Accomplishing your goals sometimes costs money. If it's more money than you have, you can still get there with a lender's help. Of course, it will cost you in terms of interest paid over the life of your loan, but you can come out ahead.

Having good credit makes everything work better for you. Imagine it like a snowball effect: if your credit starts rolling downhill, it will gather momentum and become a less pleasant ride. You could have an expensive mortgage, which means you cannot afford a newer, reliable car. If the car breaks down, it costs money to fix. Because you maxed out your credit cards, you can't make the payment on it. You can imagine the rest of the scenario.

If you have good credit while you are taking out major loans, you have a better chance of paying off the loan with your credit intact. Your interest costs will be lower, so you won't have to take money away from other resources. Likewise, you will have the flexibility to move around and choose among lenders. They will compete to do business with you, so if they're not treating you right, you can just leave.

Chapter 9

Good Credit Behavior

Managing your credit is an ongoing process. If there are errors or blemishes, of course you need to fix those. However, you can't just fix it and forget it. You have to continually follow good habits that will keep your credit in tip-top shape. This section highlights some of the most important behaviors that should become second nature to you.

Pay on Time

The single most important thing you can do to maintain or improve your credit is pay on time. If you're not on time, lenders assume that you're having problems that could lead to a default. The longer you pay on time, the better your credit will get.

Keep in mind that the goal of credit-scoring models is to predict whether or not you are likely to pay more than ninety days late. Why so much emphasis on a late payment? It's an indicator of much more serious financial trouble and potential loss to creditors. There is an easy way and a hard way to determine if somebody will pay ninety days late. The hard way: create a complex formula that runs through their credit files and spits out a likelihood of late payments. The easy way: the person lets you know by paying ninety days late.

Paying on Time Pays Dividends

Making timely payments will help your credit. According to Fair Isaac, approximately 35 percent of your FICO credit score is based on your payment history. If you can keep up with payments and avoid any delinquency items, you're helping a substantial portion of your score. Credit-scoring models look to see how many past-due items are on your report, how long since they've been reported, and how significant the dollar amounts are. If you never make a late payment, you won't have these items weighing down your score.

If you must pay late, try to get the payment in within thirty days of the due date. If you can manage this, your lenders may not report your late payment to the credit-reporting companies. If this is not possible, see if you can beat the sixty-day deadline.

Likewise, if you've got a clean payment history, it's easier to catch a break when you get into a jam. Suppose you're on vacation or you change bank accounts. The confusion could cause you to make a late payment. With a history of consistent on-time payments, this mistake won't be devastating. Your credit history will show that you've been responsible before, and you're likely to be responsible in the future.

How to Pay on Time

As with most aspects of managing your credit, you have to work a little to make sure you get your payments in on time. The easiest way to get the work done is to automate it.

Online bill-pay services can do a lot of work for you, so that you're less likely to make late payments. In their most basic form, they allow you to get your bills paid with a few mouse clicks. After that, you're done; the bill-pay service prints and mails a check. You can even schedule the payment to go out in a few weeks so that you pace yourself, or wait until you know you'll have sufficient funds in your checking account.

Keep in mind, you should always schedule your payment to arrive a week or so before the payment due date. Because you're not using your lender's preprinted envelopes and forms, they may process your payments manually, which can take more time. If you have any doubts, send a test check or call your lender to see if they'll process the payments for you.

If you want to really automate things, you can set up a system that simply pulls money from your bank account without you having to do anything. Some lenders call this an online bill pay or easy-pay system. You simply provide them with a voided check (or just your bank account number and routing information), and they get the money from your account when it's due. Of course, you have to be careful to keep sufficient funds in your bank account, and inform your lenders when you change banks.

Keep Long-Term Relationships

Some surprises are great, but your creditors, potential employers, and insurance companies probably want to minimize surprises. They like to have contracts that explain what should happen, and when. By having a history of long-term relationships, you demonstrate predictability and consistency. If you've been consistently good, then your credit will be good.

We've Done Business Together Forever

In some ways, your credit is just a bunch of lenders telling each other about their experiences with you. Your job is to have a good reputation among these lenders. One of the best ways to do this is to have a successful long-term relationship on file. In essence, you want a credit card company to be your advocate and say, "We've done business together forever." Note that if you play the balance-transfer game—transferring balances from one card to another to take advantage of introductory rates—it's harder to have long-term relationships.

Some creditors don't report everything to the major credit-reporting companies. For competitive reasons, these creditors want to keep you a secret; you're a good, profitable customer. While this helps them avoid competition, it doesn't help you manage and improve your credit. Shop around for lenders that will tell the truth, the whole truth, and nothing but the truth.

As you go through life, you should select one or two major bankcards that you'll keep forever. They should be with big name lenders that will continually report to the major credit-reporting companies. Treat these lenders as long-term partners, because that's what they are. Pay on time, pay at least the minimums, and don't jump ship just because your rate changes.

Staying Together

If you are unhappy with rates or service from your older credit cards, call them and ask for a better deal. If they won't accommodate you, consider using them as little as possible. There's nothing unfair about this. The free-market system says that if they're not competitive, you shouldn't use them as often. Likewise, as time goes on and your credit improves, you become less and less of a liability for them. You're less likely to run up debts and default. They make less profit off you, but at a lower risk.

When you decide to stop using one of your older cards regularly, you should be careful. Some credit card companies will cancel your card if you are inactive for too long, because you've become unprofitable. It's a good idea to set up an automatic monthly charge on the account (examples might be your wireless phone bill, or other subscriptions or memberships), and pay most of it off in full. The card companies make a little money on each transaction, and paying a few dollars in interest each year is a small price to pay for good credit.

More Than Just Credit

You can show long-term stability and predictability in several areas of your life. The major credit-scoring models take a close look at your credit accounts and how long they've been around. However, other automated credit-scoring models (and real people, too) look at other aspects of your life.

Your employment history is important in many cases. Credit applications often ask how long you've been with your current employer. They're looking to find out if you are a stable employee, and if your level of income has been somewhat stable. If you change jobs right before applying for credit, consider informing the lender how long you were at your previous employer.

Residence history is also important, and it typically shows up on a credit application. Again, stability can indicate that your payments will be more predictable. If you keep moving, creditors will wonder why—could you not afford the place you got into? A long time in your current residence can help outweigh some other blemishes on your credit if a real person is looking at the application.

Communicate with Lenders

Communication is key. You probably know this to be true in your personal relationships, and communication comes in very handy in the professional world as well. For some reason, consumers still haven't caught on that communication with lenders can be really helpful.

Red Sky in Morning

"Red sky at night, sailor's delight. Red sky in morning, sailor's warning." This ancient wisdom helped sailors know about bad weather ahead of time so that they could prepare for the worst. Like them, you should keep your eyes on the horizon to see what's coming at you. If things are going to get tough, then get ready.

You know better than any of your creditors how your financial health is. You know when you lose your job, suffer a family tragedy, incur major medical expenses, and so on. Use that knowledge to communicate with your lenders. If something happens that's going to make it hard to pay bills, be proactive and tell them up front. You might be surprised how easy it will be.

There are several ways to communicate with your lenders. One way is to make a late payment, or no payment at all. This tells them something, but the message isn't very clear. Another way to communicate with lenders is to pick up the phone, tell them what's going on, and ask if they can work with you.

Thinking Like a Lender

When you miss payments, your lender doesn't know what happened. Are you unwilling to pay the debt? Are you out of money and declaring bankruptcy? Are you still alive? They want to know what's going on because they've got money at risk. If it's just a temporary thing because of some financial hardships, they'll be relieved to hear that.

Remember, lenders don't want you to default on your loans. Although it may not always seem like it, lenders will work with you to make sure you can successfully pay off your debts. Consider the alternative: if you file for a Chapter 7 bankruptcy, your debts might be liquidated. In such a case, your lender could lose money forever. If they have to constantly contact you or take more aggressive steps to collect the money, it costs them money. From a lender's perspective, it might be more efficient to just work with you and wait until you're able to pay your bills.

Getting a Workout

There are a variety of ways that you can work out a deal. The most important thing to know is that you actually can work out a deal. Furthermore, it's best to take action early. By doing so, you can help keep the situation from getting worse than it needs to be, and you'll have more negotiating clout with your lenders. Consider how lenders will view these two situations:

- A borrower with a history of paying on time calls and says, "I just lost my job yesterday, and will be short on cash for the next several months. It will be hard to pay you. Is there anything we can do?"
- A borrower has not made his payments for the last three months. He has received notices to remind him and requests to call the lender. He finally calls and says, "Sorry I've been late paying. Cash flow has been tough since I lost my job. Is there anything we can do?"

Who do you think is going to have it easier? In addition, the proactive person will probably pay less in late fees, and the situation might not appear on her credit report.

Possible Workout Options

When you ask for help, your lenders might work with you in a variety of ways. In general, you can ask them to waive any fees that they've charged you or would charge you in the future. Additional fees will only increase your debt load and make it harder to pay them off.

Lenders might allow a temporary forbearance, which means you can stop making payments, or make smaller payments, for a specified term. When you know your problems are temporary, forbearance makes sense. At the end of your forbearance, you might have the opportunity to pay back what you missed in one lump sum. Or, you can add the missed payments on top of the existing loan balance, and get those paid off at the back end of your loan.

Another way to get up to date with your lender is to start a repayment plan. You might add a small amount to your normal periodic payments so that you pay off any past-due balance over time. As long as you're making payments on time and settling the debt, your lenders will be happy.

FACT

Working out programs and open communication reduce the likelihood of home loss by 80 percent. Freddie Mac conducted a 2004 study to determine the value of foreclosure alternatives like repayment plans and loan modifications and determined that it was a win-win situation. Consumers avoid the stress and costs of foreclosure, and lenders avoid the hassle and loss of revenue.

Finally, you can consider changing the structure of your loan. Sometimes, agreeing to different terms can lower your monthly payments and make it easier to take care of the debt. One way to do this is to extend the term of the loan. Keep in mind that this doesn't help you out when you look at the big picture, it's more of a short-term solution. If you extend the number of years you're paying, you'll also increase the total amount of interest you pay over the term of the loan.

Pay Now, Argue Later

Sometimes things don't work out. It's frustrating when somebody asks you for money they didn't earn or that they're not entitled to. Should you pay them or stand firm? Some common examples of this dilemma are:

- You bought a product that didn't work
- There's an erroneous charge on your credit card
- You feel swindled by a lender who got you a bad deal
- Your health insurance company is supposed to pay for a treatment, but hasn't
- You don't believe you owe the government taxes

- Your ex-spouse is uncooperative so you shouldn't have to pay child support
- Your ex-spouse racked up debt that you shouldn't have to pay

How Much Does Principle Cost?

Have you ever heard somebody say, "It's not about the money, it's about the principle?" This is typical in a case where somebody has the money to pay for something, but they refuse to pay because they're dissatisfied or upset about how things are working. Refusing to pay can be personally rewarding, and it can sometimes serve as leverage to get things done the right way. However, refusing to pay can also damage your credit.

When you have disputes with lenders, vendors, or service providers, beware of dragging your credit into it. The costs of fighting a battle can be huge. If you're committed to sticking to your guns, know what you're putting on the line.

A bittersweet truth about the credit world is that creditors have a lot of power over customers. If they report negative information about you, you can have major problems. You can miss out on job opportunities, you may have higher interest rates or be unable to get a loan, and you might not be able to renew or purchase insurance. Of course, this power is what makes the whole system work. The system gives borrowers a compelling reason to pay off debts as agreed. The message is, "If you don't pay, you're going to have trouble elsewhere."

A Conservative Course of Action

If you want to be careful about your credit, consider paying any debts and settling the details later. By having the debt paid, you gain two advantages. First, nobody can ding up your credit by reporting you to the major credit-reporting companies. Second, you prove that it really is not about the money—it's about the principle.

When it comes to medical bills, make sure you know how your insurance company operates. Getting a claim covered can be more painful than surgery, and can take months or years. Find out exactly what they require to get your treatments paid. If you can pay the service provider and then work with the insurance company for reimbursement, you may get faster results. Instead of letting a bunch of uninterested parties handle the affair, you can stay on top of things and call for accountability.

If your debt has been turned over to a collection agency, you need to be very careful. In such a case, pay now and argue later may not be the best course of action. In fact, it could backfire. Pay now and argue later is a strategy to keep you out of collections and avoid damage to your credit reports.

Charge for Long Life

To use credit most effectively, you should buy things that last. Another way of looking at this is to avoid using credit to buy things that have a very short life. A rule of thumb: you should be able to pay off the debt by the end of the item's useful life. People who follow this rule are able to stay on top of their debt. This section is not intended to lecture you about spending habits; rather, you should simply understand the concept about the lifetime value of your purchases.

What's a Long Life?

Before you charge something or apply for a loan, consider how long you'll enjoy the benefits of the item. For example, consider a night out on the town—perhaps some cocktails in a classy setting, a gourmet dinner, a show, and a cab ride. It can be very tempting to use your credit card for a night of luxury. However, consider how long you'll be paying for that one night. You can't relive it except in your memories, but the debt is on your cards.

If you make the minimum payments, it can take decades to pay off a debt. Do you really want to pay for your night out for the next twenty years?

What if you want to have another night out? It is okay to splurge on yourself from time to time, but borrowing for things that come and go will get you into a hole quickly.

If you're going to borrow, borrow for things that will give you value for the entire time you make payments on them. A house is a great example. Sure, you have to make payments for many years, and you might never own the thing outright, but you get to live in it and participate in any market appreciation.

Upside-Down Cars

Another example might be your automobile. You sometimes hear that somebody is "upside down" on their auto loan. What does it mean to be upside down? It means the loan amount is greater than the auto's value. If you sold the car at current market prices, you would not pay off the loan balance. This happens when the car loses value faster than the debt is paid down. If you need another car and you're upside down, the only way to get one is to take a loss on your current car and add more debt. Again, you're not getting ahead, you're falling behind.

Now that you know the concept, look at everything you are thinking of charging or purchasing with the help of a loan. Which will last longer, your enjoyment of the item, or your debt? If the debt will far outlive the item, reconsider the purchase.

As with the night on the town, people get upside down on their auto loans due to shortsightedness. Too many auto buyers look at their monthly payment when they consider a purchase. One way to lower your monthly payment is to lengthen the term of your loan. That's fine if the auto will last at least as long as your loan. If it doesn't, your debt outlives the item you purchased.

Be Involved

The best habit you can develop is to be actively involved in managing your credit. Don't worry, it really doesn't take that much time. You simply have to decide that you're going to take charge, and then do it.

Get Informed, Stay Informed

You are already taking great steps in the right direction. By reading this book, you now know more about improving your credit than the average consumer. The world is full of inaccuracies and myths, and consumers who don't pay any attention to their credit. This is not your problem.

As time goes on, laws and lending practices will undoubtedly change. New credit-scoring models will emerge, and noncredit-related scoring will increase. As that happens, keep your ears open and find out how it works. You can only benefit by staying up to date on how your information is managed.

Know All of the Scores

Starting now, find out what everybody is saying about you. There are many different types of scores floating around, and you are being graded. Be aware that you have more than just one credit score. First, there is the FICO credit score, the granddaddy of them all. This is used in the majority of lending decisions, but not all of them.

QUESTION?

Which credit score is the most important?
The one that your prospective lender is using. You can have the best score at one of the credit-reporting companies, but your lender may be pulling a lower score from a different company, or using its own proprietary formulas. Find out how your lenders will judge you.

Each of the three major credit-reporting companies issues its own scores as well. Based on differences between the information kept at these companies, your credit scores can vary. In fact, you might even purchase a credit score from a major credit-reporting company, but not know if it is your FICO score or a proprietary score. Get as many details as you can before you purchase scores.

Besides credit scores, there are a variety of privately developed scores that help businesses figure you out. They predict how profitable you will be, how likely you are to default or declare bankruptcy, how likely you are to make insurance claims, and more. These scores typically are not available to you, but you might see them become available in the future. If so, make sure you take advantage and understand how companies view you as a consumer.

Read the Fine Print

You already know that agreements can contain some nasty provisions. However, most people still do not read the fine print. Instead, mail from the credit card companies goes right into the shredder (or worse, the trash can). If you don't understand what you are getting yourself into, you can get blindsided by something that you should have seen coming.

Along the same lines, you should always glance over your credit card statements for any red flags. You want to make sure the interest rate they are charging you is the same as what you expected it to be. Likewise, look for unexpected fees, especially late fees if you did not pay late. Finally, check for charges that you did not initiate. If you find anything unexpected, you should contact your card issuer immediately and get it fixed. You can save yourself expensive fees, expensive credit damage, and expensive, time-consuming identity theft.

If you can stay on top of your loans and your finances, your credit should show improvements. Develop the habits that allow you to have a strong foundation, so that when surprises pop up, your life will be a little bit easier.

Chapter 10
Playing with Fire

Managing your credit is more than just checking your credit reports and scores periodically. You need to be in the habit of avoiding pitfalls. You need to sense it when something is happening that can negatively affect your credit. With that in mind, this section covers some behaviors that warrant your attention. If you ever feel like taking one of the actions discussed here, proceed with caution. Come back to this chapter, reread it, and sleep on it before you make a decision.

Co-Signing

Co-signing puts you in a position where you apply for a loan with somebody else. Typically, you are helping that person get a loan that they would not be able to get without your help. By co-signing, you tell the lender that you'll personally make sure a loan gets paid back. Co-signing a loan is extremely dangerous. If you're going to do it, you should weigh the consequences heavily. You will be held responsible if the borrower you co-sign for fails to make payments in full and on time.

ALERT!

In other parts of this book, readers who are trying to build or rebuild credit are encouraged to ask another to co-sign for them. This can be a really touchy subject. Co-signing helps one person get a loan at the expense of risking the co-signer's credit. This section details the risks involved from the co-signer's perspective.

Why Would Anybody Co-Sign?

Co-signing is a really nice thing to do for somebody. Perhaps you've already heard that it's risky, but it happens all the time. Why? There are several situations where co-signing on a loan might make sense. In general, people co-sign as a favor to somebody else. We all hate to see others suffer, and co-signing on a loan can reduce the suffering of others.

Co-Signing for Children

Parents often co-sign loans and accounts for their children. This is a way to help the child start building credit and using credit products. Without a co-signer, your child might be stuck without access to money. If your child can get a loan, chances are that the interest rate will be higher than you'd like to see. How is a higher rate going to help your child get out into the world on the right foot? By co-signing, a loving parent can help a child get a better deal.

Before co-signing on a child's loan, parents should at least consider some alternatives. Generally, parents are trying to accomplish one of the following when they co-sign:

- Help the child start using credit and understand the concepts
- Get the child a first credit account
- Buy a car and have the child make payments
- Help a child rebuild credit after some hard times

While these are lofty goals, co-signing is not the only way to get results. Instead, consider giving money to your child, and keeping your good credit out of the equation. While you may not like the idea of giving the money away, you can structure things so that you're simply helping with the loan.

For example, let's say you're going to help your son get his first credit account and decide to co-sign on a major bankcard. If your son can't pay all the bills, the creditors will ask you to make up the shortfalls. What's worse, if payments come in late or get skipped, you might have negative entries show up on your own credit report. As you know, this will lower your credit score. Finally, the account could end up in collections, and this is a major black mark on your credit!

Co-signing is not the only way to help a child build or rebuild credit. With some creative thinking, you can simultaneously accomplish the goals of helping your child and protecting your credit. Before making a decision, discuss your child's basic goals and find a win-win solution.

What if you had helped your child get a secured credit card instead? You can walk into your bank or credit union with your child and open one up in just a few minutes. You make the original deposit that the bank uses as collateral. Next, the bank issues a secured credit card that your child can use anywhere.

This is a win-win situation for everybody: your child gets a credit card at competitive rates; the bank is happy because they have a new customer, and they're not taking much risk; and you have not risked one of your most valuable assets—your credit—helping your child learn some of life's hardest lessons.

Keep in mind, the world is unpredictable, and remember how you were when you were young. Try to keep your credit separate if possible.

The Secrets of Co-Signing

Co-signing puts you on the hook for another's debt. Most co-signers don't know that the lender can try to collect debt from you without taking all possible steps to collect from the primary borrower. Remember, lenders want to take the path of least resistance. If they have any trouble collecting from the person with bad credit, they'll go after the person with good credit.

According to the Federal Trade Commission, three out of four co-signers are asked to make payments on loans gone bad. These numbers should not be surprising. The bank already knew that the primary borrower was a risk, that's why they required a co-signer. If somebody needs you to co-sign, odds are good that you'll be asked to pay.

Co-signers are just as responsible for payment as the primary borrower. This includes lawsuits, garnished wages, repossessions, and penalty fees. Remember that repossessions and collections can stay on your (the co-signer's) credit report for up to seven years.

If You Insist on Co-Signing

Given all the risks, you might be reluctant to co-sign for anybody. However, there are occasions where you may feel that co-signing is the right thing to do. Perhaps you'll have a child or loved one in the midst of extreme challenges. If you decide to go down that road with them, take some steps to make sure you're protected. By staying on top of things, you can keep the situation from spinning out of control. Here are some ideas to help manage your risk:

- Ask the lender how much it will cost if you have to pay off the debt
- Get statements or duplicates mailed to your house so you know if payments are late
- Get a written agreement that the lender will call you immediately if there is a late payment
- Avoid pledging any valuable property, such as your home or auto, for the loan
- If you sever your relationship with the borrower, get the loan refinanced without your name as soon as possible

If you do choose to co-sign on a loan, these precautions might not keep you out of trouble entirely, but they will help mitigate the potential damage to your credit rating.

The Balance-Transfer Game

Everybody loves a good deal. In the credit card world, there are good deals and bad deals. The best deals will involve a really low interest rate on any balance you're carrying. There are other less-important factors as well. For example, it's nice to avoid paying annual fees, earn some type of reward, and have flexibility and protection features in your credit card. However, the rate is what is most important.

When you have decent credit or better, you'll have a lot of folks banging on your door to offer you their version of a great deal. Often, you get solicitations to transfer your existing credit card balances to a new card in order to enjoy a lower interest rate on those balances. Another tactic is to offer you a low interest rate on new purchases going forward, so everything you buy has low or no interest applied to it. Sometimes the credit card companies will offer you a low rate on existing balances and future purchases at the same time. While these offers are tempting, they probably won't help your credit.

Knocking Down the Score

Each time you apply for one of these low-interest accounts, your credit score suffers. First, the lender may add an inquiry to your credit report, meaning they're taking another hard look at your credit history to see what type of risk you are. Yes, they say you are preapproved, but they will do some additional homework to decide how much to lend you.

ALERT!

Applying for new credit cards adds trade lines to your credit report. One or two balance transfers as you eliminate your debt won't ruin you. However, if you make a habit out of transferring balances as the introductory rate expires, you'll end up with lots and lots of accounts after a while. You'll also have a high number of inquiries.

If you've got too many accounts out there, lenders worry that you might decide to use those accounts to rack up more debt than you can handle. Will closing the accounts after you're done taking advantage of the offer help? Perhaps. If you just close your accounts, you're taking two risks. First, if you just transfer balances and then close accounts, you'll never end up with long-lived credit accounts in good standing. Lenders like to see evidence of a relationship that has worked well, and you won't have that. In addition, closing an account that you just transferred elsewhere will result in your credit-utilization ratio going up. In other words, you'll appear as if you're using a greater percentage of your available credit, which doesn't help you.

Is It Really a Solution?

Does the balance-transfer game really do anything to help you? While it can reduce your borrowing costs temporarily, it's not a long-term solution. You don't reduce your total debt, you just shift it elsewhere. Granted, you may make some payments and reduce the debt a little. However, unless you have a plan to completely knock that debt out, it will always be there. If you have such a plan, how much will you really save by playing the balance-transfer game?

Finally, your debts may be a sign that you need to change your behavior. If you're simply changing accounts and keeping the debt, it means that you're either spending too much or making too little. Figure out a solution to your budget issues, and the debt will take care of itself.

Home-Equity Loans

Home-equity loans are, as the name suggests, loans against the equity you have in your home. They allow you to borrow fairly large amounts, and the interest rate is typically more attractive than what you can find on a credit card. Why do they let you get a really big loan at a really low interest rate? Because you're putting your home up for collateral. This is a low-risk loan for the bank. They know they can sell your house and collect their money if necessary. Therefore, you'll probably make that debt a priority, and pay as agreed, if your home is on the line. This type of loan can result in debt elimination, or a complete disaster.

Debt Consolidation

Some borrowers use home-equity loans as part of a debt-consolidation program. For example, you can get a large home-equity loan and use the proceeds to pay off several smaller debts. This can sometimes work out nicely.

Home-equity loans can have expenses that take away some of your savings. You might have to pay closing costs, appraisal fees, and more. Make sure you know all of the costs in detail. Then, run the numbers and see if it's worth your trouble, and the extra risk of putting your home on the line.

Let's assume you have several large credit card debts, and you're paying a high interest rate on all. You could transfer the balance to other credit cards, but you decide not to for reasons we've discussed in this chapter. Instead, you might take a home-equity loan and pay those debts off. By replacing several unfavorable loans with one loan, you can simplify your life. Furthermore, you'll probably reduce your borrowing costs—the home-equity loan should have a lower interest rate than the rates on your other debts. To add to your savings, you might get a tax deduction for the interest you pay on the home-equity loan. This is starting to sound good, right?

Pitfalls of Home-Equity Loans

While they make sense in some situations, home-equity loans can hurt you. As with playing the balance-transfer game, you don't really eliminate any debt when you perform debt consolidation with a home-equity loan. Also, you get into big trouble if you can't make payments for some reason. Life is full of unknowns, and it's all too common that a sickness or tragedy gets borrowers off track. If you're going to miss payments or default on a loan, it's much better to default on an unsecured loan like a credit card than on a loan secured by your home.

Going Bankrupt

Bankruptcy laws allow people to start over with a clean slate. If you simply can't pay your debts, you may consider filing for bankruptcy. Bankruptcy can get you a lifeline, but it's not always the best thing to do for your credit.

How Bankruptcy Works

When you file for bankruptcy, the courts keep your creditors at bay. After taking an inventory of your assets and your ability to pay, you figure out what type of bankruptcy is best. The courts might require that you liquidate certain assets, pay off as much as you can, and then free you from paying what's leftover. Or, the courts might set up a process where you pay off what you can over several years. In any case, you get to start over from scratch—at a cost.

As you investigate bankruptcy, be sure to talk with qualified counselors. Don't make the decision on your own, and consider the motivations of anybody who offers you advice. A good place to start counseling is Consumer Credit Counseling Services. This organization has offices throughout the United States.

How Bankruptcy Hurts You

Bankruptcy appears in your credit reports for seven to ten years. As you might imagine, this is not an item that lenders look favorably upon. A past bankruptcy tells them that you defaulted on some type of debt, from another lender just like them. The cause of your bankruptcy will not earn you much sympathy. If you have a bankruptcy on your report, lenders will worry about you.

With bankruptcy items on your credit reports, you won't have access to the best deals out there. Lenders may deny your applications, or they may offer you a loan with unfavorable terms, like a higher interest rate or lower spending limit. While you may be able to get a mortgage, you'll pay a lot more in interest because of that higher rate. Overall, declaring bankruptcy will cost you for years to come.

Before You File for Bankruptcy

A lot of folks end up in a situation where bankruptcy is the only viable option. If you need to file for bankruptcy, then you need to file. However, you should consider the alternatives if any exist. Filing for bankruptcy is irreversible—even if you change your mind and decide not to go through with it, your records will show the bankruptcy for seven to ten years.

The best thing you can do before filing bankruptcy is try to work things out with your creditors. They really don't want you to go through bankruptcy and have their debt discharged. Let them know that you've fallen on hard times and that you really want to pay off the debts.

You should ask for more time to pay, a lower interest rate, forgiveness on some of the debt, and so on. It never hurts to ask; the worst they can do is say no. Try to negotiate a settlement amount that will make them happy and make them leave you alone. A settled debt will look better on your credit reports than a bankruptcy.

Keep in mind that bankruptcy won't help you with every type of debt. For example, tax debts and a few other types of debt will not be discharged. As you decide whether or not bankruptcy makes sense, be sure you understand which debts will not be affected by a bankruptcy. If the majority of your debt cannot be discharged, bankruptcy is a bad idea.

Cash Advances

Cash advances are always tempting, and come in a variety of forms. You may notice that your credit card company sends you a sheet of blank checks periodically. They encourage you to use these checks as a cash advance. You can use the money absolutely any way you want. You can transfer balances, you can make a deposit to your checking account, or you can buy an item that you've had your eye on.

Another version of cash advances is the ATM cash withdrawal. Instead of using your debit card to get cash, you can use a credit card. Of course, that means you can borrow to get the cash if you don't have it available. As with the preprinted checks, you can use this money any way you want. Cash advances are powerful and they can add a lot of convenience, but they're generally a bad idea.

Cash Advances Versus Other Loans

When you think about it, a cash advance should be just like any other loan. However, credit card companies and finance companies treat cash advances differently. They fall into a separate category from purchases and balance transfers. That separate category typically has a higher interest rate than any of the other categories.

Why would they charge you more interest on cash advances? As we discussed, you get a lot of flexibility by taking cash advances. One of the reasons they charge more is that flexibility usually costs money. Next, cash advances might not work the same for credit card companies. Take the example of the sheet of checks you get: the credit card company has to print and mail you the checks, as well as process the check differently. It's a piece of paper, not an electronic request like most credit card purchases. Finally, credit card companies may not earn any transaction fees on cash advances. It is a different beast, so they charge differently.

When you use cash advances, you can get yourself into trouble. Often, you'll have a nice credit card with a very competitive rate on purchases or balance transfers. When you read the fine print, you'll find that cash advances have a much higher rate. Furthermore, the credit card company can apply your payments to whichever category they choose: purchases, balance transfers, or cash advances. If you make a payment, typically you'll find that the credit card company pays down the category with the lowest interest rate, which usually isn't the cash-advance category. You have to pay off everything else on your card before you can start chipping away at the cash advance you took long ago.

Alternatives to Cash Advances

As a general rule, you should avoid spending beyond your means, especially when it comes to smaller items or items with a short lifespan. However, there may be times when cash flow is tight and you'll need to free up some money. In particular, you sometimes have situations where you can't charge something, but you really need to pay for it. Instead of using cash advances, you might just get creative and try to get those dollars from somewhere else. There are no good ways to do this, but here are some ideas to make the best of a bad situation.

You might think you're taking a short-term loan when you use a cash advance. Being the responsible person that you are, you figure you'll pay the money back quickly, because it's got a higher interest rate. However, you usually have to pay off all other balances with a lender before they will start putting your payments toward the cash advance.

If you have no choice but to borrow, at least make the most of it. If you put a cash advance on top of other credit card debt, you'll get eaten alive unless you can pay everything off quickly. You might consider using a different lender for a cash advance. Perhaps you have another credit card, or an offer for a cash advance. Then, pay off the cash advance quickly and get back to work on any other debt.

Another way to free up some cash is to charge everything and hoard your cash. This strategy takes some preparation and planning. If you've got income, you change your spending method to keep the income. Charge everything possible that you would normally pay cash for, and use the cash you accumulate for whatever your needs are. Note that this is a very risky approach, and it is only appropriate for a short-term situation with light at the end of the tunnel. Even with the best intentions, you might find those debts you racked up on your credit card statement years down the road.

ALERT!

Don't count your chickens before they hatch. If you work out an arrangement with your creditors, get it in writing. After you've settled the debt, get more written documentation that the debt has been settled as agreed, and that you don't owe them anything more. Then you can breathe easy. Keep copies of these letters forever.

Payday Loans

The worst type of cash advance is a payday loan or paycheck cash advance. These businesses loan you money for short periods of time. Unfortunately, the interest rates are extremely high—several thousand percent per year is what you might expect. If you ever use one of these loans, do not make a habit out of it. As with debt-consolidation programs, you need to identify whether or not you are living beyond your means. If you are, cash advances will not help you, they'll only get you in a deeper hole.

Fashionably Late

Like most of the other behaviors discussed in this chapter, late payments are a sign that something is wrong. If you didn't already know it, you should not pay late, because it will mess up your credit. However, if you ever get into a tight spot, it's important to know how to do it right.

Talk to Your Creditors

Creditors appreciate hearing from you if you're going to be late with a payment. Think about it from their perspective—they usually don't know you, they just have a big computer tracking everything. It could be that you've decided not to pay them, it could be that you've run out of money, it could be that you just forgot because you've been busy, or it could be that you've dropped off the face of the earth.

If you're going to be late, do your credit a favor and let your lenders know. Ask them for an extension, or just let them know not to expect the money on time. When you lend money out to people, you tend to dislike surprises, because they usually aren't good surprises. Lenders don't like bad surprises either, so don't keep them in suspense, just pick up the phone and fill them in.

How Late is Too Late?

If late payments are bad, then really-late payments are really bad. It's never too late to pay money that you owe, but you should try to minimize the damage to your credit. Late payments are usually measured in increments of thirty days. For example, most reporting tracks whether you pay more than thirty days late, more than sixty days late, or more than ninety days late. As you can probably imagine, the later you go, the more it bothers the lender.

From this, you can tell that it's best to pay within thirty days if you're going to pay late. That keeps you from crossing the thirty-day threshold and being reported as more than thirty days past due on a payment. This doesn't mean your lender won't charge you late fees and take other steps to penalize you, all it means is that your credit reports will likely be in better shape.

Occasional late payments, even thirty days late or more, might not be reported to the credit bureaus. Don't take advantage of it, though. Lenders give you a break because they know that everybody makes mistakes. If you start to make a habit out of late payments, they'll report each and every one.

Sometimes lenders don't even report late payments to the major credit-reporting companies unless you go over sixty days late. Again, you can minimize the damage by staying under sixty days. If you really have to push it, then stay under ninety days. Otherwise, creditors will think you're a serious risk, and it will certainly be on your credit reports for a long time to come.

Chapter 11

Quick and Easy Bad Ideas

Credit reports and credit scores are confusing. Scores are based on complex mathematical formulas, and the formula ingredients are top-secret. While your credit is based on a combination of factors, there are some very fragile pieces. Shattering those pieces can have a dramatic impact. This section focuses on common mistakes that can quickly damage your credit and your financial health. Some of this is counterintuitive: you might think you're doing the right thing, but it ends up hurting you.

A Credit-Shopping Spree

One way to quickly damage your credit is to shop for credit. Every time you submit a credit application, the prospective lender pulls your credit and creates an inquiry on your credit reports. It's important to manage the credit-shopping process and minimize the damage to your credit.

You should not let your fear of inquiry-damage limit your comparison shopping. You can save a lot of money on big-ticket items by getting a better loan. The key is to shop rates within a short period of time. The people who design credit-scoring models realized that shopping loan rates before making a major purchase is actually a good idea. As a result, mortgage and auto loans get special treatment.

This is one of those catch-22s in life. It is important to get a good rate on any loan you are considering. The best way to make sure you are getting a good rate is to compare rates among various lenders. However, the more you compare, the more inquiries you have on your credit reports.

According to Fair Isaac, the FICO credit score ignores all mortgage and auto-loan inquiries made within the last thirty days. So, if you make your purchase within thirty days of your first inquiry, your credit should not be affected. What about after thirty days? It's not like you'll never get another loan. Outside of the previous thirty days, the FICO model treats all mortgage and auto loan inquiries made within fourteen days of each other as one inquiry. The newer FICO scoring models are even more forgiving: they extend the fourteen day period to forty-five days (there are different FICO models out there being used by different companies).

If you fail to keep your inquiries within a short period of time, your credit will suffer. Consider a shopper who compares rates over several months. In addition to being extremely thorough and well-prepared, this person is damaging her credit. Undoubtedly, her score will be lower, and the loan less favorable, on her last inquiry than on her first inquiry.

Lots of Brand-New Credit

Brand-new credit can be useful, but dangerous. When you're increasing your credit capacity (that is, the amount of credit available to you), you should pace yourself. Opening up too many new accounts in a short period of time will hurt your credit score. New credit is especially important if you have a limited credit history, or if you're recovering from previous financial problems. If you're a seasoned borrower with a clean record, new credit is less damaging. Nevertheless, you need to know which pitfalls to avoid.

Length of Credit History

The length of your credit history accounts for 15 percent of your FICO credit score. This piece of the pie looks at how long you've had credit in general, and specifically how long you've had a given account. If you open too many new accounts in a short period of time, you lower your average account age. Since a higher average account age is better than a lower one, you lower your credit score. If you need more credit capacity and intend to use it wisely, consider asking your existing lenders to increase your credit limit. You'll avoid inquiries and new accounts.

New Credit

New credit accounts for 10 percent of your FICO credit score. New credit refers to the number and type of accounts that you've recently opened. In addition, this part of the scoring model looks at your inquiries: how many you have had in the last two years, and what type of inquiries they were. As you might imagine, a high frequency of unsecured credit inquiries is bad.

FACT

According to Fair Isaac, borrowers with six or more hard inquiries in their files are eight times more likely to file for bankruptcy than those who don't have any inquiries. Of course, a borrower deemed a higher bankruptcy risk will pay higher interest rates—if she can even get a loan.

As with managing your average account age, consider asking your existing lenders for a credit-limit increase. By doing so, you can avoid new credit altogether.

Take 10 Percent Off What?

A lot of people damage their credit around the winter holidays. While shopping for gifts at a department store, it's not uncommon to be offered a 10 percent discount for opening a credit account with the store. This is an attractive deal—10 percent off of $250 is $25. If you do this at several retailers, you can save a bundle.

The deal gets much less attractive when you look at the damage to your credit score. Every hard inquiry takes a few points off of your credit score, and multiple inquiries in rapid succession can be a sign of credit trouble. Remember, these are not mortgage or auto-loan inquiries, these are inquiries for unsecured revolving credit. You don't get a fourteen-day window with that type of inquiry.

Creditors want to lend money to seasoned veterans. They feel safer about giving you money if they can be confident that you'll follow the terms of your agreement and repay according to those terms. If you've got a good history, don't close those accounts and let them fall off of your credit report.

In addition to the inquiries, you open several new accounts rapidly. Also, you now have more credit capacity that you can use to get yourself in trouble. Before you take one of these offers, consider your credit. Saving a few dollars is nice. However, you might end up with higher interest rates on bigger loans and see those savings more than disappear.

I Never Use This Account

You might have several credit accounts that you never use. Perhaps you have found better accounts, or you simply have more credit than you need, so you let those accounts lie dormant. While you would get less mail if you close the account, you should think twice before doing so. What's more, closing these accounts in an effort to improve your score could actually backfire.

Better with Age

You already know that part of your FICO credit score, and plenty of other credit scores, is based on the average account age of your credit accounts. Typically, the dormant accounts you have will be the oldest ones. If you close those older accounts and keep new accounts open, you risk dropping your average account age. You will likely see a corresponding drop in your credit score.

If you decide to keep dormant accounts open, make sure that the lender does not ruin your plans. When you fail to use the account, you just cost money to the lender, and they don't like to have unprofitable customers. Make a habit out of using the account for small purchases periodically, and pay down the majority of the balance.

Also, items on your credit reports have more significance if you have a thin credit file. In other words, a credit file without much history or without many accounts. By keeping old accounts around forever, you keep your file from becoming thin. Yes, they'll be around for seven years even if you close them, but after that you could get thin. Depending on how your credit history looks, you might be setting yourself up for a lower score seven years into the future.

Using Part of what You've Got

Another factor of your credit scores is credit utilization. This is similar to the economic concept of capacity utilization: if a factory can produce 10,000 widgets a month, but it's only producing 5,000 widgets, it's at 50 percent of capacity utilization. Think of your credit in the same way. If you've got credit limits totaling $10,000, but your balances add up to $5,000, then you're at 50 percent utilization.

Some folks think that closing all of your dormant accounts will make you look better. There is some logic to this: if you have $20,000 of unused available credit, then lenders will worry that you might just go ahead and use all of that credit. If you rack up $20,000 in debt overnight, you'll probably be in over your head and you become a default risk.

However, it's often better to let sleeping dogs lie. Let's say you do have $20,000 of available unused credit and your total balances add up to $5,000. You're at 20 percent utilization ($5,000 used out of a $25,000 total capacity equals 20 percent), and this is a pretty good place to be. If you close most of those accounts to bring your available unused credit to $5,000, then you all of a sudden jump to 50 percent utilization ($5,000 used out of a $10,000 total capacity equals 50 percent), and this is higher than you want to be. Your score will drop simply because it looks like you are getting into trouble.

Timing is Everything

Sometimes it can make sense to close accounts that you are never going to use again. However, you need to know what you are doing when you do so. If an account charges a steep annual fee, and it is a newer account relative to the other accounts in your history, go ahead and close it. Just be careful about the timing—you don't want to go on an account closing spree just before making a major purchase. It is worth it to pay an annual fee if it means your mortgage rate or auto loan rate might be a little bit better. Again, if you have a thin credit file, proceed with caution.

Debt Comes Out of Retirement

Everybody makes mistakes. Old delinquent debts can cause a conundrum. If you have previously defaulted on a debt, you have to decide how you want to handle that default. If you now have the means to pay back a debt you never repaid, you might feel better if you do so, and that's a decision you make based on your personal beliefs and your current situation.

Collectors Come Calling

You might get some help bringing the issue up on your list of things to do. Debt-collection companies often buy defaulted debt, and attempt to collect the money due from the original borrower. Many of these debt-collection companies are reputable businesses. They run a legitimate operation, are well aware of the laws that regulate their industry, and they follow all of the laws.

However, there are also a few bad apples out there. The bad ones get all of the press, and there is a good reason for that: they take advantage of people's fears and lack of knowledge. What's worse, they knowingly break all of the laws designed to protect regular consumers.

If You Choose to Pay

There may be cases where you made mistakes in your youth, but now you are in a position to actually pay off the debts. This is an admirable position to take. When you do pay, make sure that paying the debt will not damage your credit.

ALERT!

Most people would agree that paying off old debts is the right thing to do. Nevertheless, you have to be very careful about how you do it because of some unintended consequences. Even though you repay a debt and prove yourself as a better borrower, your credit can suffer.

Before paying anything, get written agreement from the collectors that they will report the debt to be paid in full as agreed, not as settled or charged off. Keep in mind that the bad apples might not actually stick to the agreement, and you might have further legal battles down the road. However, if you're dealing with a reputable collector, this may be an acceptable strategy.

If You Will Not Pay

If you cannot or will not pay a debt, make sure you are extremely careful about what you say and do. The first step is to know who you are dealing with, and get the facts on your debt. In general, you should say very little on the phone, and request that all inquiries and communication be done in writing.

By knowing the facts and knowing your rights, you can figure out who you are dealing with. Find out from a reputable source what the laws are surrounding your debt. A good place to start is a local consumer-law attorney. If the debt is old enough to be outside of the statute of limitations, note how the collectors act: if they demand payment and threaten to sue, you're dealing with a dishonest firm. Remember, no matter how old the debt is, they can always ask for the money. However, they can't necessarily bring cases against you.

What's the Danger?

How could old debts, whether you are going to pay them or not, do additional damage to your credit? After all, the damage is done when you default on the debt for the first time. Your delinquency is added to your credit files, and for years to come you get lower credit scores and higher loan interest rates because of the default.

The danger is that certain actions can make bad debts look more recent than they should. Recent activity on your credit report is much more important than old activity. Having one missed payment this month is more significant than having one missed payment five years ago. Likewise, inquiries made this month are more significant than inquiries made last year.

Remember that paying off collection accounts does not remove them from your credit history and your credit reports. These accounts will appear for seven years, although having paid them off is better than the alternative. Best case: see if the collectors are willing to remove the entry altogether, or have it under the original lender's name.

In a worst-case scenario, you could bring back old debts that have already fallen off your credit reports. If a delinquency is more than seven years old, it's probably off your credit report, so it doesn't affect your credit scores and nobody can see the item. However, if you pick at old wounds, the debt can reappear on your reports. In some cases, simply acknowledging the debt with a collector or making a payment could bring it out of retirement. If you have suffered through seven years of poor credit scores and watched with relief as the item fell off your reports, it can really hurt to have the issue resurface.

Default-Rate Mania

How are credit cards like dominoes? If one gets off balance, it can send the rest of them off balance as well. As you already know, missing payments is bad for your credit. Your score will suffer if you have too many late payments or recent missed payments. However, it's not just your score that will suffer.

Inquiring Minds

Credit card companies constantly check your credit reports to see how you are doing. These inquiries are soft pulls which don't affect your credit score. They want to make sure that you are not getting too crazy with your obligations elsewhere. From their perspective, if you get in over your head, you're likely to default on the money you borrowed from them.

How often do they check your credit? It depends. Some lenders check monthly or quarterly, while others check once a year, if that. You can generally assume that the bigger organizations (like large credit card companies) will check your credit more often. Small, hometown establishments like little credit unions are likely to check less often, but you never know.

Feeding Frenzy

What happens if these inquiring minds find a problem on your credit reports? Things can get out of control really fast. Of course, it depends on the lender, and your agreement with that lender. With many credit card accounts these days, you have a universal-default clause in the contract.

Nevermind if you don't remember reading that in your original contract, credit card contracts change all of the time. The disclosures you receive periodically in the mail is probably where you will find some language about your universal-default clause.

So, what does universal default mean to you? It is a fancy way of saying, "If you mess up one of your accounts, you might as well have messed them all up." Assume you have several credit cards: Card A, Card B, and Card C. For whatever reason, you miss a payment on Card A. Surely, the Card A company will not be happy about this. They will slap the customary late payment fee on your account and send you a letter warning you not to do it again. They even go so far as to report the late payment to one of the major credit-reporting companies. No big deal, right?

Actual language from a credit offer disclosure: "We may change the rates, fees, and terms of your account at any time for any reason. These reasons may be based on information in your credit report, such as your failure to make payments to another creditor when due, amounts owed . . . or the number of credit inquiries."

If you have universal-default clauses over at Card B and Card C companies, it is a very big deal. On routine maintenance checks, the Card B and Card C companies notice that you made a late payment to Card A. As a result, they raise your rate much higher than it was the day before (perhaps they start charging you 30 percent now). You never made a late payment to Card B or Card C, but they're raising your rates. Why? Universal default.

The concept of universal default is this: If you default anywhere, you default here. Your credit card company is telling you not to default on anybody else's debt. Otherwise, your credit card company will take it personally, and assume that you meant to default on their debt. In your contract, you will notice what happens if you miss a payment. Typically, they explain how they will take away any promotional rates and raise your rate.

Vicious Cycle

If you have a meaningful amount of credit card debt, you can imagine how the situation would quickly spiral out of control. Because you miss a payment on Card A, Card A, Card B, and Card C would raise your rate. As a result, the amount of money you owe them would increase more rapidly, because of high-interest costs. Next, you'd have a hard time paying Card B. Card B charges a late fee, which adds to your balance, and so on. Ultimately, you might have to default on one or more of the loans. This scenario would be very bad for your financial health and your credit history.

Credit-Counseling Pitfalls

Having good credit can be a bad thing. Based on your good name, everybody offers to lend you money because they figure you can pay it back. For any number of reasons, you can wind up in debt up to your eyeballs. What to do then? Ask for help. However, even your "helpers" can put you in a worse situation. There are good helpers and bad helpers—if you get involved with a bad one, it can be devastating to your finances, not to mention your credit.

Downtown Scammerville

The credit-counseling world is full of shady actors. It makes sense if you think about it: people who are down on their luck are easier to swindle. Likewise, when you are desperate, you are grasping for a handhold and will grab onto anything that seems to have potential.

Some debt-counseling organizations are legitimate and helpful. However, some are worthless, and others are criminal. If you wind up with a bad apple, your situation will go from bad to worse. In the most extreme cases, debt counselors will pocket your payments that are supposed to go to your creditors. In other cases, they actually forward the money to the creditor, but they make late payments. Finally, some of these companies charge hefty fees and provide very little value.

Avoiding the Worst Ones

If you decide to seek help, find a reputable counselor. Shop around and see what type of feeling you get from various counselors. If they pressure you with a debt-management plan where you pay through them, keep shopping. A great first step is the National Foundation for Credit Counseling (*www.nfcc.org*). Some NFCC members refer to themselves as Consumer Credit Counseling Services.

ALERT!

Watch out for impostors. There are a lot of organizations with names very similar to Consumer Credit Counseling Services. Coincidence? Not likely. These organizations are trying to snatch distressed borrowers. If you are confused about whom you're dealing with, start with the National Foundation for Credit Counseling and ask for a local counselor.

How do you know if you are dealing with a rotten apple? Look for some common tipoffs in the form of bogus claims.

We Remove All Negative Items

It is not possible to remove items from your credit report if they are true. The best thing you can do is make them less negative.

Eliminate Debt via Obscure Laws

Yes, your debt is a legal obligation, and you are supposed to pay it back. Some debt-elimination companies try to "educate" you on laws that would invalidate your debts.

Pennies on the Dollar—and No Credit Damage

If you settle for less than you owe, it will affect your credit. It may be a viable option, but you will have to deal with it for the next seven years.

Raiding Retirement Resources

One quick way to wipe out debt might be to raid your retirement accounts. For years you may have taken hard-earned money out of your paycheck so that you can live well in the future. Well, is the future now? Should you take that money and put it to good use today?

A Sore Thumb

When you look around at how you can pay off some debt, a retirement account often sticks out like a sore thumb. With a near-empty bank account, your savings for the future can be a tempting stash. Your 401(k), IRA, or other retirement account has been earning money tax-deferred for all of these years, so why not dip into it? There's probably enough in there to make a huge dent in your debt.

In general, it is a very bad idea to crack your retirement nest egg to pay off debts today. First, you won't get your hands on every penny in that retirement account. Unless you have a good reason for taking the money out before age 59½, you might have to pay a 10 percent penalty on the money you take out. On top of that, you'll likely owe income taxes if the money was put in the account pretax, or you took a deduction. Sure, you might be able to get a check for your entire retirement-account balance, but you will owe the government next April.

Protected Assets

Another reason to avoid taking money from your retirement accounts is that those accounts are protected from creditors. Your creditors will tell you or ask you to cash out your nest egg, but they cannot force you to do so in most cases, especially in employer-sponsored retirement plans like 401(k)s. Those plans are regulated by the Employee and Retirement Income Security Act (ERISA). Even if you declare bankruptcy, your assets in ERISA plans are safe. You should not abuse this protection, but you should use it if it applies to you.

Your retirement savings may be all that you have after a financial crisis. They may take years to accumulate, they are extremely difficult to replace, and it is a tragedy to lose them during hard times. If you lose all of your other assets, you should at least count on having your retirement savings to help you in your later years. Cashing out your retirement may appear to be a quick fix, but it is generally a mistake over the long term.

Chapter 12
Building Credit

Credit scores reflect known information about you. If nobody knows anything about you, then you're not a good candidate for credit. Unfortunately, it is a "no news is bad news" situation. There should be a healthy helping of data about you and your creditworthiness available for all lenders to see. In this section, we'll look at how you can start building your credit record, how you can rebuild bad credit, and how you can get favorable information added to your reports.

What's the Big Deal?

How do you get credit without a strong credit history? This is one of the grand mysteries in life. Nobody wants to give you credit unless you already have a good background of using credit wisely. However, if you had that background, you wouldn't need their help.

Improving your credit might require that you simply build a credit history to spread the word about yourself. Building credit is the process of adding favorable information to your credit files, and doing the things that lenders like to see. Remember, this is a marathon, not a sprint. By pacing yourself, you will get to the finish without getting hurt.

ALERT!

Some people believe that paying cash for everything is the best way to manage money. While the concept of having enough cash to pay for what you buy is admirable, failing to use credit is foolhardy. If you never use credit, you might not be able to get it when you need it.

Using credit does not have to be expensive. Indeed, you can pay your credit card balances in full every month, and you will not pay a penny in interest. However, your creditors will know that you are a responsible person. They will know that they can count on you, and you'll be able to count on them in an emergency.

The skills you learn in this chapter are like powerful magic: they can be used for good or evil purposes. Once you build a nice-looking credit history, it will be really, really easy to get a lot of money. Don't go over to the dark side and misuse your powers. You will lead a much simpler life if you only use credit when you need it, and pay it off when you don't. Be sure to follow all of the good credit habits discussed elsewhere in this book. Ultimately, you should think of these techniques as "the ones that worked so well I quit using them."

Who Needs Credit?

Everybody ought to have a decent credit history. In times of trouble, your credit may be all you have, and it can keep you from getting into deeper trouble. If you don't have a strong credit history, you should start building one now. Nobody is going to give you any substantial money if you do not have credit. Lenders are scared of losing money, so they try to make wise lending decisions.

Give the Kid a Chance

There are a variety of reasons that you might not have any credit history. Many people go through this in their lives. For young adults who are just setting out on their own, there is no credit history. If you are in this position, it is now up to you to make your mark on the world. Just avoid making any negative marks.

If you are a parent, consider helping your children build credit before they leave the nest. They will have it much easier, and borrowing in their earlier years will be less expensive. Perhaps most importantly, giving your child a chance to use credit in a limited capacity can teach them some valuable lessons. When they are out in the world, unsupervised, they are going to get a lot of offers for credit. Some will be good offers, but some might fall into the category of predatory lending. If your child is educated and has a decent start on a credit history, it is less likely that she will get caught in the worst traps.

Welcome to the United States of America

Recent arrivals to the United States also find themselves without credit. Not only do they have to learn customs and a new locale, not to mention a language, they have to do it without credit. Other countries often have ways of judging their citizens' creditworthiness, but those metrics do not always work in the United States. Here, most lending decisions are automated; they pull a credit score and say "yes" or "no." Because of that, new arrivals need to get into the system and play by a new set of rules. Granted, there are institutions that make lending decisions without using automated processes, but not many.

Till Death Do Us Part

Some marriages do not work out. While the emotional costs are huge, there is also a great financial cost. What's worse, one of the parties might have been the sole credit user in the family. If credit cards, mortgages, and auto loans are only in one spouse's name, the other spouse probably does not have much of a credit score. Left on his own, he might have to build credit even though he's been using it for years.

A more tragic possibility is that the spouse who used credit passes away unexpectedly. A surviving spouse will have a hard time all around. Of course, one way to protect against these challenges is to make sure that everybody has some credit in their name. Keep a well-aged account open and in good standing.

I Had Some Credit, but It Broke

In addition to those without credit, individuals with bad credit can use the same techniques. In such a case, you might be rebuilding your credit after some hard times. The concept is the same: by taking steps to show lenders that you're responsible, you can earn access to better deals.

Don't believe that you're stuck with the hand you were dealt. Your credit is always a work in progress. You can create it, improve it, destroy it, and rebuild it. It might take time and patience, but you will eventually earn trust if you do the right things.

Building and rebuilding credit takes time. However, you can see improvements over several months. After several years of credit-building behavior, you will find access to attractive loans and terms that you never knew were available. Keep in mind that the ugliest parts of your past will disappear from your credit files after seven to ten years. If you are building a good reputation in the meantime, your credibility should skyrocket once those items fall off your reports.

Building Credit-Ability

As you build credit, you are building credibility. From a lender's perspective, credibility means "credit-ability." In other words, the lender is asking: "If I loan this person money, will I get it back the way I want to get it back?" Note that you are not trying to deceive anybody here. You know you can handle the responsibility, so let the rest of the world know. As you go through this process, think of your credit as a brutally honest friend who always tells the truth about you. If you have been doing well, you will know. If you made a few mistakes, you can be certain that you will hear about them.

Starting from Scratch

If you do not have the bare-bones foundation in place, you will have a hard time getting anywhere. Do you have a checking and a savings account? If not, it is time to get with the program. Many lenders do not accept cash anyway, so open a free checking account at the very least.

Having money saved up is a major credibility builder, especially if you want to borrow from the institution that has your savings. Make regular monthly deposits, similar to a monthly debt payment, and you look even better. Another advantage of having a stash of cash is that you can use it for a down payment on an installment loan. Why does that help? It lowers the total amount of money they lend you, and it also lowers your required monthly payment. These factors increase the likelihood that you will be able to pay off the debt.

As always, you need to think like a lender. Consider all of the different ways you can convince them that you are likely to pay on your debts as agreed. If you have a stable employment and residence history, that might help. Before you move or change jobs, see if you can take on a little bit more credit. If you move first and then apply, you might scare them off.

Base Hits, Build on Successes

The goal of building credit is to have small successes, and build on them. You are not trying to get a zero-down mortgage as your very first loan. If you do manage to get one, it will probably cost you more in fees and interest than it should. Try to apply for credit that you feel reasonably confident you can get. Otherwise, you might end up with a higher-than-normal concentration of inquiries in your credit files. When in doubt, ask the lender for their opinion. Don't always take no for an answer though, sometimes the only way to find out is to submit an application.

Offers that say "You're Preapproved" are not entirely accurate. The lender will likely make a hard inquiry into your credit to determine whether or not they wish to do business with you. Look for clues that you might or might not be able to get an account before you apply for it.

When you are just starting to build or rebuild credit, everything is just a little bit more important. The things you do have a greater impact on your credit than the same actions might have for a seasoned credit user. Therefore, be especially careful at this point. If you do not feel like you should take on additional loans, you are doing the right thing by holding back.

Got Better? Get Better!

Don't forget to pat yourself on the back periodically. When your lenders first gave you a shot, they were taking a risk. Therefore, they probably did not give you the best possible deal available, and there's nothing wrong with that. It's only fair that lenders who take risks deserve to earn a little more. How do things look today? Are you less risky now, based on your more robust credit history? If so, speak up.

See if you can qualify for better loan terms after you've built a good reputation. If you have credit cards, pick up the phone and ask them for a better rate. You might be surprised at what you hear. If you got a mortgage, talk with a trusted mortgage broker to see if there is any sense in changing your mortgage terms. You might now qualify for a more attractive loan. Of course, if interest rates are not cooperating, it might not do you any good to change right away.

In general, don't forget that you are moving forward and improving your credit score. You should periodically see the benefits of all the hard work you are doing. Ask for better deals. Don't forget to shop around for auto insurance every few years. Your improved credit might help you in a variety of ways.

Secured Loans

One of the most effective ways to build credit is by using secured loans. The loans are secured because you pledge some type of collateral—like money in a savings account—to the lender in exchange for using their credit card. If you should fail to pay the money back, the lender knows that they can take your collateral.

Secured loans will get your foot in the door so you can start using credit. Lenders give you a chance, and you can build on your successes.

The bank knows that you are good for the money because they're holding it in your account. They'll freeze your account so that you can't take the money out, but this is a small price to pay for the chance to get good information in your credit report.

Secured loans are not a bad thing. In fact, the holy grail of all loans—the home mortgage—is a secured loan. In exchange for your home-purchase funds, your lender has the right to take back, or foreclose on, your house if you fail to pay as agreed.

Secured Credit Cards

One of the most powerful credit-building moves you can make is to use a secured credit card. A secured credit card offers the ability to use a standard credit card at little risk to the lender. To do this, you make a deposit into your bank or credit union account. Then, you apply for a secured credit card with the same dollar limit as your deposit. You must apply for the card from the same institution that has your deposit. For example, if you deposit $500 into a savings account, you might apply for a credit card with a $500 limit.

Your secured card acts just like an unsecured credit card. You can use it in all the same places, and nobody except you and the bank will know that it's a secured card. Keep in mind that the bank is taking some risk, so they'll likely pull your credit just to make sure you won't get out of hand. Even though the card has a limit, it is possible to charge more than the limit, and doing this will get you in trouble.

ALERT!

When using a secured loan, make sure that your institution will report the loan to the major credit-reporting companies. The whole point of using a secured loan is to build or rebuild your credit, otherwise you'd just spend the cash without depositing it first. If your bank doesn't report your loans, shop around and find an institution that will.

Expanding the Foundation

Once you have a secured credit card, it is essential that you use it responsibly. Use it in moderation, and pay down the balance every month. Use the card even if you have the cash to pay for what you are buying—the key is to show others that you can use credit. If you do this, lenders will eventually see you as an attractive borrower.

As time goes on, you should be able to increase your access to credit. Perhaps you can have the bank raise your limit above the amount that you keep on deposit. This will improve your credit score by decreasing your credit utilization, and it will be a stepping stone to even greater loans. Ask about a credit-line increase every six to eighteen months until you have received several increases.

The best time to ask for an increase is when you are only using a small portion of your available balance. Otherwise, your lender might think you've fallen on hard times and you are becoming a default risk. Of course, you should not use your full credit line when you are building credit—you're just showing them that you can handle the responsibility.

Secured Auto Loans

In addition to credit cards, you can use an auto loan to help build your credit. The concept is similar to the concept of a secured credit card. However, your deposit might not be large enough to pay the whole cost of your automobile. That's okay, because the loan is secured by your deposit plus the auto itself, the bank should be able to get its money back if it repossesses the car.

The auto loan shows up as an installment loan on your credit report, so you can add some variety and spice to the items in your history. In some cases, your financial institution might not pull your credit history if you use a secured auto loan—this is more likely at smaller institutions and credit unions. This means you can reduce hard inquiries, as well as get a loan no matter how bad your history is.

After you open a secured credit card account, you should try to find a way to open an installment type of account, like a secured auto loan. Credit-scoring models look more favorably on installment accounts, and they also reward you for having different types of credit.

Utilities

While they may not be in your classic credit score, your relationships with utility companies can help you or hurt you. Telephone, energy, and cable companies that you've worked with keep data on your payment history. Establishing utility accounts and paying on time will open the door to increasingly better loans and better credit.

Be sure to get utility accounts in your name if you need to build credit. If one spouse of a married couple has a limited credit history, they should put utility accounts in that spouse's name. Likewise, if you live with roommates, see if you can get the utility accounts in your name to help with your credit. Of course, having the accounts in your name means you are on the hook for paying all of the bills.

A Different Kind of Score

Experian has a credit score developed specifically from your relationships with utility companies. Their Telecommunications, Energy, and Cable

(TEC) Risk Model uses information from utility accounts to predict how likely you are to pay on time. While utility companies obviously have an interest in this score, people with little credit history are increasingly judged with the same information.

FACT

Innovations like the Telecommunications, Energy, and Cable (TEC) Risk Model allow vendors and lenders to score millions of additional consumers. Previously, these consumers were excluded from offers because nobody knew what to do with them. Imagine how many people use mobile phones and pay electricity bills, but have never used a credit card.

Likewise, the Fair Isaac Corporation uses has a credit score that incorporates information from utilities and other service providers. The FICO Expansion Score makes credit scores—and credit—available for consumers who previously could not be scored.

Keep Your Nose Clean

Utilities are also essential in keeping your credit squeaky clean. If you've failed to pay bills you owe, your debt could be sent to a collection company. Collection items are especially damaging to your credit history, and an unpaid utility bill can leave a black mark on your credit for seven years. As always, communicating with your utility providers before a problem gets out of hand is the best route. They would rather work with you than send your account to collections.

Another reason to stay current on utility bills is that you may have an opportunity to use your payment history as negotiating clout. While many lending decisions are automated, some lenders still make decisions the old-fashioned way. If you can show them a steady history of on-time utility payments, an uncertain lender may give you a shot at a better loan.

Using a Co-Signer

A co-signer is somebody who shares a credit account with you. If you don't have credit, or if you have bad credit, lenders will consider the co-signer's credit strength when making a decision. It's important that your co-signer has better credit than you do, otherwise using a co-signer won't help you at all.

Who should you use as a co-signer? As the old saying goes, start with friends, family, and fools. You'll need to find a close person who trusts you, has good credit, and is willing to stick their neck out for you. For younger people, parents are a good first choice. Ask your parents if they'd be willing to help you out and co-sign for a credit card or a loan. To sweeten the deal, offer to have statements sent directly to them so that they can see it if you should miss any payments.

ALERT!

Using a co-signer is a major responsibility, so don't take it lightly. If you fail to pay debts that your co-signer helped you get, the lenders go after your co-signer. Lenders will demand payment, and add negative items to the co-signer's credit report. If somebody does you a favor by co-signing, repay the favor by repaying your loans as agreed.

If your parents cannot or will not co-sign, look to a spouse next. Your spouse's credit might help you get your foot in the door with a good lender. Recent arrivals to the United States often establish credit when their spouse (if she is a U.S. citizen with a credit history) co-signs for them. Finally, siblings might take you under their wing and sign for you.

If you can't find a co-signer in your immediate family, you'll have to branch out and find a friend to do you a huge favor. Proceed with caution; ruining somebody's credit is a surefire way to end a friendship.

Keep in mind that financial experts often warn people not to co-sign on a loan. There is good reasoning behind this. If the lenders will not give you money on your own merit, your friends and family should have reason to hesitate as well. Don't take it personally if a friend will not co-sign—some people just can't afford to take the risk.

Use the Big Names

You could be the best borrower in the world and nobody would know it. Being responsible and paying debts off is good, but letting everybody know about it is even better. If you're taking steps to build a strong credit history, make sure the word gets out. The best way to do this is to use large financial institutions as you build or rebuild credit. These institutions are more likely to report to the major credit-reporting companies, thereby adding positive information to your credit report.

One way to make sure your loans are getting reported is to ask. Simply find out which credit-reporting bureaus your lender uses. If they don't report their loans, see if you can find a lender that does. It may be that you can't find a lender that routinely reports loans. In that case, ask them if they'll report your loans to the bureaus; all they can do is say no.

QUESTION?

Will debit cards help my credit?
No, debit cards do not show up on your credit reports, even if the card is a big-name card like Visa. Debit cards simply pull from your checking account, so it's not the same as a credit card. Keep in mind, if you mishandle your debit card you can still get a bad reputation.

Another way to leverage the big names is by using credit accounts at large department stores. Find out if they report to the bureaus. You will find that the older and more established stores do report on your account. Getting a credit card with a department store is usually quite easy, so take advantage if it is an establishment where you would normally shop. Of course, you should always pay your balance off in full with this type of account. The interest rates are usually not the best, and you can easily forget about department store accounts.

Finally, you can try for a credit card that works at one of the big gas stations. These cards have less-restrictive rules, so they might give you a chance. Again, you do not really want to carry balances on these cards. Instead, you simply want them to make reports to the major credit-reporting companies.

Chapter 13

Making Bad Scores Better

No matter what you've heard, it is possible to improve your credit on your own. If your credit needs some improvement, this section will outline the steps you need to take. You can systematically look at a few important factors in your credit and make adjustments where necessary. Slowly but surely, you and your lenders will see an improvement in your credit and your credit scores. Then you can use techniques found elsewhere in this book to keep your credit in tip-top shape.

Get Current

Perhaps the most important thing you can do when you're tuning up your credit is to get current on all of your bills. If you are behind on any payments, new lenders will wonder how you can pay them if you're already missing payments elsewhere.

Payment History

Your payment history is one of the most important pieces of the credit-scoring puzzle. Payment history describes whether or not you pay your bills on time. If you pay late, how late do you pay? This is extremely important information for potential lenders. In fact, the FICO credit score is designed to predict whether or not you will pay late. Why do they care so much about your payment history? If you pay late, you become more likely to default.

As 35 percent of your FICO credit score, your payment history is the most heavily weighted factor (followed by amounts owed at 30 percent). It measures a number of characteristics in your payment history:

- How many past-due items you have in your reports
- How much behind you are (how many dollars)
- How far behind you are (how many days past due)
- How recent your payment problems are
- If there is a bankruptcy—if you have completely defaulted

It is important to know that more-recent items are more important to your credit score. If you had a few late payments three years ago, it won't help your credit. However, those three-year-old payments will not hurt you as much as a more recent blemish. Therefore, the longer you pay your bills on time, the more your scores improve. Keep paying bills on time over the years, and you will most certainly see improvements in your credit.

Work It Out

If you are currently behind on a credit account, see if your lender will work things out with you. Ideally, you want them to stop reporting you as delinquent. If you can work out a payment plan that is acceptable to them, they may report that you are paying as agreed. This can be a win-win situation for all parties involved. Remember that the creditor does not want you to go bankrupt, they just want their money back. How do you set up such an arrangement? Make them an offer. Either call or write, and state that you would like to pay a certain dollar amount each month to satisfy your debt. All they can do is say yes or no. If you don't get a favorable response, you can always try again. Be persistent; you might find that different customer-service representatives view things differently.

QUESTION?

How late is a late payment?
Lenders have varying definitions of late. Your agreement probably states that payments must be received by a certain time on a certain day. If you are a few days late, it may not matter. Paying more than thirty days late is a really bad idea.

Staying Current Made Easy

Because your recent activity is so important, it is essential that you don't fall behind. You don't want to see your progress wiped out by a simple mistake. With that in mind, you should take steps to make sure that simple mistakes don't happen. The easiest way to prevent mistakes is to automate your life. Set up a link between your credit accounts and your bank account. Typically, all you have to do is send a voided check to your creditor to get this done. Then, they can go get the money you owe them every month. You don't have to sit down and write a check, you don't have to hunt down a stamp, and you don't have to watch the calendar for due dates.

Correct Mistakes

You may have heard computer programmers saying, "Garbage in, garbage out," refering to the fact that computers will only do what they are instructed to do. Programmers write instructions for computers in a given programming language, or code. The computer does not interpret what the programmer is trying to accomplish. Instead, it just follows the code.

Your credit is similar. If the inputs (information added to your credit reports) are garbage, then the output (your credit score, or any human-based lending decisions) will also be garbage. Therefore, it is essential that your credit reports are completely accurate. While it's possible that a mistake will affect your credit favorably, it's much more likely that any mistake will hurt you.

Use Less of What You've Got

Credit is a good thing. It allows you to do things that you may not be able to do with your own personal savings. It gives you a safety net in the event of an emergency. But it's possible to have too much of a good thing. Having too much birthday cake can have adverse effects on your health, and using too much of your credit can be harmful to your credit.

How Important Is It?

The "amounts owed" category is the second-most important factor in your FICO credit score. It accounts for 30 percent of the score, and it looks at how you are using the credit available to you. Are you maxing out all of your credit cards? If so, lenders may worry that you've fallen on hard times and might stop paying your bills. They also want to know how you are doing with different types of loans. If you have paid a $200,000 mortgage down to a balance of $6,000, then you are a seasoned and disciplined borrower, which makes you more attractive.

How Much Is Too Much?

If your credit is not as good as you would like it to be, it may be that you are borrowing too much. Take a look at your credit accounts, particularly revolving-credit accounts like credit cards, and see how close you are to your maximum limit. If your card has a limit of $5,000 and you have a balance of $4,000, then you are using 80 percent of your available credit (4000 is 80 percent of 5000).

In general, you should strive to use 35 percent or less of your available credit. How can you accomplish this in the example above? You need to pay down the balance so that it is at or below $1,750. Alternatively, you could ask for a credit-limit increase. Either way, you want to keep your account balance as low as possible in relation to the account's limit.

Grab your credit card statements and find the maximum credit limit. Now, multiply the maximum limit by 0.35. This will solve for 35 percent of your card's credit limit. If your balance is any higher than 35 percent, you should pay down the balance or get a credit-limit increase on that account.

Note that this does not work the same way with installment accounts. Mortgages and auto loans are viewed differently. If you look at your credit report, it will show your original loan amount as the maximum credit limit. If it is a brand-new loan, you will obviously have a large balance relative to the limit. This will not damage your credit in the same way that a high relative balance on a credit card would.

Common Mistakes

In an effort to improve their credit, some people actually mess it up. The "balances owed" category is especially perilous. You might be tempted to simply open new accounts and leave them with a zero balance. Granted, this would reduce the percentage of available credit that you are using. Unfortunately, the strategy would probably backfire and lower your credit scores. Inquiries into your credit would reduce your score, and the average age of all of your accounts would also go down. Instead of improving your credit, you would damage it.

Another frequent mistake is the act of closing unused accounts. People worry that having too much credit capacity available makes them appear risky in a lender's eyes. Or, they may simply want to clean up old accounts— to get less mail, or just to organize. If you do this, you will wipe out all of that available credit. As a result, you'll be using a greater percentage of your available credit, even though you haven't borrowed any more. Like the strategy above, this strategy can sometimes reduce the average age of your credit accounts.

Time Heals Some Wounds

Some things get better with age. This may apply to your credit. If you have negative items in your credit history, there's probably nothing you can do to remove them. Don't worry though, these items cannot haunt you forever. Over time they will fall off your credit reports, and they will not be used in credit scores.

Seven Years of Bad Luck

Breaking a mirror will get you seven years of bad luck. Oddly enough, you get the same thing for making serious mistakes with your credit. You can beg and plead, and you might get lucky, but negative information will generally appear on your credit reports for seven years, including:

- Late payments
- Chargeoffs
- Accounts in collection
- Missed payments
- Chapter 13 bankruptcy

Note that a Chapter 7 bankruptcy will appear on your credit reports, and lower your credit scores, for ten years. Chapter 7 hurts creditors more, so it lasts longer.

All of those juicy details about you don't just disappear. Your successes and failures are kept in databases by the major consumer-reporting companies. However, these companies are restricted from reporting the negative items after seven or ten years. The Fair Credit Reporting Act limits how and when these companies can report on you.

Exceptions to the Rule

While you have some protection under the Fair Credit Reporting Act, there are exceptions. Tax debts, for example, will not go away unless you pay them off. The government wrote the law, so they get to make the rules. After you pay off a tax debt, the delinquency will appear on your credit reports for seven more years. Another exception to the rule involves high-dollar transactions. You can find more detail in the chapter about the Anatomy of a Credit Report.

ALERT!

You should examine your credit reports to see if there is any outdated negative information. Somebody may have incorrectly reported the date on one of your accounts, whether by accident or on purpose. If the account is too old, write a letter and get the information removed.

Myth of the Disappearing Act

A widely spread myth is that you can pay someone to remove items from your credit reports. Of course, the goal would be to remove negative items that are lowering your credit scores. Shady credit-repair companies often claim that they can do this. Unless the negative items are errors, they are promising more than they can legally deliver. If anybody makes promises to the contrary, it's a sure sign that you are dealing with a scam artist.

Basic Credit Improvement

If you think about it, improving your credit is pretty easy. You just have to do the things that make you attractive as a borrower. You don't need to use any fancy tricks, you don't need to pay for a system, and you don't need to spend precious hours on the process. What you do need to do is simply pay off your debts as agreed.

Sunk Cost

In the field of Economics, there is a concept called the "sunk cost." The sunk cost is a cost you have already paid, and you cannot get the money back. For example, pretend you are playing poker and you have an extremely weak hand. Assume that through the course of this hand, you have chipped in $20. Suddenly, you get another card and realize that you probably won't win this hand. You have to make a choice. Do you stay in the game or do you fold?

You should base your decision solely on whether or not you think you will win the hand. However, your $20 in the pot may nag at you. You may have the following thought: "I've already put in $20. I should just keep playing (and adding to the pot) to see if I can get it back." Of course, that would be the wrong course of action. Your $20 is most likely gone, and you need to look forward, not backward. While this is a relatively simple example, multimillion-dollar businesses struggle with the same problem. It is difficult to let a sunk cost go.

Keep It Simple

Use your best judgment when you think about your credit. If you wanted an executive summary of the best ways to improve your credit, it would read something like this:

- You can't change the past; focus on the future
- Start small, and work your way up
- Variety is the spice of life—use different types of loans
- Everything is best in moderation, including debt
- Always pay at least the minimum on time
- Check your credit reports at least once per year
- Credit is like your brain—use it or lose it

Looking Forward

Just like the best businesses, you should look forward when making decisions. Of course, you can learn something from your past experiences.

Most notably, you may have learned what not to do. However, do not dwell on those experiences, and don't let them drag you in the wrong direction. All of your future decisions should be decisions that will improve your situation going forward.

FACT

You will enjoy the process more, and you'll probably have better success, if you use a simple, basic approach to improving your credit. Just develop some habits that will keep you out of trouble. With each day, it will get easier, and soon you'll be surprised at how good your credit score really is.

If you have made mistakes in the past, there's nothing you can do to correct those mistakes. Your best bet is to use credit responsibly. Without a doubt, people will notice. Your credit reports will show that you are a responsible borrower. In turn, your credit scores will increase. If you can simply focus on doing the right things going forward, your credit will follow.

How Long Does It Take?

Rome wasn't built in a day, and your credit won't blossom overnight. It can take months or years for you to see substantial results, but you will see results.

Slam Dunks

There are a few things that will immediately improve your credit. For example, if you remove erroneous information (like somebody else's delinquencies or bankruptcy), you will drastically change the nature of your credit profile. Run a credit score before and after removing the bad information, and you'll see a difference.

Another way to make a nice dent toward better credit is to look at your amounts owed. If you are using 80 percent of your available credit, your score will suffer. If you have the funds available, consider paying down your debts so that you are using no more than 35 percent of your available credit.

Granted, this may not be an option, but if you have the money to do it, it will make a big difference in how lenders view you.

Your Mileage may Vary

The amount of time it takes to improve your credit will depend on your individual circumstances. For example, if you had a recent bankruptcy, it will take several years for you to see improvements. On the other hand, you can rebound from one late payment after several months of on-time payments. In general, you might expect to see improvements in your credit scores after six to nine months of good behavior.

Why It's so Slow

The process can be painfully slow. You might think that in this day and age things could happen more quickly, and you might be right. However, the system is not set up to update quickly. Consider the process involved when you pay down your balances. First, you write a check and mail it to your credit card company. The credit card company processes your payment, and credits your account. Now you have a lower balance. Next, the credit card company has to report your account information to the credit-reporting companies. If they only make these reports monthly or quarterly, the whole process can take several months.

Rapid Rescoring

There is one way to get dramatic results in a short period of time. There is a legitimate service called rapid rescoring that sometimes gets used for mortgages. If you use one of the slam-dunk techniques discussed above, your mortgage lender may be able to accelerate the rescoring process. They use special relationships with the credit-reporting companies to get things done quickly. They can update your credit reports and generate a new credit score in as little as thirty-six hours. As you may have guessed, there is some cost involved. Whether you write a check for it or not, you are paying for it somehow.

Borrowing in the Meantime

It could take months or even years to see improvements in your credit. What are you supposed to do during that time? You probably need debt, and it would probably help you to use debt—remember, you can't have good credit unless you can show that you're good with credit. Therefore, you need to find a reasonable way to get access to credit. You should start by using the strategies described in the chapter on Building Credit.

There are a number of card issuers that focus on borrowers with bad credit. These cards claim to issue credit to anybody and everybody regardless of your credit history. They even report your activity to the credit-reporting companies, which helps you build credit. These may work, but watch out for high fees.

Any credit available to you might not be at the most attractive terms. You may have to pay higher interest rates, and you may have a limited number of choices. If so, work with what is available to you, and then work your way up the food chain. Just be careful, predatory lenders come out of the woodwork when you have poor credit. If you get stuck with a bad deal, it can cost you a bundle, and it will be more difficult to improve your credit.

Credit Repair

Sometimes you need the help of an outsider. You can't be an expert at everything, so you might use the services of a credit-improvement expert. The right credit-counseling agency can truly help you improve your situation. However, the world of credit counseling and credit repair is full of scam artists.

A Helping Hand

Not every organization that claims to help you improve your credit is a bad one. There are organizations that actually want to help you, and they will charge a fair and reasonable rate. In fact, you might not pay anything out of pocket—the agency gets paid by your creditors. One of the most respected organizations that offers counseling services is Consumer Credit Counseling Services (on the Web at *www.moneymanagement.org*). This is a nonprofit organization with a history of helping people.

Unfortunately, Consumer Credit Counseling Services's reputation is a little too good. The world is full of businesses with names that are suspiciously similar to CCCS's name. Those other businesses may not have your best interests at heart. In fact, many of these businesses pose as nonprofit organizations, but profit is their main motivation. In early 2006, the IRS revoked the tax-exempt status of many of these so-called nonprofits. After an audit of sixty such organizations, the IRS found that at least thirty were bogus.

File Bankruptcy Today!

A lot of so-called credit-repair agencies are just bankruptcy attorneys in disguise. There is nothing wrong with bankruptcy attorneys, as long as they identify themselves as such. Unfortunately, many of these attorneys get folks in the door with false advertising. They claim that "credit problems are no problem," or that they can "wipe out your debts." Not surprisingly, their expert opinion is often that you should just file for bankruptcy.

Beware of agencies that only want to put you into a debt-management program (DMP). A good agency will take a holistic approach to improving your financial life. The one-trick ponies are only interested in setting up a DMP so that they can collect fees. Speaking of fees, never pay one until you understand what you are getting.

A New Identity

Some credit-repair companies tempt you with the promise of a clean slate. Imagine starting over, shaking off the chains of your past credit problems. Some organizations suggest that you can do this by creating a new identity. You apply for an Employer Identification Number (EIN) from the IRS, and use that in lieu of your Social Security Number. Because the EIN is a brand new number, your credit history is not attached to it. Of course, this is illegal, and breaking the law won't make your life any easier.

Twist Your Lender's Arm

Some credit-repair agencies should actually be called credit-damage agencies. They suggest that you play hardball with your lenders. These agencies suggest that, by failing to pay your bills (on purpose), you signal that you are out of money. You should do this even if you have the money to pay your bills. As a result, your creditors assume that you are on the brink of bankruptcy. This makes it easier for you to offer them less than you owe. They are more likely to accept the offer, figuring that something is better than nothing. Unfortunately, these tactics are more likely to damage your credit than to help you out.

Do-It-Yourself

Instead of taking your chances, you might be better off doing it yourself. The techniques you learn from this book will help you make progress toward better credit. If things get too complicated or too difficult, you can always go for help.

Chapter 14

Correcting Credit-Report Errors

Errors happen. While the credit-reporting system often works perfectly, sometimes you're penalized because of inaccurate information. In these cases, you may feel that "innocent until proven guilty" no longer applies. You may have to work extremely hard to get these errors corrected. This section details credit-report errors: how they happen, why they're so frequent, and what you can do about them. You'll find a step-by-step approach that you can use to get errors removed.

14

An Easy Way and a Hard Way

If you are lucky, you might be able to get errors fixed the easy way. If one of your creditors is the source of an error, you should try to get them to stop reporting erroneous information. A phone call may be all it takes. You can bring a mistake to their attention, and ask that they correct it. Once their records are correct, that information will flow through to the credit-reporting companies.

If you are not so lucky, you will have to go through the unpleasant process of disputing errors in your credit report. Credit-reporting companies say that they do not create records on you—all they do is repeat what others report on you. If you cannot figure out who is reporting something derogatory about you (if it is not one of your accounts that simply has an error), then you have to sort it out with the credit-reporting company.

Everybody Makes Mistakes

Errors can come from a variety of sources. When you have errors on your credit report, it can be extremely frustrating. To help you through the process, it is important to take a big-picture view of the situation. This will help you see where errors may be coming from, and it will help you focus your attention so that you can get results.

On the Bright Side

If it makes you feel any better, consider how the system works as a whole. Credit reporting and credit scoring probably helped you get credit quite easily. Were it not for the credit-reporting process, getting loans would take a lot longer. In addition, lending decisions might be biased, allowing for discrimination or poor judgment on the part of lenders. Finally, with the advent of scoring and risk-based lending, loans are available to a wider population.

To say that fixing errors in your credit report can be frustrating is a major understatement. The process can be absolutely mind-boggling if it does not go smoothly. It can take months, years, or even a lifetime. You might feel like you're beating your head against a wall, and you might even lose your faith in humanity. There are a lot of really disturbing stories out there, so just be aware that others have been down this path before you, and most of them eventually found success.

FACT

Errors on your credit report represent a glitch in the system. Periodically, things go wrong. Credit reporting happens on a huge scale. The seemingly small percentage of errors can result in major headaches for millions of consumers. If you find yourself a part of this group, remember to keep the big picture in mind.

The Lender's Perspective

When trying to solve a problem, it is best to understand the perspective of all parties involved. You have a goal, and you may be in the right, but other interested parties have their own motivations. Consider the lender's perspective when it comes to credit-reporting errors. Like most businesses, lenders want to operate as efficiently as possible. In other words, they're trying to save money. As a result, they may not devote extensive resources toward ensuring that your credit reports are accurate.

Leaving Money on the Table

Credit-report accuracy happens to be in the lender's best interests. Consider the outcomes of inaccurate credit reports. If a responsible borrower has errors in her credit report, she will look less attractive as a customer. While she may have never made a late payment, her credit report may indicate otherwise. Perhaps it shows several accounts past due, and a recent bankruptcy.

If these errors were not a part of her credit report, lenders would love to have this person as a customer. She pays her bills on time, as agreed. Therefore, she would be a profitable customer. Unfortunately, the creditors do not know this because of her marred credit report. They deny her applications for credit, or offer her rates that are simply not acceptable. As a result, they lose a customer, or at least they fail to gain a profitable customer. The lenders leave money on the table when this happens.

Risk to Principal

Now, consider an opposite example. Imagine a borrower who has had a hard time meeting his debt obligations. He has paid his bills late in the past, but only on one of his accounts, and it has been several years. The other six accounts on his credit report are sparkling and immaculate. Like the borrower above, his credit reports are inaccurate. However, instead of showing somebody else's derogatory information, the errors on his report make him look more attractive as a borrower.

As you navigate through your credit and fix errors, consider the objectives of all the parties involved. By knowing what they want and how they operate, you will have knowledge to help yourself solve problems. Ultimately, credit-report accuracy benefits everybody.

Because of the appearance of a strong credit history, credit-scoring models grant this borrower a fairly high score. Lenders decide to offer him credit, and they offer a fairly generous credit line. Unfortunately, they're taking a risk that they don't even realize. There is a decent chance that this borrower will not pay his debts as agreed. As a result, the lender will have to spend time and money trying to collect on the debt. In a worst case scenario, the borrower will default altogether and the lender will have to take a loss.

In the Real World

You just looked at two examples of how erroneous credit reports can hurt lenders. It may seem that either example is equally probable. In the real world, things don't work out that way. First, lenders are more scared of losing principal (the second example) than they are of missing out on a good customer (the first example). How might this influence their decision-making process?

Accurate credit reports would benefit everybody. Consumers would be judged on a fair basis, and lenders would have an accurate picture of who they are dealing with. It is amazing that lenders cannot devote more resources toward ensuring credit-report accuracy. Regulators, lawsuits, and consumer advocates do most of the heavy lifting.

FACT

Errors in your credit can come from several sources. A creditor or information provider could report inaccurate information about you. You should try to fix that with the creditor. Credit-reporting companies are also guilty: they sometimes mix and match data incorrectly and cause errors to appear on your reports.

What about the Agencies?

Lenders are responsible for the information that ends up on a credit report. However, they are not responsible for all of the errors out there. The credit-reporting companies play an important role in creating and correcting any errors. Sometimes these companies are referred to as credit bureaus or credit-reporting agencies. The three largest ones in the United States are TransUnion, Equifax, and Experian.

The credit-reporting companies store information that is sent to them by your creditors. Your creditors might send monthly updates on each of your accounts. This information is stored in massive computer systems. While you might imagine that the credit-reporting companies keep your credit report, that is not exactly accurate. They keep records of the account updates sent by creditors. Whenever somebody asks for your credit report, the credit-reporting company creates one by joining all of the records that seem to be yours.

Common Errors

A credit report can have a lot of different types of errors in it. Information comes from a variety of sources, and it comes in at different times. All of the information is compiled and joined into one place. Because of the complexity involved, it is not surprising that errors happen. Some types of errors are more frequent than others. This section highlights some of the more common errors, as well as a few of the not-so-common errors. If you have errors in your credit reports, start by looking for these culprits:

- Transposed Social Security Numbers (123-45-6789 instead of 123-54-6789)
- An authorized user is listed as the account owner
- Transposed first and middle names (John Paul Doe instead of John Doe Paul)
- Nicknames create mix-ups
- Names are spelled incorrectly
- Similar names get mixed together
- Similar but different Social Security Numbers get mixed together
- Different generations get mixed together (Paul Jr.'s accounts with Paul Sr.'s)
- Outdated delinquencies still appear (bankruptcies older than ten years)
- Multiple listing of the same account (especially delinquent accounts)
- Illegally reaged collection accounts
- Customer erroneously listed as deceased

Some of these errors can be extremely persistent. Even after getting them removed, they might pop up again. If they keep coming back, you really need to dig into the details and find out where they're coming from. Either a creditor keeps reporting the release information about you, or the credit-reporting company keeps mixing you up with somebody else.

Studies Show

A variety of different studies have attempted to understand how accurate credit reports really are. The results vary. However, studies performed by independent or government bodies (in other words, not by a private company who might be biased) all show that credit reports are full of errors.

These errors might be present in all of your credit reports, one of them, or none of them.

A 2004 study by the Public Interest Research Group showed that 29 percent of credit reports had serious errors. These were errors that would result in a creditor denying your application for a loan. For example, failure to pay (or pay on time) a bill, or an erroneous public record (such as a bankruptcy, tax lien, or judgment) would fall into this category. This same study found that 54 percent of credit reports "contained personal demographic identifying information that was misspelled, long-outdated, belonged to a stranger, or was otherwise incorrect" ("Mistakes Do Happen." National Association of State PIRGs. 2004).

ALERT!

If you are ever denied credit, ask for a copy of the credit report (or credit score) that was used in the decision. It is not illegal for your lender to disclose this information, although they may have promised the service provider that they will not do so. This report may differ from the one you will get on your own.

Other studies have also found errors to be quite common. A 2002 study by the Consumer Federation of America looked at differences between your credit reports from the three major credit-reporting companies. Not surprisingly, your credit score differs depending on which credit-reporting company supplies the data. This is because not all lenders report to every credit-reporting company. However, the differences are still quite dramatic. Thirty-one percent of people had credit scores that differed by fifty points or more. Five percent had scores that differed by 100 points. Fifty or 100 points is enough to change the interest rate that you pay on a loan.

Do You See What I See?

When a company takes an adverse action against you, such as denying your application for credit, you are entitled to a free copy of your credit report. Unfortunately, you may not see the exact same credit report that your lender looked at. Further, you may not see all of the information that was used in calculating a credit score. How are you supposed to figure out what caused the denial of credit?

Credit reports are generated whenever somebody asks for one. The credit-reporting companies don't just keep them lying around, sitting on a shelf ready for quick delivery. They are created in response to a request. Depending on how the request is made, the delivered report may be more or less accurate.

When you get a copy of your credit report, you are probably quite specific in providing your personal information. You know how to spell your name, and you get your Social Security Number right. The credit-reporting companies require you to prove that you really are who you say you are. However, they're not as restrictive with lenders. A lender can get your credit report with your name and Social Security Number only. Because the lender is less specific, the credit-reporting company is less restrictive in weeding out records that don't belong to you. Therefore, it is likely to be less accurate.

Who Do Reporting Companies Work For?

As you gain a clearer picture of how errors work, you should take a close look at the credit-reporting companies. What are their motivations? Who do they work for?

The Customer Is Always Right

Credit-reporting companies work for their customers. Their customers include anybody who buys credit reports and credit scores from them. For the most part, their customers are lenders. Lenders pull your credit anytime they need to evaluate your creditworthiness, like when you apply for loans. In addition, lenders check your credit periodically. They check to see if you're falling behind on other accounts or racking up too much debt, among other things. Credit-reporting companies make a lot of money from their lending customers.

In addition to paying the credit-reporting companies, lenders provide information. They report on their customers regularly. Since credit-reporting companies sell information, they love the organizations that give it to them.

Of course, lenders report to the credit-reporting companies to discourage borrowers from defaulting. Some lenders do not report anything unless you fall behind, but the reputable ones report both good and bad information.

Credit-reporting companies do not want to do a bad job for their customers. What's the worst thing that could happen to a lender? A borrower could default—declaring bankruptcy and getting a liquidation of his debts. If this happens, the lender is unable to collect any money. Therefore, credit-reporting companies want to make sure that they expose any potential risks. They would rather portray a consumer as more risky than less risky.

Pesky Consumers

Consumers, on the other hand, are more of a nuisance. If they ever call at all, it's with a complaint. They seem to think that there is an error somewhere that needs to be fixed. However, credit-reporting companies only report information that is provided to them. They don't make the stuff up, right? Yes and no.

QUESTION?

Do I have a right to dispute inaccuracies in my credit reports?
Yes. Under the Fair Credit Reporting Act, you have a right to have accurate credit reports. You can take action to get errors fixed, including contacting credit-reporting companies, disputing errors, and bringing lawsuits against organizations that violate your rights. Don't let anybody tell you otherwise.

The credit-reporting companies use some artistic license when they figure out how to group account records together. Most of the time, it works beautifully. Just imagine how difficult it must be to provide a record on an individual. People get married and change their names. They use different versions of their name on different account applications, and they move across the country. To add to the confusion, the creditors may provide them with incomplete or incorrect information. The credit-reporting companies have to contend with all of these challenges.

The Floodgates

When things go wrong, people tend to complain, and the credit-reporting companies are inundated with disputes. Consumers claim that a delinquent account is not theirs, or is not delinquent. They claim to be alive when their credit report clearly says that they are deceased. They claim all sorts of things. All of these claims must be investigated, and that takes resources. Since these consumers are not paying customers, you can imagine how eager the company is to satisfy their needs.

In his book *Credit Scores and Credit Reports*, Evan Hendricks explains in wonderful detail how credit-reporting companies "investigate" disputes. Read this book if you would like to understand the nuts and bolts of your credit reports (you'll also be saddened and angered by some of the accounts in the book, which should motivate you to manage your credit). After boiling down the numbers, it turns out that an employee has about 1.66 minutes to handle a dispute. In order to manage this volume, credit-reporting companies use an automated system to verify accounts with the reporting creditor. As Mr. Hendricks noted, a better word to describe the process might be compare. If the record at the creditor is similar enough to the record at the credit-reporting company, no correction is made.

Disputing Errors Step-by-Step

When disputing errors, you should err on the side of caution. Your initial request to have an error corrected might be all it takes. However, you should act as if it will not. If you are systematic and thorough from the beginning, your life will be easier in the event that you run into trouble.

Under the Fair Credit Reporting Act, the credit-reporting companies and your creditors must resolve your dispute, whether favorably or unfavorably, within thirty days. If they fail to do so, they must permanently remove the disputed information from your files. Your job is to dispute information that you feel is inaccurate, and follow up to make sure that the issue is resolved.

Write a Long Letter

You can use the mail, Internet, or phone to dispute any errors. Which one should you use? In this day and age, you might suppose that the Internet is the most efficient and effective way to correct errors. However, your best bet is probably to use snail mail—it is easier to document and prove your actions if you use the mail. If time is of the essence, you might try one of the other methods.

Everything you send should be sent via certified mail, return receipt requested. This will help you verify that your materials made it to the intended destination, and you will have a paper trail that you can use to document your activities. It only costs a few dollars, and gives you proof that you have sent correspondence asking that the error be corrected.

Mark Twain once commented, "I didn't have time to write a short letter, so I wrote a long one instead." Do not make this same mistake with your dispute letters. Keep them extremely short, and to the point. Furthermore, you should not use a nasty tone. A real person will read your letter, and you need their help. If the normal dispute process does not work, you're going to need a lawyer—you can leave the nasty verbose documents to them.

What to Say

Your brief letter should contain all of the relevant information needed to resolve your dispute. You can find a sample letter, which you can use as a template, in the appendix of this book. As an alternative to crafting your own letter, you may be able to download a dispute form from the credit-reporting company's Web site. Presumably, the standardized format will allow them to handle your dispute efficiently. If you choose to write your own letter, make sure you include the following:

- Name
- Current and previous addresses

- Social Security Number
- Date of birth
- Full account number and name of creditor in question
- Specific reason for dispute
- Signature
- Date

Along with your letter, you should include a photocopy of your entire credit report with the items in question highlighted. Your credit report will have information that may be useful to the credit-reporting company. Highlighting the items in question helps to make sure that nobody gets confused. Most importantly, you should enclose supporting documentation. Prove to them that the credit report is wrong. You should not send originals of any document. Make photocopies of your supporting documentation, because you may need to use it more often than you think.

Where to Send

Send your dispute package to the credit-reporting company, or companies, that has erroneous information on you. These companies have special addresses for disputes, which you can find at the bottom of your credit report. If you are reviewing your credit report online, you may have to click on a link to get more details about the dispute process at that particular company.

After you send in your dispute kit, do not send anything else to the credit-reporting company for at least thirty days. If you send something else in, they can restart the clock and once again take thirty days to get back to you. In addition, they may flag your dispute as frivolous if you contact them too often.

In addition to sending your dispute to the credit-reporting company, you should send a complete copy to the creditor in question. Although your dispute is supposed to go through the credit-reporting company, you may nudge things along by contacting the creditor as well.

Make an Appointment

After you submit your dispute, the issue must get resolved within thirty days. The credit-reporting company should notify you that the error was corrected, or that the information was verified as accurate and will not be removed. In order to keep things moving, you should make sure that this happens. If you have not heard from the credit-reporting company within forty days, you should contact them. Set a reminder in your computer, mark your calendar, or do whatever it takes to make sure that you stay on top of this.

If they have not responded within forty days, you should remind them of your original dispute, and include photocopies of documentation such as United States Postal Service receipts proving when they received it. Note that they have not responded, so the information must be permanently removed. Again, you can find a sample letter in the appendix of this book.

Call in the Experts

If the dispute process does not work for you, you may need to get help. The Fair Credit Reporting Act has made things a lot better than they used to be. Consumers have more power to know what is in their credit reports, and to get errors fixed.

Get a Lawyer

You might get results if you bring a lawsuit against the credit-reporting company. You have the right to sue them if they do not abide by the Fair Credit Reporting Act. If you choose to go this route, be sure that you use a lawyer who is well schooled in the Act. A good place to start searching is the Web site for the National Association of Consumer Advocates (*www.naca.net*). You may be able to find a law firm in your area with the required expertise.

Shame Them Publicly

If you are the outgoing, creative, or well-connected type, you may be able to shame them into doing the right thing. If you can get a celebrity or other influential person to plead your case, this may help. Media outlets may be able to shine a burning spotlight on the credit-reporting companies and get you some attention. Or, you can use your imagination to find ways to expose any injustices that you are suffering.

Write Your Officials

Since you have already gone to the trouble to document errors and write to the credit-reporting companies, you could send those letters to regulators and officials. If you send a letter to the Federal Trade Commission, they will forward your correspondence to the credit-reporting company in question. That might send a message that you mean business. Likewise, you might alert local officials. They may take an interest because you're in their community, and help to draft laws that will better protect people like you.

Document, Document, Document

It is essential that you keep meticulous records of the dispute process. By documenting everything, you protect your rights under the Fair Credit Reporting Act. You can prove that you appropriately notified the credit-reporting companies and gave them ample time to correct errors. If you need to bring a lawsuit against them, or if you want to publicize your plight, you'll need to be able to prove everything.

By keeping records and documenting everything, you not only build a legal case, you're also more likely to follow a systematic process that will yield results. You will know exactly what you have done, and what needs to be done next.

Keep copies of absolutely everything. Until your issue is resolved, you should consider anything related to the error extremely valuable information. Keep organized files of all of your disputes and communications with the credit-reporting companies. If possible (and legal in the relevant states), record any phone conversations on the matter. Keep track of how much time you spend, how much extra you have to pay because of any errors, and whether or not you have been denied credit or insurance.

Chapter 15

Setting Kids Up for Success

Think of all of the things you strive to teach your children. You teach them how to tie their shoes, play well with others, and ride a bicycle. To instill good habits and discipline, you probably require that they keep their room clean. As they grow older, you teach them more complex life lessons and value systems. How much time and energy do you spend teaching these things? In most families, it's a lot. Often, financial education is an afterthought, if it even comes to mind at all.

Get 'Em While They're Young

Teaching your children about credit at a young age is important. It is one of life's most valuable lessons. While it may seem shallow, financial skills can make your child's life a lot easier. Of course, money cannot buy happiness, but money problems can cause a lot of unhappiness. Do not think of it as teaching your children how to be rich. Instead, think of it as teaching them to stay out of trouble.

ALERT!

You already know that bad habits are extremely hard to break. If you have ever struggled with a bad habit, you know this from first-hand experience. The best thing you can do for your children is help them develop good financial habits and make smart choices about money, so they won't spend their way to financial ruin.

The best way that you can teach your children how to handle money is to be responsible with it yourself. Lead by example, and they will pick up cues and behaviors from you over the years. If you are thrifty, responsible, and avoid unnecessary debt, your children are likely to be the same way. If you are irresponsible and spend more than you have, your children will almost certainly do the same. Consider a major fringe benefit of setting a good example: you will have good credit. You won't have to deal with the same headaches and costs that a person with bad credit does.

Life Lessons about Money

Life presents plenty of opportunities for you to help ensure that your children have good credit behavior. If you pay attention, you can probably find several instances every day. You can use your own spending, you can use your children's spending, or you can use hypothetical examples to help teach these lessons. If you are a parent, you have no doubt come across some items that seem to be overly expensive. For infants, diapers can make a huge dent in the budget. Next, small children typically want a nice selection of the best toys. Then, fashion takes its toll. Finally, your children may move on to the most expensive source of parental financing—higher education.

As you move through the stages in life, look for ways to help your children develop the behaviors they will need for the rest of their lives. For example, you may be faced with the prospect of spending $100 for a pair of jeans or shoes. Even if you are going to buy the product, try to find a way to throw some education into the mix. Explain that you are taking $100 out of your budget for this purchase, and it has to come from somewhere. Highlight some of the things that you may have to cut back on because of this.

Cards for Kids

Some parents find it useful to give their children a credit card. For younger kids, this might be a secured credit card or a debit card. They watch you use your credit card every day, so you might as well start helping them understand how it works. Otherwise, they may just be under the impression that the "magic card" allows you to get whatever you want. If you go this route, you should be sure that the card will limit excessive spending.

If you have a card with funds earmarked for your children, you can use it with them. You don't need to give it to them so they can run around town with it—use it with them when you are shopping. Together, you can monitor how much you have to spend, and where your money is going.

Some companies offer cards specifically for the purpose of teaching your children about money. Some of these can be very useful, although you should watch out for fees. The best ones limit purchases and decline any transaction that goes above the limit you designate. If you pay your children any type of allowance, or if you pay them for some type of work they do, you can just make deposits into their credit card account. Many of these services allow you to monitor your child's spending online if you think that will be helpful.

Joint Users

You can even use credit cards to help build your child's credit. One way to do this is to open a joint credit card account with your child. Both of you will be account owners, however, you don't have to give a card to your child. The purpose of the account would simply be to build up a solid credit history in the child's name. The child's credit report will show years and years of responsible use on a revolving debt account. Of course, you want to make sure that the bills always get paid on time. Once your child is ready for her own card, you can either remove your name from the account (if the credit card company allows this) or have her open a brand new account. Either way, she will have started her foundation of good credit.

Cash Only

Some parents are appalled at the idea of giving anybody under the age of eighteen a credit card. For some, cash is the only way to go. You can see how much you have, and it hurts just a little bit more to hand over cash than it does to swipe your plastic. The psychological impact of digging into your wallet and pulling out those green bills is certainly greater. If you are of the same mind, your child may have no use for credit cards. However, money is becoming more and more electronic. Many people operate their budget responsibly using credit cards and electronic payment systems. The choice you make will depend on your preferences.

Watch Out for the Joneses

One of the best lessons you can teach your children is to avoid envy. If they try to keep up with the Joneses, they're bound to have horrible credit. Advertisements and peers can have a dramatic influence over young people. Help them be so comfortable with themselves that they do not make bad choices. If you look at average savings rates in the United States, you can only conclude that people in general do not make smart financial decisions. As a result, they're living above their means. If your children do not understand this, they will want to have a lifestyle similar to that which they see in the glamorized world. Of course you have to splurge occasionally and enjoy life, but you should help your children develop realistic expectations that are in line with your circumstances.

Give Them a Jump Start

A wide variety of organizations have dedicated themselves to teaching children about financial responsibility. Often, they tout themselves as "financial literacy" advocates. Many of these are quite good, and some of them have free information for parents, teachers, and children. If you're looking for a resource that you can use to help educate children, the Jump$tart Coalition is a good place to start.

QUESTION?

Who can teach financial literacy to my kids?
If the teachers at your child's school can not, or will not, teach financial literacy, try searching around in your community. A parent of your child's classmate may have some expertise and be willing to share it. Likewise, you can ask local financial advisors for assistance.

The Jump$tart Coalition for Personal Financial Literacy is a not-for-profit organization based in Washington, DC. The goal is to promote financial literacy for students from kindergarten age all the way up to college. After conducting a number of surveys, the group found that the average high school graduate does not have basic personal finance skills. As a result, a young person's first experience with a credit-issuing company is often a bad experience. For example, a college freshman may rack up debt and find himself unable to pay the bills. To combat this, the Jump$tart Coalition finds ways to promote financial education.

Resources, Resources, Resources

You can find handy resources in a lot of different places. Many financial companies offer educational resources as a public-relations strategy. You can find turnkey programs developed for teachers to use in the classroom, complete with handouts, posters, quizzes, and lesson plans. Likewise, you can find Web sites that are created for young students. These programs usually feature interesting characters and places in an effort to keep childrens' attention.

Where do you find these resources? The Internet is full of them, but you can use the Jump$tart Coalition's Web site (*www.jumpstart.org*) as a point of departure. There, you'll find a clearinghouse of free resources and links to other programs promoting financial literacy. Whether you use these tools as part of a class or one-on-one, you can help your child improve her chances against financial mistakes.

The More the Merrier

As you expose yourself to the world of prepackaged financial-literacy programs, select a few that may be useful in your child's school. If you can find a teacher or a volunteer willing to teach a class on financial topics, take advantage of it. It is easier for your child to be responsible and resist financial temptation if his peer group is also financially literate.

Off to College

Someday, your child may head off to college. This is a rite of passage for many young adults. For the first time in their lives, your children live away from home for an extended period of time. They have more freedom to make their own decisions, and make their own mistakes. They learn a lot about the ways of the world as they are exposed to different people and different ideas.

Unfortunately, they're also exposed to a lot of marketing. During the opening days of a school year, you can hardly walk across campus without being bombarded by offers for a free T-shirt if you sign up for a credit card. Credit card companies aggressively market to college students for a variety of reasons. The ones with good intentions are simply trying to get a foot in the door with a lifetime customer. As a person goes to college, his needs evolve; a credit card can fit in nicely. Credit card companies can also have shady motivations. They can prey on the fact that college students have still not learned some important lessons about money, and they're more likely to have a live-for-the-moment mentality. They figure that a loving and understanding parent will bail out a child who charged too much.

ALERT!

Food and entertainment expenses can add up fast for a new college student. With a busy schedule and a new group of friends, it is easy to build up debt. College students might do best to keep a credit card for emergencies only, and pay cash for routine food and entertainment expenses.

Setting the Foundation

For most students, handling their own finances is part of the college experience. This may be the first time in their lives that they have made important financial decisions. The things they do now can affect them the rest of their lives. Someday they will most likely want to settle down and buy a home. Likewise, they will need to purchase their own auto and homeowner's insurance policies. The quality and affordability of loans and insurance will depend on how they handle their credit from day one. This fact is often overlooked with all of the excitement around going to college.

Should You Co-Sign?

As you send your kids off to college, you may wonder if you should co-sign on a loan with them. If they do not have any existing credit history, they may need to borrow your credit history in order to get a credit account. Granted, there is probably a way that they can open a credit card account, but it might not be a good one—perhaps there is a high interest rate on balances, or hefty fees. Co-signing can be extremely risky, as you saw earlier in this book.

Before you co-sign, consider some alternatives. One of your best choices might be to open a secured credit card for your child. You can make a deposit to a bank account, and get a credit card with a limit as high as your deposit. Not only does this protect your credit, it helps your child build a healthy credit history. Another alternative is to open a brand-new card with your child as an authorized user. You can make sure this card has a low credit limit, so you can avoid any big surprises.

If you decide to co-sign with your child, proceed with caution. Obviously you love and trust your children, but you should be cautious so that both of you don't end up with damaged credit. Have duplicate statements mailed to your house, and make sure you can login to check the account on the Internet. You don't need to snoop around in your child's private life, but you do have a right to make sure that the account is being managed properly.

Student Loans

Higher education is not cheap. The costs can include everything from tuition and fees to pizza and sweatshirts. For some parents, a child's education wipes out an entire lifetime of saving. There's not much relief on the horizon. In fact, the costs of higher education have been increasing faster than wages for years, and by now education has a strong lead. What's a parent to do?

Putting Yourself Through College

Students have been putting themselves through college for a long time. Some parents consider it character building, and some parents simply can't afford to pay the costs of higher education. There are living expenses, textbooks, additional fees, and more. If middle-aged parents can't manage the costs, students are even worse off. As a result, many resort to student loans. Some estimates suggest that the average student leaves school with about $20,000 in debt. For many, $20,000 is nothing—they've got a lot more than that to contend with.

It's an Investment

When you look at the big picture, taking out loans might actually be a good idea. If you take the view that higher education is an investment, it is probably money well spent. It is no secret that people's incomes rise along with their level of education. However, that does not mean it makes life easy for anybody. Students are faced with a hefty monthly payment at a time in their careers when they can least afford it.

Look at the bright side. As far as loans go, student loans are probably the most forgiving of all types. They can be structured so that your child has decades to pay them back. In addition, students can postpone or alter their required monthly payments based on hardships they face. In general, student loans are considered good debt, because they are installment loans and they provide a lifetime of value for the student.

If your child must borrow for college, student loans are probably the best choice. These loans have special features. They have flexible repayment options, including the ability to slow down payment during financial hardships. Your child might even be able to spread the repayment period over twenty-five or thirty years, depending on her balance.

Give Good Guidance

If you want to set your kids up for success, you have to give them some guidance. You have been around the block a few more times than they have, so share some of your wisdom with them. Granted, young adults don't always want to listen to their parents, so it is up to you to find a way to communicate with them effectively. Help them understand that the easy money they're borrowing today must be repaid over many years.

Help them keep their debt at a reasonable level, given their future earning potential. If necessary, counsel them to work part time during college to help pay the bills. The pay-as-you-go option is not as much fun, and it might take longer, but the luxury of entering the workforce without student loan payments is priceless.

Grown-Up Kids

Once your kids are all grown up, they may be completely self-sufficient. However, some children end up in difficult financial situations from time to time. They may lose a job, suffer from an accident or sickness, or lose it all in a business venture. If this ever happens to your children, they may come asking you for financial help.

In previous chapters you learned how co-signing works. It is simply a way for a person with good credit to assist a person with not-so-good credit. Presumably, you'll have better credit than your children if they come asking for help. Should you co-sign to help them get a loan? Co-signing is always risky. Before doing it, you should evaluate any alternatives. If you want to help your children, you can simply give them money, or loan it to them at an attractive interest rate. This is much safer than co-signing, and it may solve your child's problem.

You should do whatever you can to avoid co-signing. Even if you feel comfortable that your child will repay as agreed, you never know what will happen. In the event of an accident, sickness, or death, you may find yourself responsible for a loan. See if you can avoid co-signing by gifting or using another creative strategy.

If the loan is bigger than you can afford to gift (a home purchase for example), you may have to get more creative. You can take the loan out in your name only, and have your child make payments to you. If she is unable to do so, you'll know what's going on, and you won't have late payments affecting your credit. The downside of this approach is that if you're forced to sell the property, you'll be forcing your child out of her home. This would not be a pleasant experience.

ID Theft Is for Kids

Identity theft is reaching epidemic proportions. While you should be vigilant about watching your own identity, you must also monitor your child's identity. It does not matter how young the child is—identity thieves don't know, and they certainly don't care. Later in this book, you learn all the details about identity theft, and how to detect it. You should routinely and continually take steps to protect your identity. While you're at it, get in the habit of taking the same steps to protect your child's identity. Check their credit reports, and protect documents that contain their sensitive personal information.

Chapter 16

Love, Marriage, Divorce, and Credit

Credit sticks its nose into every facet of life, including love. With roughly half of all marriages ending in divorce, half of all marriages risk a credit disaster. This section talks about love and credit. You'll know what to do if things go sour.

So, What's Your Score?

If you're of the belief that there is only one soul mate for every person, you might want to add an important characteristic to your list of requirements. As you may have already guessed, a person's credit should be compatible with your credit. While it may seem silly, this can make or break a relationship. It can also break the bank in the worst circumstances. While there may not be institutionalized uses of credit for finding a mate, plenty of anecdotal evidence shows that some folks want a mate who has good credit.

Lending, Insurance, and Love

Having a general idea of your lover's financial situation just makes sense from a financial-planning perspective. You need to know where you are, where you're going, and how to get there. Open communication is the only way to accomplish that. You'll need to know sooner or later, so you should have conversations about money before you get married. You don't necessarily need to look at your sweetheart's credit history, but you should know enough to guess what it looks like.

As you get to know someone, observe how he uses a credit card. Does he use it for every purchase, even $1? This could mean that he is living beyond his means. Does he live in a house, or drive a car that is way too nice for his income? That might suggest some unrealized yearnings that will bring trouble in years to come.

If you think about it, this makes perfect sense. Credit says something about your behavior. It says different things, depending on whom you ask. For an insurance company, information in your credit files says whether or not you will be an expensive client for them. For a lender, the information is useful in predicting whether or not you will pay your debts as you agreed to in a contract. For potential lovers, credit can also say a lot. To some, your good credit might mean that you're boring, predictable, and generally not much fun. To others, your bad credit might mean that you're irresponsible, hard to get along with, and dishonest.

Just like you can tell a lot about a person by the way she treats a waiter in a restaurant, you can also tell a lot about a person by the way she handles credit.

Studies Show

If you think this is a little bit over the top, you might be right. However, it is important to know about the factors that affect somebody's credit before you get too serious. Money issues can cause major problems in a serious relationship. In February 2006, Fair Isaac Corporation's consumer site, myFico.com, released a study that showed just how important financial responsibility is.

The survey was clearly a ploy to generate awareness about credit scores from myFico.com just around the time that singles were suffering from Valentine's Day solitude. However, the numbers really do not lie. People value a mate who is responsible with their credit. Take, for example, answers to questions about various personal traits. When asked to select traits that were more important than the others in sustaining a relationship with a spouse or significant other, the answers came out as follows:

- 53 percent—Being faithful to each other
- 52 percent—Being honest
- 22 percent—Being financially responsible
- 18 percent—Having a sense of humor
- 10 percent—Sexual compatibility
- 13 percent—All of these

This is shocking, right? Even some "old reliable" answers—having a sense of humor and all of the above—came in under financial responsibility. There are a number of other fascinating findings, but one last example should suffice. The study asked respondents what would be the most important advice they could give if they were counseling a friend on a potential mate. It turns out that it's more important to know if the potential mate has a good credit history than it is to know if she wants to have children or is on good terms with family members.

How's Your Credit?

Given the gravity of good credit, it might be tempting to ask any potential mate for a copy of their credit reports and a FICO Score. You would not be the first person who has suggested this. Some financial advisors tell their clients to compare credit histories before tying the knot. However, you'd better be careful. While it's important to know *in general* how responsible your mate is, pulling out the credit reports is extreme. You can probably end a good relationship by demanding that your sweetheart produce a credit report.

When You Tie the Knot

When you get married, you make a vow to spend your life with another person. You have found the one you want to be with, and you'll do what it takes to make it through good times and bad times. If you've ever been to a wedding, you have probably heard the line about staying together, "for richer or poorer." If that shows up in common wedding vows, then money must be important to a marriage.

FACT

A woman does not have to have her husband apply jointly with her on credit accounts. Before the Equal Credit Opportunity Act, some lenders actually required a woman to get her husband on a loan before granting credit. Presumably, she would not be able to make the payments herself—even if she had a job and sufficient income.

Merging Lives, Merging Credit

Marriage is a merging of your lives. You decide to do things together. Some people say that you think with one mind and feel with one heart. As far as your credit goes, you still have two credit reports. This can be a good thing or a bad thing, depending on your credit. Some people think that marriage automatically merges the credit of both spouses. However, you should think of credit histories as separate, but sometimes combined. A good way to keep this straight in your mind is to remember that Social Security Numbers are a major factor in sorting out credit records. When you get married, you don't merge Social Security Numbers, you each keep your own.

If two spouses keep separate individual accounts, one spouse's credit cannot affect the others. Sometimes a person with good credit marries a person with bad credit. In such a case, the couple has to manage loans so that they always get the best deal. For example, you might have one spouse do all of the borrowing in the marriage. While this strategy keeps interest costs down, it may not be ideal (you'll see why later in this chapter).

Sometimes, it is not possible for one spouse to do all the borrowing. For larger loans, like home mortgages, one person's income may not support the loan. Lenders want to see that a borrower can reasonably make the required payments and provide for basic living expenses. They try to ensure this by keeping the required payments under a certain percentage of the borrower's total income. If it's a really big payment, you might need more than one income.

A bride-to-be should let her creditors know if she changes her name due to marriage. She does not have to use accounts in her new name, but doing so will keep things simple. Even if she changes names, she should keep one or two individual accounts open as the only borrower on the account.

Obviously, two working spouses will contribute to the family's living expenses. So, you might expect that you could just show a borrower that you have two incomes to support the payment. However, borrowers want both spouses to become personally liable for a loan, and both of their credit histories will be considered. From a lender's perspective, they don't know (or care) what will happen in the future. One spouse could leave or die, but the lender still wants the loan to be repaid.

A Helping Hand

If one spouse has considerably better credit than the other, the spouse with good credit can help the spouse with bad credit. Assume that a husband has bad credit, but he has the good sense to marry a woman with good credit. The woman likely has various accounts with a clean history. If the man is added to the account—as a joint account holder, for example—his credit reports will inherit the on-time payments of his wife. When added to the mix of the man's previous credit use, this new account spruces things up nicely. Over a period of several months to a year, his credit score is likely to improve. You can do this with a spouse or anybody else you want to help, but you should be careful not to let them ruin your credit.

Everybody Needs Credit

In the past, men took care of all of the money matters. While women might have known a thing or two about finances, everything officially happened in the man's name. While that may have boosted male egos and kept the status quo, it did nothing to help women. Times have changed, but there are still married couples that only have credit in one person's name—usually the male's.

As you know from other portions of this book, having and maintaining credit is a process. You can't just do it once and forget about it. Likewise, it's a use it or lose it proposition: if you don't use your credit, it will go bad. If one partner in a marriage stops using credit, they are setting themselves up for trouble down the road. First, one half of all marriages end in divorce. Also, people die. Men tend to die younger than women, so it's usually a woman that's left as a widow.

If you really love somebody, you should help them build credit. Let's say you've married a nice young individual who does not have a great history. One of the most romantic ways to show your love is to help your honey get good credit. If something should happen to you, how would your spouse ever get a loan?

No matter what the reason for separation, you have to have your own credit so that you can be self-sufficient. If you don't use your credit for several years, lenders will wonder whether you are worth the risk. Always keep an account or two open, or use accounts jointly. This will ensure that you have the credit you need if something happens. See Chapter 9 for additional ideas on how to keep long-term relationships with your lenders.

In the Unlikely Event of Divorce

While it might never happen to you, it's probably worth knowing how a divorce might affect your credit. Consider this an intellectual exercise, or useful information that you can pass on to your friends.

Just as marriage is a merging of two lives, divorce is where you separate your two lives. This is no small task. Depending on how long you have been together, you might have to unwind a really messy ball of twine. If you find yourself faced with this task, one of the things you need to remember is your credit. Divorce and credit don't mix well. The most important thing you can do is try to keep the lines of communication open. Both of you could suffer if things go awry. While you may not want to talk to each other, you owe it to yourselves to clear things up correctly.

Some people think that getting a divorce means that everything automatically gets split up: the assets, the debts, everything. This is not the case. In fact, a divorce only splits up the marriage, and everything else has to be done manually. If you have a joint credit card account, for example, you still have a joint credit card account after a divorce. You might not be married anymore, but the account hasn't changed. Therefore, you need to get rid of the joint account so that you can continue toward closure of your marriage.

Settling Debts

When you decide to call the whole thing off, you need to diligently manage all of the existing debts from your marriage. There is an easy way and a hard way to do this. The easy way would be to communicate openly and agree on how things will get settled. The hard way, of course, is to play hardball with each other. Of course, this is a really difficult time emotionally. It may not be easy to keep emotions out of any financial discussions. Furthermore, your ex may not make that possible at all. However, you need to make sure that things get done correctly.

A Plan of Attack

During or before the divorce proceedings, you should figure out who will be responsible for which debts. You can do this any way you like. The most important thing is that everybody knows what they need to take care of. When dividing up debts, it is a good idea to make the user of the asset the responsible party. For example, suppose you have a home mortgage and an auto loan. Whoever will live in the house should take care of the home mortgage. Whoever will drive the car should take care of the auto loan.

By having the asset user make the payments, you make it so that the responsible party has an incentive to keep the debt current. If you have a nasty divorce, and you're supposed to make the payments on your spouse's automobile, it can be tempting to withhold payments and wait for the car to be repossessed. Of course, this strategy would damage your credit, though it might be rewarding emotionally.

FACT

Different states have different ways of handling debts. If you are going through a divorce (or are considering a divorce), it is imperative that you speak with a qualified attorney who knows your state's laws. You may be surprised at how debts are handled, and how they affect support payments and asset divisions.

After you decide who will pay for each of the debts, update the accounts. If you will continue to live in the house and make mortgage payments, you should be the only one on the mortgage loan. To accomplish this, you can call your lender and ask to have your ex removed from the loan. It may be necessary to refinance the loan, essentially replacing it with a brand-new loan. This takes time and money, but the closure and reduced risk for all involved more than compensates the expense. If there are monetary expenses, figure those into the total divorce settlement. Nobody has to win or lose; you just need to tidy things up.

In the same vein, assume that your ex-spouse will drive the car and take over payments for the auto loan which was in both of your names. It is very important that you get your name off the loan. Again, your spouse may need to refinance or find some other way to accomplish this, but it is worth the time, energy, and cost.

Refinancing

For mortgage loans, you will most likely have to refinance the loan. Why? If you applied jointly when they gave you the loan, they looked at both of your incomes when determining if you could make the payments. With both of you as borrowers, the mortgage lender could count on two incomes, and could go after two people in case of a default. If you just remove somebody from a loan, the risk to the lender increases. They would rather have you apply for a new loan, with new terms that reflect the new level of risk. If your single income is not enough to support the payments, they won't grant you the loan. From their perspective, your ex was responsible when you initiated the loan, and they're not going to let her off the hook unless you alone can make the payments. Now, if you remarry and have a dual income, or if your income actually is enough to support the payments, refinancing should not be a problem.

The Bad News

If you must go through a divorce, hopefully it will be as easy as possible. Ideally, you will come to agreements smoothly and quickly. However, it doesn't always work out that way. If there is any tension in a divorce, you need to be on the lookout for dangers to your credit.

Account Users

Sometimes a person puts a spouse on a credit account as an authorized user or account user. An account user is authorized to use the account, but that person is not responsible for paying back any debts. In other words, they can charge stuff, but they don't have to pay it back—the account owner does. If your ex-spouse was an authorized user, you need to change that. Again, divorce applies to your marriage, not your credit accounts. Your ex is still an authorized user, and you may not want that to be the case. If he has a charge card that you are responsible for paying on, he can still use it after a divorce. If he racks up a lot of debt, that is your problem, not his—unless he is a joint account holder, then it's a problem for both of you.

Remember that your lenders are not a part of your divorce settlement. They're just some innocent bystanders who lent you some money. Although they probably hate to see you suffer, their main priority is to get their money back sooner or later.

Imagine this worst-case scenario: Your ex-husband is an authorized user on an account that is owned by you. After a divorce, you've been really busy, and haven't gotten around to cleaning up all of your accounts. He still has his credit card, and there is $10,000 of available credit on the account. He uses the card for a vacation or two, and maybe some new toys, like expensive bicycles. The next time you get a statement, you see $10,000 of new purchases. You call your ex and ask for the money, and he is not cooperative. You can fight all you want, but the credit card company says that you are responsible. If you refuse to pay, your credit suffers (and your husband's will as well, but he's not on the hook for repayment). The lesson: get your financial affairs cleaned up immediately.

But the Divorce Says . . .

Even if the divorce agreement says that your ex-spouse is responsible for paying a debt, the creditors aren't part of that agreement. If your name is on the account and it does not get paid as agreed, your credit will suffer. Granted, your ex may have violated the terms of the agreement—and you may be able to recover damages from her—but the creditors will still report the account as delinquent if you fall behind. You might be better off keeping the debts current yourself by paying what your ex is supposed to pay (assuming this fits into your budget), and then going after the money later.

Unilateral Action

As a joint account holder, you do not need your spouse's permission to do things on an account. Therefore, your best bet might be to call the creditors for any account that is held jointly (or with your spouse as an authorized user) and close the account. You can reopen accounts in your name only, and you won't run the risk of having another person racking up debts on the account.

ALERT!

Remember not to get too crazy with closing and opening accounts. If you try to open too many new accounts in a short period of time, your credit will suffer because of all the inquiries. As preventative medicine, keep individual accounts in your name before the divorce, and only open the accounts you need after a divorce.

Who's Debt Is It?

Usually, you can assume that any debts that you are not a joint holder on are not your responsibility. Usually. However, there are a number of states that think otherwise. In community-property states, any debt incurred during the marriage can be considered joint debt. Your creditors might not have you on as a joint holder, but you need to be aware of this for your own financial planning. You will need to budget for payments on those debts that the state says are yours.

Don't Make It Worse

Divorce will not be a pleasant experience. You may have a million things to do when you are managing a divorce, and your credit might not be your top priority. However, your credit can suffer during a divorce, and it might just be the thing that helps you stay afloat after the whole thing is over. Make your credit a priority, so that you have one less thing to recover from. Plenty of divorces lead to bankruptcy. It is often because the loss of combined incomes (or one income that supported everybody) is too much of a strain. However, others go into bankruptcy because the divorce went badly. These bankruptcies could be avoided.

Chapter 17

Special Topics for Your First Home Purchase

Buying your first home is an overwhelming experience. You hear all kinds of jargon, and you're faced with a million choices. Because your home is such an important purchase, you want to do things right. This section highlights some of the topics that apply to your credit and your mortgage loan. By preparing yourself and your credit, you can make the process much less stressful and much less expensive. Instead of scrambling for a loan that you can live with, you can negotiate for the loan you deserve.

Mistakes Now Are Costly

When you're getting ready to buy your first home, you need to be really careful. Any mistakes that you make right now can throw you way off track. Because you're getting ready to take out a large loan—probably one of the largest loans of your life—you need to get the best terms possible on that loan. As you'll remember from earlier in this book, monthly payments are a function of just a few ingredients: your interest rate, the loan amount, and the amount of time over which you will repay the loan. If something goes wrong when you're getting the loan, your interest rate could go up. If that happens, your monthly payments will rise, and you might even price yourself out of the market. If you don't get the best interest rate you can get, you may end up paying thousands of extra dollars in interest over the life of your loan.

Perks for First-Timers

You may hear a lot about first-time homebuyer programs. These programs offer some special benefits to people who are buying their first home. The actual benefits you get depend on the program. These programs may be offered by local governments and organizations. For the most part, these programs offer some sort of subsidy to make homeownership more affordable for low- and middle-income families. They may offer attractive loan terms, or make it easier to get into a house with a smaller down payment.

Are They Worth It?

First-time homebuyer programs can be useful for some. However, they are not the right choice for every first-time buyer. These programs often come with a variety of strings attached, because they are designed to help people with specific financial characteristics. You should certainly investigate any subsidies that you may be eligible for. However, these programs have less value if your credit is good. With a FICO score above 720, you're probably better off in a standard, unsubsidized mortgage loan. If your score is below 680, you'll want to take a good hard look at first-time homebuyer programs.

FACT

In addition to subsidized loans, you may get some tax incentives as a first-time homebuyer. For example, you may be able to take $10,000 from an IRA for your first home purchase without an early withdrawal penalty. Check with a tax adviser for details, and see IRS Publication 530 for some additional ideas.

Qualifications and Restrictions

In order to use the first-time homebuyer program, you typically have to qualify. To meet their requirements, you may have to have an income below the specified level. They try to limit these programs to those in need. In addition, you'll most likely find limits on the cost of a home that you can buy in the program. You'll be limited to the lower-cost homes in your area. You should also be aware that these programs don't allow for the full spectrum of loans in the marketplace. You might be limited to one or two types of loans—most likely you'll be able to do a thirty-year fixed-rate mortgage. Finally, if you decide to sell your house too soon, you may have to pay recapture taxes. All things considered, it can be difficult to qualify for these programs and make them work well. Nevertheless, they are a perfect fit for some borrowers.

Check Your Credit

When you decide that you are ready to purchase a home, you should check your credit immediately. This is the time when it can make a lot of sense to pay for credit reports and credit scores. In general, you should try to give yourself at least three months to deal with any issues in your credit reports. This means that if you want to buy a home in July, you should start checking your credit reports in March. You will certainly have surprises coming at you from several directions. Don't let your credit be one of them.

Spruce It Up

When you receive your credit reports, look for anything that will lower your credit scores. In particular, search for any errors: accounts that are not yours, erroneously reported late payments, and negative items that should not appear in your reports. If you find any errors, start the process of getting them corrected as soon as possible. You may have to dispute them several times before they are removed, and you might even need to hire a lawyer. If you're going to go through this hassle, it's better to do it at a leisurely pace. You don't want a simple credit-reporting error to keep you from buying a home.

You should also look for some easy-to-fix items that might lower your credit scores. If you're using a high percentage of your total available credit, see if you can get that percentage down before you get a mortgage. Again, the sooner you do this, the better. Just because you pay down a balance on your credit card, does not mean that the credit card immediately reports your new balance to the credit-reporting companies. It takes time, and you should give them at least a month.

If time is of the essence, you may be able to improve your credit, and your credit scores, in just a few days. Through a process called rapid rescoring, your mortgage lender may be able to hurry things along at the credit-reporting companies. If you are correcting mistakes or making quick fixes to your credit reports, rapid rescoring may help.

Pay Down or Down Payment?

As you get ready to buy your home, you may consider accumulating funds for a down payment. It can take months or years to accumulate enough money to have a significant down payment. If you save up the money, but you also have credit card balances, you're faced with a difficult decision. Should you use that money for a down payment, or should you use it to pay down your credit card balances? The answer should depend on what will benefit you the most financially.

If paying down your balances will substantially improve your credit score, you might get a much better rate on your mortgage. As a result, you might save substantial money on your monthly payments, and also on total interest costs throughout the life of your loan. Before you make a decision, run the numbers and see what's best. You'll need to take into account how long you plan to stay in the house and make payments, and whether or not your down payment can help you avoid private mortgage insurance (PMI).

You should also keep in mind that interest payments on your home mortgage may be tax deductible. If you use your savings to pay down your debts, you'll need to get a bigger loan. In a sense, you are using money from the mortgage to pay down your credit card debts. As a result, the interest payments that you would have been paying to the credit card company become tax-deductible interest payments. Before you go with this strategy, check the tax laws to make sure that your mortgage interest will be tax deductible.

A Good Time to Close Accounts?

When you get ready to make a home purchase, you will be busy sprucing up your credit to make your loan more attractive. You may run across something that says you should close your old, unused credit card accounts. The theory is that having too much available credit card capacity will hurt your credit scores. As a result, some people recommend closing those accounts before you apply for a mortgage.

QUESTION?

How much of my available debt should I use?
In general, you should try to use 35 percent or less of your total available credit. This sends a signal to lenders that you are comfortably meeting all of your monthly obligations. The percentage of debt you're using is part of the "amounts owed" category in your FICO score.

In fact, you will do more harm than good if you follow this strategy. By closing your inactive accounts, you reduce the total amount of credit available to you. This has the effect of making it look like you're using a greater percentage of all the credit available to you. The credit-scoring models interpret this as a sign of trouble—if you're getting maxed out on your credit, you might soon default on the debt or make late payments. Therefore, closing those old accounts hurts your credit when you're trying to improve it. Some mortgage brokers and real-estate agents suggest this strategy with the best of intentions. Unfortunately, they end up leading you down the wrong path.

Should You Wait on That Purchase?

You buy a home at a time in your life when you are settling down. You finally reach the point when you can afford to own your own place. Perhaps you're at this point in your life because you've secured a decent job, or because you've developed responsible spending habits. In any case, you're probably not trying to buy a house when you're flat broke. Indeed, this is probably a time in your life when you're buying several nice things for yourself.

ALERT!

Cutting your spending will do more than just help your credit. When you finally buy your first home, you'll need every penny you can get your hands on. You'll need new furnishings, decorations, and other things to fill those empty rooms. You might even experience an expensive event not long after you move in, such as a plumbing or roofing issue.

In the months and years leading up to your first home purchase, you should be careful what you buy. Making large purchases can lower your credit score. A brand-new plasma TV could cost you a lot more than the purchase price—it could cost you thousands of dollars in interest over the life of your mortgage. It may be difficult to restrain yourself at this time in your life; after all, you finally get to enjoy the fruits of your labors. However, as you approach the time when you'll buy a home, hold off on spending. Wait until after closing to buy those home furnishings and luxuries.

A common pitfall that catches first-time homebuyers is the car payment. Shortly before buying your home, you may be tempted to buy a nice new car. Unfortunately, the payments associated with a newer car can jeopardize your mortgage. Lenders will look at a number of ratios to determine what type of loan you qualify for. One of those ratios is your ratio of debt payments to monthly income. If a high percentage of your monthly income is already heading out the door to pay for your car and other items, how are you going to make your mortgage payments? A new car is one of those things that you should wait on if you're considering buying a home.

Shopping Rates

When you apply for a mortgage, you obviously want to get the best interest rates. How do you know what the best interest rate is? You'll have to shop around and apply for loans at a variety of different institutions. Each time you apply for a loan, the lender will want to pull your credit to see how risky you might be as a borrower. As you may recall from earlier in this book, each time somebody pulls your credit for the purpose of getting a loan, your credit suffers just a little bit. These hard inquiries can be a tipoff that you are having financial difficulties. How can you shop around and not damage your credit?

Forty-Five Shopping Days

If you're going to shop around for the best mortgage rates, you should do so within a short period of time. The newest FICO credit-scoring models allow you to shop rates within a forty-five-day period without counting all of the inquiries. Instead of counting all of these inquiries individually, they are treated as one single inquiry for a mortgage loan. Therefore, you should focus your rate shopping into just a few weeks. If you drag the process on for too long, you'll actually see the rates get higher and less attractive.

You can get an idea of how much your mortgage rate should be without getting your credit pulled. If you know what your credit score is, you can find some good estimates. Ask your bank or credit union what their rates are like, and check national publications and Web sites such as *www.bankrate.com*.

Good Loans from Good People

To get a good loan, it is essential that you have good credit. However, good credit by itself does not guarantee that you'll get the best loan available to you. You need to have a knowledgeable expert help you get the right loan. If you don't already have a person or institution in mind, you'll need to find a good mortgage lender who will act in your best interests. You need a person who will leverage your credit, however good or bad it may be, and get you the best terms possible. How do you find such a person? Much like searching for any other professional, you should ask around. Check with your friends, families, and coworkers to see if they have had positive experiences with anybody. Interview the person to make sure you will work well together, and don't be forced into making decisions before you're ready.

When Your Credit Improves

Mortgage loans come in many different varieties. There are different structures of products, and there are different tiers. Attractive borrowers—those with the best credit—fall into the tiers with the best-available terms. As you may imagine, unattractive borrowers get less attractive terms. They may have higher interest rates, prepayment penalties, and a limited number of loan choices.

When you get your first mortgage loan, you may not qualify for the most attractive loans because of your credit. However, as the years wear on, your credit will hopefully improve. At that point, it may make sense for you to replace your mortgage with a better one. You really need to do some math to see if this makes sense. If you can actually get a better interest rate along with a flexible loan, it may be worth your time, energy, and money. Refinancing may look attractive, but don't forget that there are costs involved. You may have to pay points, legal fees, and more. Take those into consideration as you decide what to do.

If the Going Gets Tough

After you buy your home, you may fall on hard times. Perhaps an accident or sickness will put a big dent in your budget. Perhaps you'll lose a job that you felt quite comfortable in. No matter what the case, you may find yourself in a situation where it is hard to make your mortgage payments. If you are unfortunate enough to end up in this situation, don't let it get worse. Call your mortgage lender immediately, and find a way to work something out until you get back on your feet.

The best way to handle a challenging situation is to be proactive. If it looks like you'll have a hard time making your mortgage payments, communicate that over the phone, not through missed payments. Your lender would much rather hear from you, and work something out, than have to hunt you down and find out why you didn't make your payment. If you are proactive and you call before you miss any payments, your lender will be much more flexible. They may allow you to skip a few payments, pay less than normal for a while, or restructure your loan so that it is more manageable for you.

Paying Off Delinquencies

If you have delinquencies on your credit reports, your mortgage lender may ask that you pay those delinquencies off. For example, there may be accounts in collections that you've never managed to pay, or a lender may have charged off a debt that still appears on your reports. Some mortgage lenders want these issues to be resolved if they are going to grant you a loan.

Paying off old delinquencies should improve your credit, not damage it. Supposedly, the credit-reporting companies have fixed things so that this does not occur. However, this is a fairly recent fix. Therefore, you may want to play it safe for the next few years. If you have to pay off a delinquency, do it at closing.

If you find that a mortgage lender is asking you to pay off old delinquencies in order to get a mortgage, proceed with caution. If the delinquency is from three or more years ago, you should insist on paying the item off at closing. If you pay it off before closing, the account will have recent activity on it, and it could damage your credit. Note that delinquencies are bad no matter what, but old delinquencies on accounts are not as bad. If your credit is damaged from paying off one of these delinquencies, your mortgage loan could be affected. Furthermore, if the home purchase does not go through for any reason, you will be stuck without a home, and with worse credit than when you started.

Chapter 18

Spending Plan

You need to keep your credit in tip-top shape for your entire life. The easiest way to do this is to control your spending and prepare for the unexpected. In order to get your credit in shape and keep it there, you should follow some type of spending plan. In general, you'll want to meet all of your obligations, have a little fun, and stay out of trouble. In this section, you'll see how a spending plan can help you do that.

You, Incorporated

The best way to manage your money is to think of yourself like a business. From this day on, you should consider yourself owner and president of You, Incorporated. If you'd like, you can certainly come up with a more creative and descriptive name. The point is that you should think of your finances the same way that a business views its finances. Of course, if you have a spouse or other family members in the picture, they would be cofounders of the enterprise.

Businesses really do have the same financial issues as individuals. Money comes in, money goes out, and they try to build on successes. There might be a few businesses that have a lot money, and they're not even sure what they should do with it all, just like wealthy individuals. However, for the most part, businesses have to manage their finances wisely, just like you.

Just the Facts

Managing your personal finances like a business may help you to view things objectively. In other words, you can look at the numbers and see where money is going without involving your emotions. Of course, emotions are important, and you should be able to spend on things that make you happy. Nevertheless, there is no harm in taking a big step back and looking at your cash flow with an objective set of eyes.

Just Don't Call It a Budget

You may be getting suspicious that this spending plan is really just a budget. As a matter of fact, you will be using some of the same concepts, techniques, and ideas that you would use in creating and working a budget. However, budgeting is no fun. The word "budget" is just another way of saying that you will deny yourself the things you enjoy because they cost too much. Instead of using a budget, you will use a much more sophisticated spending plan. A spending plan is not about denying yourself anything; it is about finding ways to meet all of your needs.

Preventative Medicine

You may be familiar with the idea of preventative medicine. Lots of Health Maintenance Organizations (HMOs) these days stress the importance of preventative medicine. The bottom line is that healthy habits help you avoid getting sick in the first place. The same is true for your financial health and your credit. Developing good habits and following a spending plan can help you avoid financial hardships. Granted, accidents happen, and there are some things that we cannot control. Nevertheless, you should try and manage the things that you have some control over. Barring any major catastrophes, good habits will keep you out of trouble.

Your spending plan is an important part of your overall financial health. It is just as important as your credit score, retirement savings, insurance protection, and every other piece of your financial puzzle. All of these pieces work together as one—if one of them is not working properly, it can ruin the other pieces as well.

Your spending plan serves as a preventative medicine in another important way. Part of your plan will be to build up an emergency fund. The emergency fund gives you a cash cushion that you can spend when times get tough. This fund can help you protect your credit in two important ways. First, you'll have a cash reserve on hand so that you can continue to make payments on any outstanding loans. This helps to avoid making late payments, which can really hurt your credit. In addition, you may be able to spend some of your emergency fund before going deeper into debt. Of course, after all the dust has settled, you need to replenish your emergency fund. The reason this can help your credit is it helps you keep your balances fairly low. As you'll recall, using too much of your available credit makes you look more risky and lowers your credit scores.

Managing Your Scores

Your credit reports can give you some useful tips when it comes to managing your spending. Some of the same things that damage your credit can give you ideas on where you need to improve. Anything that lowers your credit scores should be addressed. If you think about it, this makes sense. Credit scores are designed to be an automated system for evaluating your financial health. They look for indications that you might be spreading yourself too thin. If they see these characteristics, your score goes down.

Earlier in this book you learned about some of the common red flags that can damage your credit. Take a look through your credit reports and use these red flags for ideas. Your overall financial health will improve, and so will your credit. As an example, look to see if you have any late payments. If you do, could this be a hint that you're having a hard time managing your cash flow? Build a solution into your spending plan. Likewise, are you using a high percentage of your total available debt? It probably means that you're spending more than you're bringing in. Finally, look for excessive hard inquiries on your credit reports. These can indicate that you are trying to use credit too heavily. As you know, borrowing more doesn't help, because you'll have to pay it back sooner or later.

Fixed Expenses

Your fixed expenses are an essential part of your spending plan. Fixed expenses are expenses that you have every month. They really don't change much, although some of your fixed expenses could vary slightly. Your fixed expenses are most likely monthly obligations such as your mortgage or rent, insurance premiums, membership or service fees, and auto-loan payments. You might also include some expenses that vary slightly month to month, but are fairly stable. These expenses might include your utility payments, phone or cell phone payments, or any other service that you pay for each month. It is important that the dollar amount for these charges does not change much from month to month.

Crunch the Numbers

Tally up the total costs for your fixed expenses. Once you have added all of these together, you have an idea of what you're basic monthly obligations are. These are the costs you have to pay no matter what. Whether you sit around the house, or jaunt around the world, you have to come up with this much each month. Given this information, take a quick glance at your household income. This gives you an initial preview of how you're doing.

Line 'Em Up

Now that you have all of your basic monthly expenses written down, line them up from most expensive to least expensive. If you have access to spreadsheet software, you might want to enter your budget into the spreadsheet so you can slice, dice, and sort. Microsoft Excel works quite well, and Google has offered free spreadsheet software in the past. With your monthly expenses arranged from highest to lowest, look for any surprises. Does anything stick out like a sore thumb? If so, investigate alternatives—see if there is any creative way for you to put less of your money toward that expense going forward.

FACT

There are a lot of tools on the Web that you can use to manage your spending. Some of them are even free. Search with terms like "budget spreadsheet" or "budget worksheet," and you can find some nice templates. Find one that works for you—some are very basic, and some have lots of bells and whistles.

Start Cutting

Most of your monthly expenses are probably true necessities. However, there might be some that fall into a gray area; they're not quite necessary, but they are near-necessities. Try to find just one or two expenses that you can cut back on for starters. You don't have to revamp the whole thing, just start by making improvements in one or two areas. Perhaps it's that health-club membership that you only use once or twice a week. Could you jog, bike, or lift weights with dumbbells at home instead? Maybe it's the cable bill. Do you have enough time to watch TV to make the expense worthwhile?

Variable Expenses

After you understand what your fixed monthly obligations are, take a close look at your variable expenses. These are expenses that might change from month to month. The amount you spend on variable expenses usually depends on your behavior in a given month. Consider a simple night out. Perhaps you enjoy a modest dinner and a movie. The more you do this in a month, the higher that expense is. Some months you may do it often, and in other months you may spend your evenings doing other things. Your eating out and movie expenses vary depending on your behavior.

Track Your Spending

Do the best you can to track your variable expenses. You can do this in as much or as little detail as you like. The more detail you have, the better. Some experts recommend keeping a note pad with you and making a record every time you spend money. You might also be able to make these records in your personal digital assistant (PDA) or your cell phone. If you actually record every expense, you'll have a very clear picture of where your money is going. Most people do not do this, but those who do have a much easier time managing their spending. The problem is that most people have no idea where their money is going. There's nothing wrong with that if you have a lot of money, but it only hurts you if you have to manage your spending.

It takes time and energy to track your spending in detail. Keep in mind that you don't have to do this forever, just do it for a while as an experiment. If you can track your spending for a few weeks or a few months, you should get plenty of useful information.

If you don't record every single expenditure, at least find a way to track your spending with some sort of category system. You might have categories for entertainment, lunch, dinner, gas, gifts, charitable giving, coffee, nights out, and so on. Again, the more detail you use the better. With a simple category system, you should be able to track the vast majority of your variable spending.

Just like you did with your fixed expenses, you should arrange your variable expenses from largest to smallest. Then, take a deep breath and see what you're spending your money on. Are there any shocking surprises in this list? If so, that's where you need to spend your energy. You'll need to change your behavior to spend less money on those items.

Lots of Emergencies

What if your variable spending is all on emergencies? If you tend to spend a lot on emergencies, see if you can pinpoint a common cause. For example, if your car constantly breaks down and requires emergency maintenance, you might need a new car. Run some simple numbers and see if you would actually save money by buying a new car. If you don't have the ability to buy a new car, consider saving up for one. Look for causes and alternative solutions to your emergency spending.

Emergency Fund

As a tool to protect your good credit, you'll need to build up an emergency fund. The emergency fund is a cash reserve that acts as padding—if you get hit with an emergency, your emergency fund keeps it from hurting too bad. As mentioned above, it helps you stay out of debt and stay current on your obligations. Your emergency fund is what you would dip into if you should lose your job or if you have to pay for something expensive. It is not for expensive toys or luxuries; rather, it is for expensive necessities like home repairs, medical bills, and auto repairs.

How Much for an Emergency?

The size of your emergency fund depends on a variety of factors. As a general rule of thumb, you might try for three to six months of your living expenses. Your fixed expenses will give you an idea of what your living expenses are, but you may want to build in a little extra by looking at your variable expenses too.

Three to six months of living expenses is a pretty broad range. Where should you fall into that range? It depends on how secure you feel. If you feel very secure in your job, or your ability to get another job if your current job ends, then you might be fine saving up three months of living expenses. In addition, if you are financially secure, meaning you are not living paycheck to paycheck, you can probably afford to build up a larger emergency fund.

Your emergency fund is a crucial tool for protecting your credit. It allows you to stay current on your debt payments if you lose your job, or worse. It also allows you to minimize the amount of debt you take on if something expensive happens. Making payments on time and keeping your debt balances low help to keep your credit healthy.

Your First Emergency Fund

If you are just starting to build your financial foundation, your emergency fund will probably be smaller than three to six months of living expenses. About $1,000 is a decent place to start if you are currently stretched thin. It is more important to pay down your revolving debts than to build up your emergency fund. Once you get those balances down, you can start building up your emergency fund to a more appropriate level.

Debt Payments

Your debt payments should be a high priority in your spending plan. These payments should be considered fixed expenses—no matter what happens in a given month, you have to make those payments. At the very least, your minimum required payments should be a part of your fixed budget. The reason you should prioritize debt payments is that these payments can trip you up and cause problems. If you skip a payment, it can damage your credit and send you down a treacherous and slippery slope. In addition, debt payments take money away from other important things in your life.

FACT

Your payment history accounts for 35 percent of your FICO credit score, and missed payments can make your score drop like a rock. To avoid major damage to your credit, you have to make debt payments a priority. Discipline and organization will help you get those payments in on time and maintain your credit.

Ultimately, you will want to have virtually no debt. It is a good idea to keep a few credit cards open and keep small balances on them, but this will not cost you much in interest. Remember that interest does not get you anything above and beyond what you bought in the first place, it just costs more to buy the same things. You do get the luxury of buying things before you have saved all of the money to buy them, and that can be worth paying interest for, like when you buy a home. Huge piles of revolving debt generally don't help you much.

E Is for Entertainment

Entertainment expenses are another important part of your spending plan. You have to plan to have a good time every once in a while. As long as you plan ahead, entertainment expenses should not ruin your plan. Pick a number that you can afford to spend on the finer things in life, and stick to it. These expenses are most damaging when you have not earmarked money for them ahead of time.

It can be difficult to find dollars that you can direct toward entertainment expenses. Often, the necessities take up almost all of one's income. If you find yourself in a similar situation, work on finding ways to entertain yourself on the cheap. Look for books and Web sites that specialize in frugality. You may find inexpensive entertainment ideas, and you'll probably be able to shave a few dollars off other parts of your budget.

Saving for Later

Saving for your future is another essential piece to your financial puzzle. There was a time when people did not need to worry about this. Governments and employers provided help through retirement plans, and did all of the work for you. However, those days are gone. You have the responsibility to create financial security for yourself—you cannot count on anybody else to do it for you. As a result, you need to save money for your future.

If you can't find the money to save for your future, go back and look at your spending plan. Are there any "leaks" in your budget that are costing you more than they should? A few dollars a week can really add up, especially if you have a number of years until retirement starts.

The best way to do this is to systematically save a little bit of money each month. Ideally, you would look at this as a fixed expense that must always be covered. By making saving easy, automatic, and a priority, you greatly improve your chances for success. In addition, you manage your risks by investing periodically, if investing in the markets is a part of your retirement plan. If you've heard it once, you've heard it a million times: pay yourself first. By doing so, you will find a way to make your other expenses fall into line.

Where to Start

The right way for you to save for retirement will depend on your individual situation. If your employer has a company-sponsored retirement plan, that's a good place to start. If they match your contributions to the plan, it is probably a good bet. You need a really good reason to avoid contributing when your employer matches your contributions. Above and beyond the match, you might investigate other retirement accounts. There's nothing wrong with contributing more than the minimum required to get your employer's matching dollars, so what you do beyond that is a matter of personal preference. You could investigate individual retirement accounts

(IRAs) and Roth IRAs as a next step. These types of retirement accounts may have different features and tax characteristics than your employer's plan.

Where to Find Help

Remember that the responsibility of saving for your retirement is yours. However, you don't have to do it alone. The world is full of resources that can help you get the job done. If you want to do it yourself, you'll need to read up on the basics. Start in the personal finance section of your local bookstore or library. Note that there are a lot of different philosophies and strategies when it comes to saving for your retirement and investing. If you are just getting started, simple and steady is the best way to go: figure out how much risk you can take on (if any), don't put all of your eggs in one basket, and think long term. Avoid trading strategies and any hot stock tips.

If you want to hire a professional, you can do that, too. The world is full of people who can help you manage your finances. You have to be careful if you hire someone, because there is a lot of abuse in this area. Meet with and interview any prospective advisors, and don't be pressured into making any decisions on the spot. If you ever feel uncomfortable about the person you're working with, walk away and find somebody else. The best way to find a good advisor is to ask around. Check with your friends, family, and coworkers to see if they have had good experiences with anybody in particular.

Chapter 19

Optimize Your Borrowing

Saving your pennies and borrowing wisely are the keys to having good credit. If you use products and services wisely, you have more money to spend as you need. If you are going to borrow, you should do it in the most efficient and effective way possible. This will allow you to minimize your borrowing costs, which keeps you out of some dangerous credit pitfalls. This section highlights some ways that you can borrow wisely and keep your credit in excellent shape.

Zero-Percent Interest Offers

If your credit is halfway decent, your mailbox may be flooded with offers for new credit cards. In many cases, these offers include a teaser rate as low as 0 percent. Teaser rates are artificially low rates that credit card companies offer to get you in the door. Typically, these rates expire after several months or a year, and then the account charges standard interest rates.

Free Money

Teaser rates are extremely tempting. If you can borrow money at a 0-percent interest rate, then you use somebody else's money at absolutely no cost. However, there may be a hidden cost. The lure of free money tempts people to spend like crazy and rack up significant debts. Once the teaser rate expires, reality sets in. You have to repay those debts, and the credit card company starts to charge hefty interest rates. Likewise, any late payments will cause the credit card company to take away the teaser rate and start charging higher rates.

In general, you should use these offers only as a short-term strategy. For example, if you have a credit card balance with a high rate of interest, you may want to take advantage of an offer for a 0-percent balance transfer. As long as you completely pay off that debt before the teaser rate expires, this is a wise strategy.

Surfing Cards

Unfortunately, too many people fall into the trap of surfing cards. Their intention is to use teaser rates as a long-term strategy. This is a very dangerous strategy. These people simply shift the balance from one card to the next. They open a new credit card account with a promotional rate every time their previous promotional rate expires. The problem with this strategy is that you never pay off your debts; you simply shift them from one place to another. As time goes on, chances are that your overall debt burden increases, simply because you are treating the symptom, and not the cause, and your credit only deteriorates. What's worse, a sickness or disaster could strike and you'd start missing payments. If you're going to use teaser rates, use them as a short-term strategy.

Student Loan Consolidation

If you have student loans, you may be able to make some adjustments that will help you financially. With a little bit of tweaking, you might free up some money that you can use to manage your credit. Student loans have some unique features. If you consolidate them, you can choose among several different repayment plans (how the plans work will depend on your student loan balances, among other things). If you can extend your payments over many years, your required monthly payment will decrease.

ALERT!

If you extend your student loan repayments, you will end up paying more in interest over the life of your loan. You might have an attractive interest rate, but you'll pay interest for many more years. It may work out in your favor, but you should be aware of how much you are paying.

What should you do with the money you save? If you want to improve your credit—and if you have credit card balances—then you can use those extra dollars to pay down your revolving debts. Once your revolving debts are under control, you can redirect those dollars to your student loans or some other financial goal.

Mortgage Refinancing

Your mortgage will most likely be the largest loan you ever take on. It buys you a place to lay your head, and peace of mind. Because the dollar amounts are usually so large, the interest rate that you get on your mortgage is extremely important. By shaving off a percent or less, you can save a bundle of money. If you know you can save money, refinancing your mortgage is a good move.

How can you get a lower mortgage rate? One way is to work with changing interest rates. If interest rates in general have gone down since you got your mortgage, you may be able to refinance and get a better rate. Before doing this, you need to make sure that it makes financial sense. Do the math, or sit with an honest mortgage broker. Refinancing costs money—the fees and closing costs may wipe out any potential gains. However, if all the moving parts line up correctly, it may be worth your while. If you're going to stay in the house long enough to regain those costs, refinancing makes sense.

Home Equity Loans

Home equity loans are another tool you can use to optimize your borrowing. If you have revolving debts that you would like to reduce, you can borrow against your home's equity to pay down those debts. The two main advantages of using this strategy are lower interest costs and potential tax savings.

Lower Interest Costs

A home equity loan usually has a lower interest rate than a standard credit card. This is because a home equity loan is secured by your home, and the bank can kick you out and sell your house if you fail to repay the loan. Credit cards, on the other hand, are not secured by anything. If you fail to pay them, the credit card company can sue you. However, you don't pledge any collateral when you open up a credit card account. Because the lender takes on more risk with a credit card account, the interest rate is higher. Therefore, if you shift your revolving debt to a home equity loan, the interest rate that you pay on that debt should decrease.

Potential Tax Savings

You might also get some tax savings by using a home equity loan to consolidate your debts. The interest you pay on a home equity loan is tax deductible in some situations. Essentially, this means that you don't lose all of the money you're paying in interest; some of the interest payment is effectively subsidized through your tax savings. Before you take this approach, check IRS Publication 936 to make sure that you can qualify to take the deduction.

Pitfalls of Home Equity Loans

Home equity loans can be dangerous, so you should not take the idea lightly. When you borrow against the value of your home, you're taking a serious risk. As mentioned above, your lender has the right to foreclose on your home if you fail to make payments on the loan. Is that risk worth it? You may only save modest amounts of money in exchange for that risk.

When you borrow against your home equity, you truly are "betting the farm." If you are unable to make your required payments for any reason, you risk being evicted from your house. Don't do it unless you are reasonably confident that you can afford the risk.

As with mortgage refinancing, home equity loans cost money. You need to take those costs into consideration before going forward. You might get a lower interest rate and enjoy some tax savings, but those savings could be wiped out by fees associated with closing the loan. When you factor in the risk of losing your home, it might not be worth considering. A home equity loan can help you optimize your borrowing in a few specific situations, but it does not work for everybody.

Nothing Wrong with Asking

To get the most out of your borrowing, you should ask your credit card companies to work with you. If you keep balances on your credit cards, the first thing you should ask for is a lower interest rate. By keeping a balance on your card, you are a profitable customer. The credit card company should be willing to work with you and give you a deal. To get a better rate, just call them up and ask.

Getting a Lower Rate

When you request a lower interest rate, let them know that you think you deserve a lower rate. If you have seen more attractive offers elsewhere, let them know. However, you probably won't make much ground by telling them specifically what offers you've seen. The customer-service representative on the other end of the line will simply try to overcome and rebut any arguments you make. State your case simply, tell them what you want, and ask them for a yes or no answer.

FACT

You should be polite, but firm when you ask for a lower interest rate. If you are thinking of leaving for a better deal, let them know. However, you will most likely talk with an entry-level employee who does not care about your business. If you don't make much progress, try again later or take your business elsewhere.

Getting a lower interest rate will be easier if you've been a cooperative borrower. In other words, you should ask for a deal only after you have made on-time payments for an extended period of time. If you have missed payments, they will consider you a risky borrower who they have no incentive to negotiate with. In addition, it will help you if you have a low balance on that credit card relative to the maximum credit limit. Again, you appear less risky, and there's always the potential that you'll increase your balance if they give you a deal.

Getting to No

Your credit card company may reject your request. However, don't be discouraged. A no simply means that they were not ready to make a deal when you talked with them. You can always call back in a few months, or you can take your business elsewhere. If you decide to do business with a company that is more willing to work with you, don't rush to close the accounts that denied your request. As you've learned elsewhere, it helps your credit to have old accounts with low balances. If a credit card company was unwilling to give you the deal you deserve, you can simply keep a small balance on your account and let it lie dormant.

Increasing Credit Limits

You can also ask your credit card company to increase your credit limit. This means that they will allow you to borrow more—but that's not why you would do it. Borrowing more would only mean that you have more debt to pay off in the future. Instead, you increase your credit limit so that you can increase your credit scores. By using a smaller percentage of your total available credit, you appear less risky to the credit-scoring models.

The "amounts owed" category accounts for 30 percent of your FICO credit score. In this category, the scoring models look at how much you owe relative to how much you are allowed to borrow. This category also accepts other factors, but increasing your credit limit is intended to make it look like you're borrowing less. If you keep your debt balances exactly the same, you will look better because you have more available credit.

This strategy can help even if you pay your balances off in full every month. Your credit card companies don't necessarily report that you pay your balances off every month, instead, they simply report your current balance on whatever day they happen to report to the credit-reporting companies. It is simply a snapshot in time. They might happen to report your balance the day before your check arrives to pay it off.

Your credit reports may show that you're maxing out your credit cards even if you pay your cards off in full each month. The credit card company simply takes a snapshot of your account and forwards that snapshot to the credit-reporting companies. If you use your card heavily and then pay it off each month you could be hurting your credit.

Having a higher available credit limit will help you show that you are not skating on thin ice. Another way to do this is to have a low balance on the days they report. If you can figure out when your lender reports your balance to the credit-reporting companies, you might want to pay down your balances a few days ahead of time.

Getting a credit card limit increase is easy. All you have to do is ask. You can pick up the phone, or you can even make your request online while you're logged in to your accounts.

Managing Fees

Having good credit means you can save a lot of money in interest costs. Unfortunately, lenders sometimes find other ways to get into your pocket. As a result, you have to be vigilant and manage the fees that you pay.

Waive Goodbye

Some credit card companies charge an annual fee just for the right to use their card. They also make a small percentage each time you purchase something on credit. Even if you pay your balances in full each month and avoid finance charges, you can still be a profitable customer. Therefore, there's no reason that you should have to pay annual fees. If you have halfway-decent credit, you need a really good reason to pay annual fees.

Remember that it costs at least twice as much to get a new customer than it does to keep an old one. Once credit card companies have a foot in the door with you, they have an incentive to keep you around. This means that you have some bargaining power, and you can walk away if you want. You should exercise this power, and ask your credit card company to waive any unreasonable fees that they charge you. Sometimes, you only have to call once, and they will waive your annual fees indefinitely.

If the company is unwilling to completely waive the fees, they may cover half of the cost or offer you something else. Therefore, it never hurts to call them and ask. You might not get exactly what you asked for, but you may get something else to sweeten the deal. You should ask them what it takes to get an annual fee waived—are there specific criteria that you need to meet as a customer?

Everybody Makes Mistakes

Some fees act as penalties. The credit card company may smack you with a fee if you send your payment in late. Likewise, you may be assessed a fee if you charge more than your maximum allowable credit limit. Just like your annual fees, you may be able to get these fees waived. If you are a good customer and you don't often make the same mistake, then you have a decent chance of getting these fees reversed. Call your credit card issuer, state your case, and ask that the fee be reversed.

Credit card companies occasionally waive your fees without you having to ask. However, you should certainly not count on that. Find a time when you have a few minutes to sit on hold, and call the credit card company. Explain that you're a good customer, and ask them what they can do for you.

A Healthy Mix

To have the best credit scores, you should have a healthy mix of credit. This means that you should have a variety of accounts and use a variety of credit types: revolving credit, installment credit, and real estate credit. While the specifics are a mystery, some experts recommend having two to six revolving credit accounts, and two or three installment loans.

This may make you wonder whether or not you should pay off mortgage and auto loans. If you pay these loans off and they eventually disappear from your credit reports, you may lower your credit scores. What you actually do is up to you—you may philosophically believe that you should pay off your mortgage if you have the means to do so. According to the credit-reporting companies, paying off your mortgage will not hurt your credit, but it generally helps to have a mortgage.

Chapter 20

Insure Your Good Name

Protecting your good name is just as important as building it. You can do everything right—build credit, fix errors, follow good habits, and so on—and watch all of your work get wiped out by a tragedy. Accidents, sickness, and the other guy can create a financial storm when combined with the inability to work. In a 2005 study, researchers found that about one half of all bankruptcies were sparked by a medical mishap. Therefore, you should take steps to protect yourself from unforeseen events.

The Law of Large Numbers

Insurance is simply a way to share the costs that most people incur over their lifetimes. By pooling money, it is easier for everybody to get their needs met. You may not be able to pay tens of thousands of dollars for that procedure today, but you will very likely pay tens of thousands of dollars into the health-insurance system over your lifetime. If you don't, chances are that your employer will.

The law of large numbers suggests that only a portion of people in a group will need the most expensive treatments in a given time. For example, consider stomach cancer. According to the American Cancer Society, one person in one hundred is likely to develop stomach cancer at some point in their lives. This means that ninety-nine out of 100 consumers help to pay for that one person's treatment. Don't let this bother you, the person with stomach cancer likely helped pay for a treatment you received that he didn't.

Increasingly, the law of large numbers is only part of the cost equation. Credit scores and other consumer data are also used to determine rates. You might think that your consumer data has little to do with the timing of your death or the likelihood that you get in an auto accident. Insurers disagree, and charge rates accordingly.

Insurance companies employ armies of actuaries to crunch the numbers and predict what is most likely to happen. An actuary can tell you how likely you are to get sick, die, be involved in a car accident, or suffer hail damage to your roof. They are the ones who interpret the laws of large numbers. Based on their findings, insurance companies charge you more or less based on the likelihood of a claim.

While there may be problems and inequalities in the insurance system, you are usually better off with insurance than without it. Medical care is expensive, and getting more expensive.

Health Insurance

Health insurance pops up occasionally as a major national debate. While there is no agreement on the solution, everybody agrees on the problem: too many people are uninsured or underinsured.

Catastrophes and Bankruptcy

As you already know, a bankruptcy can wreak havoc on your credit for seven to ten years. More importantly, bankruptcy is not an enjoyable experience. Before a bankruptcy, people get worried and stressed about their financial situation. Creditors call to collect their money. In a financial crisis, you would likely scale back your spending by skipping meals, dropping phone service, or avoiding visits to the dentist.

In 2005, A Journal of Health Affairs publication shed a disturbing light on the truth about bankruptcy and medical expenses. David U. Himmelstein, Elizabeth Warren, Deborah Thorne, and Steffie Woolhandler found that approximately half of the bankruptcies they studied were a result of unmanageable medical costs. You can see the details of the study at the Journal of Health Affairs Web site (*www.healthaffairs.org*).

The most startling finding was that roughly 75 percent of people who filed medical bankruptcy had medical insurance at the onset of their illness. Furthermore, these were middleclass people. Health insurance does not guarantee against major expenses; the combination of medical-care costs, prescription-drug costs, and the loss of income were found to be especially damaging. Subjects in the study lost their income for a variety of reasons. Perhaps they were unable to work or had to scale back their hours, or they took time off to care for a family member.

Causes of bankruptcy in the study included:

- 28.3 percent—Illness or injury
- 7.7 percent—Birth or addition of a new family member
- 7.6 percent—Death in the family
- 2.5 percent—Alcohol or drug addiction
- 1.2 percent—Uncontrolled gambling

With this knowledge, you should understand that it is not enough to simply have health insurance. You must have the right kind of health insurance, and it is a good idea to have other types of insurance as well. The next time you apply for benefits, make sure you consider the risks to you and your family. Finally, don't let your coverage lapse, even for brief periods of time.

FACT

Health insurance does not cover every penny of your costs. The average person who declared bankruptcy as a result of medical expenses, and who also had private health insurance at the onset of illness, paid $13,460 out of pocket for medical care.

Group Coverage

A lot of people are fortunate enough to have coverage through their jobs. Employer-sponsored insurance programs often, but not always, cost less for the end consumer. The insurance company assumes that all of the employees—through the law of large numbers—will balance each other out. In other words, some will be profitable and some will be unprofitable.

If you have group coverage through your employer, be sure to understand exactly what is covered. You may find limits or exclusions on certain treatments, such as cosmetic, mental health, or alternative procedures. These limitations can cost you dearly if you find yourself in need. If you find that there are more exclusions than you'd like, consider purchasing individual insurance to cover the gap. Some health-insurance products cover specific treatments, so you might not need a full-blown health-insurance policy for just a few items.

COBRA

If it sounds like the name of a dangerous snake, you might not be far off. In truth, the Consolidated Omnibus Budget Reconciliation Act (COBRA) is helpful for consumers. It was designed to help people who lose group coverage after an employee job loss, death, divorce, or other qualifying event.

COBRA might be the best of several unpleasant choices—it is better than going uninsured.

ALERT!

If you apply for continued coverage under COBRA, be prepared for sticker shock. Typically, employers help cover the costs of health insurance. Once you are no longer employed, the full insurance premium is your responsibility, and it will most likely be much higher than the amount you had taken from your paycheck each month.

If you lose your job, is your health insurance going to be on the top of your to-do list? For most people it usually isn't. You would most likely brush up your resume, call people in your network, and check your budget to see how long you can last without a paycheck. COBRA makes it easy to keep your group coverage for a limited time, until you can find a more permanent solution. You keep the same coverage you had while employed; however, you have to pay the full price for coverage.

HIPAA

The Health Insurance Portability and Accountability Act of 1996 (HIPAA) added protections for consumers with group health-insurance plans. The Act can help you protect your credit because it limits exclusions and discrimination in group health-insurance policies.

Since HIPAA, it is easier to make sure you do not have gaps in your health-insurance coverage. You should do everything you can to make sure you always have health insurance. If you go without health insurance for too long (currently 63 days), you risk losing access to the most complete health coverage. You might be subject to pre-existing condition exclusions and restrictions. However, you can prevent this if you keep continuous coverage and document that you have done so.

Anytime you terminate an insurance contract, whether it is an individual policy or a group policy through your job, make sure you get a Certificate of Coverage that shows the dates you were covered. In addition, you should enroll in your group health plan as soon as you are eligible. If you wait, you risk giving up some of your rights.

Temporary Insurance

Sometimes it is hard to coordinate insurance start dates and end dates. Rather than run the risk of going without insurance coverage, consider a temporary insurance policy, also known as short-term insurance. These policies cover illnesses and accidents for short periods of time, and monthly premiums are much lower than a standard individual insurance policy.

If you don't want to use your COBRA benefits, consider a lower-cost temporary plan. These plans often qualify as creditable insurance under HIPAA, so they can help you avoid lengthy gaps in coverage, which will limit your next permanent policy. Temporary plans are usually restrictive, and may exclude pre-existing conditions, but they can fill the gap so your next policy will not exclude pre-existing conditions. Furthermore, they can help you stay out of bankruptcy if you get an unexpected surprise.

Disability Insurance

Disability insurance replaces your income if you are unable to work. Once the policy kicks in, you receive payments that should help to replace lost income. As noted above, the combination of medical costs and loss of income can be devastating. Remember, your health insurance pays a portion of your medical costs; it does not make your other bills go away.

Length of Disability

Most people have short-term disability insurance through their job. This coverage likely pays benefits if you are unable to work for a few weeks or months. While this is extremely important, what happens if your disability lasts longer? You should at least consider longer-term disability insurance. When a disability goes beyond a few months, it tends to last a while. Long-term disability policies pick up where short-term policies end.

Definition of Disability

What is disability? For the purposes of disability-income insurance, disability is the inability to work. Different policies go into greater detail. For example, an "own occupation" policy considers you to be disabled if you cannot perform your own occupation. Consider a brain surgeon who uses her hands in a specialized way—if she loses the ability to operate on peoples' brains, she is considered disabled under an "own occupation" policy. Therefore, the insurance company will pay her.

If the surgeon has an "any occupation" policy, she might fail the disability test. She must be unable to perform the duties of any occupation before she is considered disabled. The insurer might point out that she can still function as an excellent primary care physician or pediatrician. She could also work in insurance sales, sanitation arts, or at a convenience store. If she has an "any occupation" policy, she might have to go to work at another job.

Causes of Disability

Disability happens for a variety of reasons. Of course, accidents usually come to mind first. However, plenty of sicknesses and other conditions can lead to long-term disability. Some of the most common culprits include:

- 24 percent—Musculoskeletal problems (for example, back pain)
- 13 percent—Circulatory system issues
- 11 percent—Nervous system diseases
- 10 percent—Injuries and poisonings
- 10 percent—Neoplasms (growths and tumors—may be cancerous)
- 6 percent—Mental disorders

FACT

It can happen to you. Roughly one-third of all working Americans will suffer a disability of more than ninety days in their lifetime. The average disability will last two and one half years. (National Association of Insurance Commissioners (NAIC), Commissioner's Individual Disability Table A, 1985).

What about Social Security?

Social Security will pay benefits to a disabled person. However, you should understand how it works before you count on it. Social Security is much more restrictive than an insurance company in defining disability. They use an "any occupation" system. You have to be unable to perform the functions of any job before you qualify for benefits. In addition, your disability must be projected to last for more than one year, or result in your death.

QUESTION?

How much will a long-term disability insurance policy pay me?
Typically, you get monthly payments of up to 60 percent of your monthly earnings before disability. Any more than that, and you might not have much reason to go back to work. The insurance company wants you to have an incentive to get better and start earning income again.

Another drawback to the Social Security system is that your payments will likely be much lower than the amount of money you need. Check your last Social Security statement or call the Social Security Administration to find out what you might expect if you become disabled. You might find that it is half of what you can expect from a private policy. If you are a high-wage earner, you will get less than half of the maximum payment from a private policy.

Life Insurance

Everybody knows what life insurance is: if you pass away while a policy is in force, your beneficiaries get a tax-free payment. Like disability insurance, life insurance can help replace lost income if a breadwinner dies. It can prevent the addition of insult to injury, so your beneficiaries' credit doesn't suffer while they are suffering emotionally from your loss.

Who Needs Life Insurance?

If you have somebody depending on you, you probably need life insurance. If you're young and single, you can get away with only insuring your own income in case you live through hard times. However, once you add other people to the mix, you need to think of them. In fact, you might consider life insurance even before you take on the responsibility of providing for others; the older you get, the more expensive insurance gets, and you might become uninsurable if you get really sick.

Thirty-One Flavors

There are many different types of life insurance available. Really, you only need to understand that there are term policies and permanent policies. Term policies remain in force for a specified number of years (or a specified term), and then they are gone. A permanent policy might last as long as you do, and it usually has a build-up of cash value over the years.

Which should you use? It depends on a variety of factors. For protecting your credit, term insurance may be adequate. Term insurance typically offers the largest death benefit, or payout, for the lowest monthly premium payment. If you only want to protect the family in case of an unexpected death, term insurance should do the trick.

Whenever you buy any type of insurance, make sure you buy it through a strong insurance company. What good is an insurance policy if the company is unable to pay a claim? One way to manage this is to buy insurance only from companies rated A+ or better. A good source for insurance company ratings is A.M. Best's Web site (*www.ambest.com*).

Term Insurance

For example, assume that a young couple moves into a new home and has two children. They buy thirty-year term insurance on each of them. If one should die, the insurance company will pay the surviving spouse a large sum of money. That spouse can then pay off the mortgage and provide child care and higher education for the children. If nobody dies after thirty years, the policy goes away. However, they may not need the large death benefit at this time—the children are now self-sufficient and the surviving spouse earns a healthy income. Furthermore, the home mortgage is likely paid off, or the surviving spouse can move to a smaller, less-expensive home and eliminate any house payments.

Permanent Insurance

Permanent policies do more than just protect your dependents for a given number of years. First, they can extend the amount of time that coverage stays in place. If you want to be sure that somebody gets a death benefit payment, a permanent policy might be appropriate. For example, you might want to ensure that your spouse never has to enter the workforce, even if you die when you are sixty-five. A permanent policy can be in place for an entire lifetime, so it is reasonable to expect that it could pay a death benefit when you and your spouse are in your fifties, sixties, seventies, or older. Depending on your household, permanent insurance can protect your credit or perform other tasks.

Life Insurance at Work

Large employers often offer group term life insurance as an employee benefit. Make sure you understand what you have. Standard group life policies are quite modest. For example, your coverage may only be for $10,000 or one year's salary. While this money will help, it is not enough to protect your loved ones. See if you can sign up for more, even though you will have to pay for the extra coverage.

The small death benefit is only one reason to look outside your employer for coverage. Another reason to shop individual policies is to have control over your life insurance. Consider what happens if you leave your job; you will most likely lose your coverage. If you become self-employed, you won't have another employer to pay for your insurance. At that time, you might be older, when insurance is more expensive, or uninsurable because of recent health issues. For these reasons, you should investigate owning your own life insurance.

Long-Term Care Insurance

Long-term care insurance provides benefits for, as the name suggests, long-term care. What is long-term care, and why is it dangerous to your credit? Long-term care refers to all the services you require above and beyond medical treatments. Some people think of it as home-health care or nursing-home care insurance, and that is a decent place to start.

The need for long-term care is greatest at older ages. However, plenty of young folks find themselves in need as well. According to the United States Government Accountability Office, about 40 percent of people (there are 13 million of them) receiving long-term care are between the ages of eighteen and sixty-four. An auto accident, a sickness, or a disease can easily qualify you for long-term care benefits.

ALERT!

There are a lot of moving parts in long-term care policies. At this point, you should just familiarize yourself with the concept so that you understand how to protect your credit. Then, you can figure out the nuts and bolts of a policy that might be appropriate for you.

Uncovered Services

Long-term care insurance covers services that are typically not covered anywhere else. Your health insurance might pay for surgery after an accident, but they will not pay for your bathing and feeding for five months after the surgery. If you are destitute, you might rely on Medicaid to pay for your nursing home. However, that means you have to "spend down" your assets first, and limit your care to those services that Medicaid will pay for.

How Do I Qualify?

Long-term care insurance kicks in when you are unable to perform certain activities. These are called the Activities of Daily Living (ADLs). If you are unable to perform two or more ADLs, your policy can start paying benefits. The ADLs are:

- Dressing
- Bathing
- Transferring (or moving from one place to another)
- Toileting
- Eating
- Continence

You may also qualify for benefit payments if you are diagnosed with a serious cognitive disease like Alzheimer's.

Long-Term Care Benefits

There are a few ways to receive benefits under a long-term care policy. The most common ones are indemnity benefits and reimbursement benefits. Indemnity benefits pay you a fixed dollar amount each day, regardless of what your actual costs are. Your actual costs could be higher or lower—if they are higher, you have to make up the difference out of your pocket. Reimbursement policies pay you based on your actual expenses, up to a limit defined in the policy.

Depending on your policy, you can receive long-term care at home or in a nursing facility. You may be able to have family members perform the duties, or you may be required to hire people with certain licenses and skills.

Auto and Homeowner's Insurance

Auto insurance and homeowner's insurance are no-brainers. If you don't already have coverage, you probably know that you should. In fact, going uninsured is difficult, because state laws and lenders often require you to have coverage. For these reasons, this section touches very briefly on auto and homeowner's insurance.

Furthermore, you have liability coverage in your auto and homeowner's insurance policies. If somebody gets hurt, the bill can climb to several hundred thousand dollars quickly. Why not let the insurance company take that risk? Yes, it costs money, but it is a small price to pay for peace of mind.

Skipping auto and homeowner's insurance can ruin your credit. Just like a bad sickness can put you in bankruptcy, auto and home repair costs can easily get into the thousands of dollars or more. The risk-to-reward ratio simply isn't favorable if you are thinking of going without coverage.

Additional Liability Insurance

Umbrella insurance is a liability insurance that pays once you exhaust your benefits under an auto or homeowner's insurance policy. If you have assets—or if people think you have assets—you should take a good hard look at umbrella insurance. It is dirt cheap, but it can save you a million.

Most homeowner's and auto insurance policies have some liability coverage, so why buy more? Umbrella insurance serves two major purposes:

- It pays above and beyond what your other policies pay
- It covers items that your other policies do not cover

Most insurance policies have a limit on what they will pay for a liability claim. For example, your auto insurance might pay up to $300,000. If you are found liable for more than that, the auto-insurance company won't pay. Where else does the money come from? If you do not have any additional coverage, it comes out of your pocket, meaning you might have to sell your assets to cover the difference. If you have additional coverage under an umbrella policy, the insurance company will pay the difference, as long as the claim fits into the policy, of course.

An umbrella policy can also cover you for things that are not covered under any other insurance policies. For example, you might want worldwide liability coverage, which some basic homeowner's and auto policies cannot offer. Likewise, you may want to protect yourself from slander or invasion of privacy lawsuits. There are other examples, but the point is that you have coverage in more areas of your life.

ALERT!

You do not need to be rich to benefit from umbrella insurance. Consider your assets: retirement-plan savings, autos, equity in your home, business interests or property—it adds up. Even if you have nothing to lose, umbrella insurance can help keep you from going into debt.

How much does umbrella insurance cost? It depends on how much you want, but it is really quite inexpensive. For $150 to $300 per year, you can get at least a million-dollar policy. You can add millions on top of that for even less. Note that the insurer typically requires that you have adequate coverage on your auto and homeowner's insurance before they will issue a policy. For example, they might require that you keep $300,000 of liability insurance on your auto policy. That way, the umbrella insurance doesn't kick in unless your liability goes above the $300,000.

The Language of Insurance

If you are intimidated by insurance, you're not alone. However, you have to keep in mind that insurance is there to protect you and help you. There may be times when it doesn't feel that way, but insurance companies help you take risks that you cannot afford to take alone.

Part of the problem with insurance is the jargon. Unfortunately, everything isn't written in plain English. This section should help you get a grasp on what those guys are talking about at the insurance company.

Deductibles

A deductible is the part of a claim that the insurance company will not pay. Essentially, it's your share of the cost. You will find deductibles in health, auto, homeowner's, and other policies. When you choose insurance plans, note that the deductible affects your pricing: the higher the deductible, the lower your premium payments. This is because you are taking on more risk with a higher deductible.

Coinsurance

After you pay the deductible, you may have coinsurance. Like a deductible, coinsurance keeps you involved in the process so that the insurance company is not writing all of the checks. The goal is to keep you from spending all of the insurance company's money for no good reason; if it comes out of your pocket, you'll make sure it's needed.

Coinsurance is usually talked about as a percentage. For example, 80/20 coinsurance usually means that the insurer pays 80 percent of costs and you pay 20-percent. Typically, you'll also have an out-of-pocket limit, which shifts any risk above a certain level back to the insurance company. For example, you might pay 20 percent coinsurance on costs up to $5000 ($1000 out of your pocket), and then the insurance company pays the rest.

Keep in mind that different policies offer different types of protection. You should be thorough when you buy a policy. If you own a business, you will probably want a policy that does not exclude your business activities and business property. Also, make sure you understand if and when legal-defense costs are paid.

Elimination Period

For long-term disability and long-term care insurance, you have something called an elimination period. This is a set period of time where your condition exists, but the insurance company hasn't started to pay you benefits yet. For example, assume you buy a long-term disability policy with a ninety-day elimination period. You have to be disabled for ninety days before they start paying you benefits. The purpose is to avoid claims where you are disabled for a short period of time. You might as well call the elimination period a waiting period.

Benefit Period

The benefit period also shows up in long-term disability and long-term care policies. It is the amount of time that the insurance company will pay benefits to you. You might have a long-term disability insurance policy that has a two-year benefit period. This means that they will pay you your monthly benefits for up to two years; after you've satisfied the elimination period, of course. If your disability is shorter than two years, that's great. However, if your disability lasts longer than two years, you are on your own.

As you may have guessed, longer benefit periods (or shorter elimination periods) result in higher costs to you. You have to pay more each month for the luxury of knowing that you have a less-restrictive policy. Some benefit periods go up until you reach age sixty-five, or whenever your maximum Social Security benefits kick in. These plans are more expensive, but they give you more protection.

Chapter 21

Protect Your Masterpiece from Thieves

It takes a lot of work to build up your good name. You do what it takes to make all of those payments on time. You build a healthy mix of credit accounts to show that you are a seasoned borrower. You manage your money wisely, and you protect yourself against the unknown. Improving your credit takes years. Unfortunately, it can be stolen and ruined in an instant. If you're not thinking about identity theft, it is time you did.

What Happens with Identity Theft

Identity theft occurs when somebody uses your identity to commit crimes. An important distinction here is that that somebody is not actually you. They lead others to believe that they are you, so you get all of the blame and consequences. Unfortunately, there are no known cases where an identity thief has committed random acts of kindness and senseless acts of beauty and left the credit to his victim. Instead, they create a variety of problems in your name. Identity theft is a serious crime, usually involving some type of fraud.

Who Are You?

Identity theft can get really complicated. The problem is that businesses, governments, and organizations don't really know who you are. They have never met you, and they could not put a face to your name. The reality of the world today is that computers keep track of things for us. There are just too many people out there; even if you are really good at remembering names, you can't remember them all.

An identity thief will take advantage of this. Even though they're not really you, they lead others to believe that they are. How do they do this? They use some distinct characteristics that are supposedly unique to you, and only you. Not surprisingly, the big ones are your name, address, date of birth, and Social Security Number. Think about it: these are the characteristics that organizations ask for whenever you apply for a driver's license, credit card, auto loan, bank account, or insurance.

If any organization that you do business with asks for your Social Security Number, see if they really need it. Some places allow you to use an alternative—they may assign you a unique customer ID, or allow you to choose one. The less you use your Social Security Number, the better.

Long, long ago, these characteristics must have held more meaning. Presumably, they were top-secret information that only you and your trustworthy business partners knew. Over time, people got lazy and began to use these characteristics more and more publicly. Colleges assigned Student ID numbers that happened to be the student's Social Security Number. Driver's licenses displayed Social Security Numbers, and Internet user names were often Social Security Numbers.

Where To Go from Here

Granted, there is some wisdom in using Social Security Numbers. A consumer can hardly remember twenty different user IDs, but they often remember their Social Security Number. The problem is that the Social Security Number is at the top of the information hierarchy. There is nothing more unique about you than your Social Security Number; at least, there is nothing practical and widely affordable at the present time. Your DNA is substantially more unique, but it is hard for the customer-service representative on the other end of the line to verify this.

Don't be surprised to see increased use of fingerprints, retina scans, voice recognition, DNA testing, and a variety of other sophisticated tools in the future. These methods will certainly make it harder for identity thieves to claim that they are somebody else. However, criminals are notoriously pesky and creative. For years, Hollywood movies have shown ways that a creative person might circumvent these security measures. Whether or not criminals will use the same methods is unclear, but there is no doubt that they will find a way to beat the system.

I Am You

In the meantime, identity theft is relatively easy. All a would-be thief needs to do is write your name, address, Social Security Number, and birthday on an application. They are now you, and because of this, they have all of the same rights and powers that you do. They can change your address, use your credit to open accounts, withdraw your money, and more. If you are starting to get nervous, that's good.

Some identity thieves assume your identity in every sense of the word. They're not just looking to steal some money from a credit card company. Instead, they want to live an entire life under your identity. These people may be in the country illegally—perhaps they just want a shot at the American dream, or perhaps they are terrorists. Some of these folks are hiding from the past. They may not want somebody to find them, like law-enforcement officials, for example. As a result, they live their life as you. They give your name and information to employers, but they usually "forget" to pay income taxes on your Social Security Number.

A Standard Case

A typical identity-theft case is just a matter of stealing money. The identity thief is somebody who does not have as much money as they would like to have. Instead of getting a job, the identity thief turns to fraud. Once they have your personal information, they start using accounts in your name. Sometimes, identity thieves will open brand-new accounts. They contact credit card companies and open new accounts in your name. They might also frequent stores that offer instant credit. For example, they may buy clothes at a major department store, or they may buy furniture from a rent-to-own establishment.

QUESTION?

Do I have to pay for charges made by a thief?
In most cases, you will not be responsible for debts created by an identity thief. However, you have to report the crime in a timely fashion, and alert your creditors. You may not have to pay the charges, but you will spend a lot of time and energy cleaning up the mess.

Of course, the identity thief has no intention of paying the bills. The whole point of stealing somebody's identity is that the victim is left with the bill. Therefore, in a standard identity-theft case, the victim finds huge amounts of debt that he did not personally incur.

Here's a Nice Account

Sometimes, identity thieves will attack your existing accounts. If they know (or have reason to believe) that you have a lot of assets, they may try to make withdrawals in your name. Your bank account and brokerage account would be prime targets. A common tactic is to change your address on your bank and brokerage accounts. That way, statements are no longer mailed to your house for your review. Then, the thief can take out as much money as he likes. You will not notice the transactions because the mail no longer comes to your house. In recent years, financial institutions have caught on to this. Most have added safeguards so that it is more difficult to pull this off. They send a letter to the old address and the new address stating that there has been an address change. If you ever get such a letter and you haven't moved lately, you should keep a close eye on your accounts for other signs of identity theft.

That Explains It!

It can take a long time to detect an identity thief. In most cases, victims are not aware that their identity has been stolen until after the thief has racked up thousands of dollars and opened several accounts. In some cases, it goes on for years. You might go several years before you apply for a new auto loan or home loan, only to be turned down because of a poor credit history. If you are not aware that you have a poor credit history, you look into your credit reports and see a jumbled mix of accounts that are not yours. Then, you have to start the cleanup process.

How Thieves Work, and How to Stop Them

Identity theft comes about in a variety of ways. The common ingredient to all cases is the fact that a thief gets a hold of your personal identifying information. Once they have that, they're ready to strike. They may sit on your information for a while, waiting for you to drop your guard, and waiting for any short-term fraud alerts to expire. Once they have your information, they can use it for many years to come.

Personal information that can be used for identity theft is all over the place. Although you are not an aspiring criminal, you should know how they operate so that you can protect yourself. Identity thieves have several tricks of the trade that they use to get the information needed for identity theft.

Dumpster Diving

A common way to get valuable personal information is a practice known as dumpster diving. As the name suggests, dumpster diving involves digging through dumpsters with the goal of finding discarded papers that contain important information. Unlike scuba diving, you don't have to travel to exotic places to be a dumpster diver. Major cities are full of them. A good dumpster diver can easily hit a hundred dumpsters in one day. If just a small percentage of consumers are careless enough to throw away important documents, the dumpster diver has a good day.

If you live in the suburbs, don't necessarily assume that you are safe. Dumpster divers might operate at a bank, doctor's office, or other institution with which you do business. Furthermore, dumpster divers can operate out of landfills and recycling facilities. It may not even be your fault—an employee may throw out a document with your information on it, and put you at risk.

To protect yourself from dumpster-diving identity thieves, you have to make sure that there is nothing there for them to find. The easiest way to do this is to shred any documents that have important personal information in them. If you don't already have one, buy yourself a cross-cut paper shredder. When in doubt about anything, shred it. If they can't read it, they cannot use it against you.

It is difficult to ensure that others who have your personal information are protecting it. Banks and other institutions can slip up, and all the shredding you've been doing might be for naught. Ask them if they have policies and procedures for protecting customer information. If they do not, consider working with somebody else.

Computer Hacking

An increasingly common form of identity theft is a result of computer hacking. Thieves might gain access to your computer, or the computers of a company that you do business with. Once they are in, they can download anything they want. If the computer happens to belong to an organization, the personal information of hundreds, thousands, or even millions of consumers may be at risk. Computer hacking is the preferred method of obtaining valuable information. As you might imagine, it is much more glamorous than dumpster diving, and the working conditions are better. When computer hackers are most successful, they get information on a large number of potential victims. This increases the likelihood that they can find somebody who has assets and good credit.

ALERT!

Be sure to keep all of your computer software up to date in order to keep your personal information safe. Hackers and computer experts constantly discover vulnerabilities in popularly used software. Software manufacturers often provide free security updates to fix the vulnerabilities. If you don't update your software, you make it very easy on the hackers.

To protect yourself against computer hackers, you need to protect your computer. The easiest thing you can do is have a good antivirus program and keep it up to date. You should also check to see if a firewall will do you any good. Follow some commonsense computing rules: don't open attachments from unknown senders, avoid visiting Web sites that you don't need to visit, and keep all of your software up to date.

There are a lot of free software programs out there that help you protect your information. Search around consumer-privacy Web sites, and you will find some good ideas. You might start with the Gibson Research Corporation (*www.grc.com*). You can learn about some of the threats out there, and you can even run tests to see if your computer is at risk. Another useful program is Spybot Search and Destroy. This program checks for common spyware programs running on your computer. Spyware is a type of computer program that spies on you as you use your computer. These programs can allow all kinds of shady characters to learn more about you.

Old computers can also be a gold mine for identity thieves. Since computers constantly improve, you may buy a new one every few years. What happens to that old computer? If you donate it, sell it, or give it away, you need to be sure that any sensitive information is permanently deleted. Even if you delete everything, the data may still be on your computer's hard drive. To permanently wipe the data out, you should use a specialized software program designed for this purpose. As an alternative, you could reformat your hard drive before getting rid of the computer.

Going Phishing

Another easy way to get information for identity theft is to use a tactic called phishing. Scammers contact you and claim to be employees of a reputable institution. They often use the names of banks and credit card companies with this strategy. For example, you may get an e-mail from somebody who claims to be an employee (or automated system) at Bank of America. The e-mail might say that they have had technical difficulties, or that something strange is going on with your account. Then, they ask you to verify your identity by sending all of your personal details: your full name, date of birth, Social Security Number, and so on. Of course, you divulge this information to an identity thief, not the bank. Much like computer hacking, phishing is fairly easy. Scammers can send thousands of e-mails just as easily as they can send one. Much like real fishing, they throw their bait out and see if anybody will bite.

Identity thieves can use computer-hacking techniques to get your information. However, it is probably still much safer to do things online (such as pay bills with an online bill-pay service) as opposed to the old-fashioned way. Most transactions and computer systems are secure. However, systems that aren't secure make it really easy for the scammers.

To protect yourself from this type of scam, be extremely cautious about whom you talk to. If somebody calls you or e-mails you asking for sensitive information, be suspicious. If the request comes via e-mail, there's a 99.9-percent chance that it's a phishing scam. Most organizations will never call you or e-mail you and ask for personal details. If it ever happens, you can simply state that you'd like to call them back just to be safe. Then, call a number that you know is a legitimate phone number to that organization—don't call a phone number given to you by the person requesting your information.

An Inside Job

Most of the methods described previously are fairly anonymous and involve thieves who have no idea who the victim is. Having your identity stolen by an unknown criminal is somewhat random, but it happens all of the time. Unfortunately, some victims of identity theft have a connection with the thief. Sometimes there is a close personal connection, and sometimes it's a business relationship.

Occasionally, you see a high-publicity case where an employee sells the information about his customers. A person at a bank or credit card company can easily get a hold of the personal details of a large number of consumers. If the employee is part of the wrong crowd, he may sell that information to somebody who plans to use it for identity theft. Unfortunately, one bad apple can do some serious damage to a bank's PR.

ALERT!

In order to access your credit report, some thieves pretend to have a permissible purpose for obtaining your credit information. They may pose as a landlord, potential employer, or financial institution as they request your reports. Once they have succeeded, they know about most of your accounts, they know your current and previous addresses, and they are ready to strike.

Sometimes the connection is even closer; family members have been known to steal each other's identity. It may be a troubled youth, or somebody in a tough financial situation. Either way, the victim feels especially violated in these cases. When the identity thief lives with the victim, it is more difficult to uncover the crime. The thief can easily intercept mail and cover his tracks.

It is difficult to prevent a dishonest insider from doing bad things. As a consumer, you are largely at the mercy of organizations that you deal with. The greatest power you have is the power to take your business elsewhere. If you suspect (or know) that an organization is not protecting your valuable information, go somewhere else. Unfortunately, they may already have information about you in their databases—the fact that your account is closed does not mean that your personal details have been deleted.

Stolen Property

Identity theft also happens when valuable items are stolen or lost. Your purse or wallet may have all kinds of useful information for an identity thief. Your Social Security Number, birthday, address, and account numbers fall right into an identity thief's hands. Likewise, the thief may steal a laptop or computer hard drive that contains sensitive personal information about a group of people. Traveling salespeople, human-resource specialists, and consultants all have important information on their computers.

Skimming

There are an unlimited number of ways that identity thieves operate. Most of the methods above involve impersonating a victim, and using their accounts. However, some thieves use a much simpler form of identity theft. All they need is a credit card number, and something to buy. They can get your credit card number in all the ways listed above. In addition, there are countless other creative ways to get valuable information. For example, the technique known as skimming allows criminals to capture your credit card number as you make purchases. There might be a hidden device attached to the machine, or the thief might have a small portable device he can use while he has your card.

How to Detect a Thief

Identity thieves can wreak havoc on your life in a very short amount of time. Before you know it, they may have opened numerous accounts, siphoned money from existing accounts, and even declared bankruptcy in your name. While they operate quickly, there are steps you can take to detect identity theft in process. The sooner you catch it, the less damage you'll suffer.

Has Anything Changed?

Keep an eye out for anything unusual. Once identity thieves start using your good name, a few subtle hints may pop up. For starters, you may find that you are no longer receiving bills, statements, or correspondence from financial institutions that you do business with. This could very well mean that an identity thief has changed your address so that you won't see what's going on in your accounts. Although it may be nice to stop getting bills from your credit card company, it's probably a bad sign.

Try to minimize the amount of sensitive personal information that you carry. It is too easy to lose or misplace something. If you have an option to keep your Social Security Number off your driver's license, exercise that option. Likewise, tell your service providers that you do not want to use your Social Security Number as a customer-ID number.

Read Those Statements

Another sign of identity theft is a series of unauthorized transactions on your accounts. This may mean that an identity thief has started using your account number to make purchases. They might be dipping into your checking account, or they may be racking-up debt on a credit card account. It is easy to give your statements a cursory glance and miss important details. Spend the extra minute it takes to look the statement over thoroughly. You might even want to check your accounts online, that way you can see transactions as they happen.

Interesting Phone Calls and Letters

There's nothing out of the ordinary about somebody dialing the wrong number—you probably do it on occasion yourself. However, make a mental note every time a financial institution calls you and it seems to be in error. In particular, you should be alert to claims that you have unpaid debts. It could be that an identity thief has racked-up bills in your name and refused to pay them, and now the collectors are calling. The same thing goes for letters about unpaid debts. You should investigate these immediately, and resolve the situation.

Application Denied

If you are ever denied for credit, insurance, or employment, it could be because an identity thief is ruining your credit. Anytime you are denied something based on your credit, you should receive a disclosure explaining that this happened. In addition, you're entitled to view your credit report. Especially if you are surprised to hear that you've been denied, take a close look at your credit reports for any signs of identity theft.

Federal laws require that you be notified whenever you are denied credit, a job, or insurance because of information in your credit reports. You will receive a disclosure stating that somebody took adverse action against you. When this happens, you are entitled to view your credit reports for free.

Lots of Inquiring Minds

As you review your credit reports periodically, pay close attention to the section on inquiries. This section has the early warning signs that can help you stop identity theft. If financial institutions, employers, and landlords are making inquiries that don't make any sense to you, it could be that they are inquiring for somebody other than the real you. This may mean that somebody is trying to open accounts in your name or otherwise assume your identity. If an inquiry does not make sense to you, find out more. Your credit report should have contact information for anybody making inquiries into your credit.

Not My Account

In addition to the inquiry section of your credit report, you should review the accounts section for signs of identity theft. If you see accounts in there that you don't remember opening, it could be that an identity thief opened that account for you. Don't assume it's just an error on the part of the credit-reporting companies. Even if it's an error, it's important that you fix it. If it's not an error, and it is in fact identity theft, the situation is even more urgent.

If You've Been Robbed

In an ideal world, the techniques described above will keep you safe. By following these techniques, it will be hard for identity thieves to steal your identity. Like most creatures, identity thieves choose the path of least resistance; therefore, hopefully they will leave you alone. Identity thieves will tend to steal identities that are easy to steal, and there are millions of other consumers out there who take no precautions whatsoever with their identity. Until the public better understands the severity of identity theft, that's probably how things will go. Nevertheless, you can still have your identity stolen, no matter how cautious you are. Ingenious scammers and careless business partners can make your worst nightmare come true.

Fraud Alert

If you find yourself in this unfortunate situation, you need to act fast. The faster you shut everything down, the easier your life will be in the clean-up process. One of the first things you should do is place a fraud alert on your credit reports. To do this, you simply contact one of the three major credit reporting companies—Equifax, TransUnion, or Experian. The company you contact is supposed to forward the alert to the other two companies. However, there's no harm in contacting them yourself to request a fraud alert, just to be safe. The credit-reporting company will require documentation from you to make sure you are who you say you are. Once the fraud alert is created, you should receive free copies of your credit reports.

There are two types of fraud alerts. One of them lasts for ninety days, and the other one lasts for seven years. If you have been the victim of identity theft, the seven-year fraud alert is probably your best bet. Keep in mind that while the fraud alert is active, lenders are not supposed to open new credit accounts in your name without contacting you first. If you actually want to open a new credit account, the process might go slowly. Lenders will proceed with caution, and they'll have to contact you (the real you, as defined in the fraud alert) before lending any money. As a result, you should make it as easy as possible for them to get a hold of you. If you have a cellular phone, include that number when applying for new accounts.

QUESTION?

Will creating a fraud alert protect me from identity theft?
The actual value of a fraud alert is up for debate. Whether or not it will prevent an identity thief from opening new accounts in your name is unclear. However, it is certainly better than doing nothing. Responsible lenders will do their part to help fight fraud, especially since it will affect them as well.

Freeze Them Out

A much stronger tactic you might use is to ask for a security freeze. A security freeze blocks all access to your credit reports until you remove the freeze. This is much more dramatic than merely placing a fraud alert on your reports, and it will certainly prevent identity thieves from opening new accounts in your name. Note that a security freeze may not be available in your state—only a handful of states allow them at the present time.

Close Affected Accounts

Next, you should close any accounts that have been affected by the identity thief. These may be accounts that you opened, or they might be accounts that the identity thief opened in your name. You can find all of these accounts on your credit reports, complete with contact information for the institution that holds the account. Call these companies and ask what the procedure is to formally report that you've been a victim of identity theft, and let them know that one of their accounts was involved. Most often, they have a special department for fraud control. If the representative you speak with sounds a bit unsure of things, ask for the fraud department.

ALERT!

Think carefully before you add a fraud alert to, or place a freeze on, your credit reports. Doing so can make it extremely difficult to get credit. If you are hoping to buy a house, for example, things may slow down dramatically, and you might miss out on buying your dream home.

You'll most likely have to submit written documentation of the identity theft. Even if they say that a phone call is sufficient, you should follow up in writing as a safeguard. As with every other letter you send that has anything to do with correcting errors on your credit report, you should send the letter by certified mail, return receipt requested. They may have a special form that they want you to use, and they may require copies of official documents, such as a police report. The Federal Trade Commission (FTC) has a model Identity Theft Affidavit that you can use with your creditors. This affidavit is available at *www.consumer.gov/idtheft*.

Once you are successful in closing the accounts affected by identity theft, ask for written documentation from the credit provider stating that the account was closed in good order. If the identity thief opened new accounts in your name, be sure to get written documentation from the creditor acknowledging that it was a fraudulent account from the beginning.

Alerting the Authorities

Identity theft is a serious crime. It involves theft and fraud, and it can make your life miserable. Therefore, you should report occurrences of identity theft to the authorities. First, file a police report with your local law-enforcement agency. Let them know that you've had your identity stolen, and provide documentation, including information on accounts affected by the theft. You should also try to file a report in the jurisdiction where the identity thief lives, if you have that information.

You should also inform the FTC that you are a victim of identity theft. While the FTC does not necessarily follow up on your case, they do keep records of identity-theft cases nationally. With enough information, the FTC and other regulators can better fight identity theft.

Appendix A

Useful Web Sites

Fair Isaac's Consumer Web site
www.myfico.com
Learn all about credit scoring.

The FTC's Web site on Credit
www.ftc.gov/credit
Information on your rights as a consumer.

AnnualCreditReport.com
www.annualcreditreport.com
This is where you get your free credit reports.

The FTC's Web site on ID Theft
www.consumer.gov/idtheft
Comprehensive resources on avoiding and recovering from identity theft.

Privacy Rights Clearinghouse's ID Theft Victim's Guide
www.privacyrights.org/fs/fs17a.htm
Detailed instructions on recovering from ID theft.

Insurance Information Institute—Insurance Scoring FAQ
www.insurancescoring.info/faq.htm
Learn more about how your credit affects your insurance.

An Overview and History of Credit Reporting
www.phil.frb.org/pcc/discussion/historycr.pdf
A report with details on how we got to where we are.

ChoicePoint's Consumer Web site
www.choicetrust.com
A consumer-reporting company that creates insurance scores and other reports.

Equifax.com
www.equifax.com
Equifax's official Web site. One of the major credit-reporting companies.

TrueCredit.com
www.truecredit.com
TransUnion's consumer Web site. One of the major credit-reporting companies.

Experian.com
www.experian.com
Experian's official Web site. One of the major credit-reporting companies.

VantageScore
www.vantagescore.com
Learn about the new VantageScore.

Appendix B

Sample
Correspondence

Sample Dispute Letter

This template may be used to send disputes to the credit-reporting companies. Note that you should always be friendly and respectful in these letters—the reader will be an employee who receives hundreds of letters a day. Rudeness will only make them care less about you, and it won't help your case in court. Finally, keep your letters extremely brief and on topic. If you want to provide a long explanation, do so with a separate attachment.

Include a photocopy of your credit report and any supporting materials—never send originals. Mark them with identifying information (like "Exhibit A" and "Item #1") to make the process as easy as possible for the credit-reporting company, and to protect your rights.

[DATE]

TO: *[CREDIT-REPORTING COMPANY]*
[ADDRESS OF CREDIT-REPORTING COMPANY]

Greetings:

Please correct the following errors on my credit report (a photocopy of the report, marked "Exhibit A," is enclosed with this letter). I'm disputing the following items:

Account: ABC Credit Card Company, account #123456 (Exhibit A, Item #1)
Reason for dispute: I never paid late. Please remove the late-payment notation.
Note: Exhibit B shows on-time payments for every month.

Account: Big Bank Auto Loan, account #987654 (Exhibit A, Item #2)
Reason for dispute: This is not my account. Please do not report it with my history.
Note: I do not live in Hawaii, and I never have.

Please investigate and correct these items promptly. Contact me in writing at the address below if you need further information from me. Please send a copy of these disputed items to the creditors listed above. If you will not send them this information, please inform me of that promptly.

Thank you for your help in this matter.

Sincerely,
[YOUR SIGNATURE HERE]
[YOUR FULL NAME]
[YOUR MAILING ADDRESS]
[YOUR SOCIAL SECURITY NUMBER]
[YOUR DATE OF BIRTH]
[YOUR PREVIOUS ADDRESSES IN THE PAST FIVE YEARS]

Sample Follow-up Letter

[DATE]

TO: [CREDIT-REPORTING COMPANY]
[ADDRESS OF CREDIT-REPORTING COMPANY]

Greetings:

I sent a dispute letter to your company on [DATE]. Because you have not responded to me within thirty days of receiving my request, my dispute must have been valid (Exhibit A shows a photocopy of that letter, and Exhibit B confirms when you received the letter via mail).

Please confirm that you have corrected the account listed below, and include a copy of my updated credit report. Please be sure that the disputed item does not reappear on my credit report.

Account: Big Bank Auto Loan, account #987654

Thank you for your help in this matter.

Sincerely,
[YOUR SIGNATURE HERE]
[YOUR FULL NAME]
[YOUR MAILING ADDRESS]
[YOUR SOCIAL SECURITY NUMBER]
[YOUR DATE OF BIRTH]

Index

The EVERYTHING Series!

BUSINESS & PERSONAL FINANCE

Everything® **Accounting Book**
Everything® Budgeting Book
Everything® Business Planning Book
Everything® Coaching and Mentoring Book
Everything® Fundraising Book
Everything® Get Out of Debt Book
Everything® Grant Writing Book
Everything® Home-Based Business Book, 2nd Ed.
Everything® Homebuying Book, 2nd Ed.
Everything® Homeselling Book, 2nd Ed.
Everything® Investing Book, 2nd Ed.
Everything® Landlording Book
Everything® Leadership Book
Everything® **Managing People Book, 2nd Ed.**
Everything® Negotiating Book
Everything® Online Auctions Book
Everything® Online Business Book
Everything® Personal Finance Book
Everything® Personal Finance in Your 20s and 30s Book
Everything® Project Management Book
Everything® Real Estate Investing Book
Everything® Robert's Rules Book, $7.95
Everything® Selling Book
Everything® **Start Your Own Business Book, 2nd Ed.**
Everything® Wills & Estate Planning Book

COOKING

Everything® Barbecue Cookbook
Everything® Bartender's Book, $9.95
Everything® Chinese Cookbook
Everything® **Classic Recipes Book**
Everything® Cocktail Parties and Drinks Book
Everything® College Cookbook
Everything® **Cooking for Baby and Toddler Book**
Everything® Cooking for Two Cookbook
Everything® Diabetes Cookbook
Everything® Easy Gourmet Cookbook
Everything® Fondue Cookbook
Everything® **Fondue Party Book**
Everything® Gluten-Free Cookbook
Everything® Glycemic Index Cookbook
Everything® Grilling Cookbook

Everything® Healthy Meals in Minutes Cookbook
Everything® Holiday Cookbook
Everything® Indian Cookbook
Everything® Italian Cookbook
Everything® Low-Carb Cookbook
Everything® Low-Fat High-Flavor Cookbook
Everything® Low-Salt Cookbook
Everything® Meals for a Month Cookbook
Everything® Mediterranean Cookbook
Everything® Mexican Cookbook
Everything® One-Pot Cookbook
Everything® **Quick and Easy 30-Minute, 5-Ingredient Cookbook**
Everything® Quick Meals Cookbook
Everything® Slow Cooker Cookbook
Everything® Slow Cooking for a Crowd Cookbook
Everything® Soup Cookbook
Everything® Tex-Mex Cookbook
Everything® Thai Cookbook
Everything® Vegetarian Cookbook
Everything® Wild Game Cookbook
Everything® Wine Book, 2nd Ed.

GAMES

Everything® 15-Minute Sudoku Book, $9.95
Everything® 30-Minute Sudoku Book, $9.95
Everything® Blackjack Strategy Book
Everything® Brain Strain Book, $9.95
Everything® Bridge Book
Everything® Card Games Book
Everything® Card Tricks Book, $9.95
Everything® Casino Gambling Book, 2nd Ed.
Everything® Chess Basics Book
Everything® Craps Strategy Book
Everything® Crossword and Puzzle Book
Everything® Crossword Challenge Book
Everything® Cryptograms Book, $9.95
Everything® Easy Crosswords Book
Everything® Easy Kakuro Book, $9.95
Everything® Games Book, 2nd Ed.
Everything® Giant Sudoku Book, $9.95
Everything® Kakuro Challenge Book, $9.95
Everything® **Large-Print Crossword Challenge Book**
Everything® Large-Print Crosswords Book
Everything® Lateral Thinking Puzzles Book, $9.95
Everything® **Mazes Book**

Everything® Pencil Puzzles Book, $9.95
Everything® Poker Strategy Book
Everything® Pool & Billiards Book
Everything® Test Your IQ Book, $9.95
Everything® Texas Hold 'Em Book, $9.95
Everything® Travel Crosswords Book, $9.95
Everything® Word Games Challenge Book
Everything® Word Search Book

HEALTH

Everything® Alzheimer's Book
Everything® Diabetes Book
Everything® Health Guide to Adult Bipolar Disorder
Everything® Health Guide to Controlling Anxiety
Everything® Health Guide to Fibromyalgia
Everything® **Health Guide to Thyroid Disease**
Everything® Hypnosis Book
Everything® Low Cholesterol Book
Everything® Massage Book
Everything® Menopause Book
Everything® Nutrition Book
Everything® Reflexology Book
Everything® Stress Management Book

HISTORY

Everything® American Government Book
Everything® American History Book
Everything® Civil War Book
Everything® Freemasons Book
Everything® Irish History & Heritage Book
Everything® Middle East Book

HOBBIES

Everything® Candlemaking Book
Everything® Cartooning Book
Everything® **Coin Collecting Book**
Everything® Drawing Book
Everything® Family Tree Book, 2nd Ed.
Everything® Knitting Book
Everything® Knots Book
Everything® Photography Book
Everything® Quilting Book
Everything® Scrapbooking Book
Everything® Sewing Book
Everything® Woodworking Book

Bolded titles are new additions to the series.
All Everything® books are priced at $12.95 or $14.95, unless otherwise stated. Prices subject to change without notice.

HOME IMPROVEMENT

Everything® Feng Shui Book
Everything® Feng Shui Decluttering Book, $9.95
Everything® Fix-It Book
Everything® Home Decorating Book
Everything® Home Storage Solutions Book
Everything® Homebuilding Book
Everything® Lawn Care Book
Everything® Organize Your Home Book

KIDS' BOOKS

All titles are $7.95

Everything® Kids' Animal Puzzle & Activity Book
Everything® Kids' Baseball Book, 4th Ed.
Everything® Kids' Bible Trivia Book
Everything® Kids' Bugs Book
Everything® Kids' Cars and Trucks Puzzle & Activity Book
Everything® Kids' Christmas Puzzle & Activity Book
Everything® Kids' Cookbook
Everything® Kids' Crazy Puzzles Book
Everything® Kids' Dinosaurs Book
Everything® Kids' First Spanish Puzzle and Activity Book
Everything® Kids' Gross Hidden Pictures Book
Everything® Kids' Gross Jokes Book
Everything® Kids' Gross Mazes Book
Everything® Kids' Gross Puzzle and Activity Book
Everything® Kids' Halloween Puzzle & Activity Book
Everything® Kids' Hidden Pictures Book
Everything® Kids' Horses Book
Everything® Kids' Joke Book
Everything® Kids' Knock Knock Book
Everything® Kids' Learning Spanish Book
Everything® Kids' Math Puzzles Book
Everything® Kids' Mazes Book
Everything® Kids' Money Book
Everything® Kids' Nature Book
Everything® Kids' Pirates Puzzle and Activity Book
Everything® Kids' Princess Puzzle and Activity Book
Everything® Kids' Puzzle Book
Everything® Kids' Riddles & Brain Teasers Book
Everything® Kids' Science Experiments Book
Everything® Kids' Sharks Book
Everything® Kids' Soccer Book
Everything® Kids' Travel Activity Book

KIDS' STORY BOOKS

Everything® Fairy Tales Book

LANGUAGE

Everything® Conversational Chinese Book with CD, $19.95
Everything® Conversational Japanese Book with CD, $19.95
Everything® French Grammar Book
Everything® French Phrase Book, $9.95
Everything® French Verb Book, $9.95
Everything® German Practice Book with CD, $19.95
Everything® Inglés Book
Everything® Learning French Book
Everything® Learning German Book
Everything® Learning Italian Book
Everything® Learning Latin Book
Everything® Learning Spanish Book
Everything® Russian Practice Book with CD, $19.95
Everything® Sign Language Book
Everything® Spanish Grammar Book
Everything® Spanish Phrase Book, $9.95
Everything® Spanish Practice Book with CD, $19.95
Everything® Spanish Verb Book, $9.95

MUSIC

Everything® Drums Book with CD, $19.95
Everything® Guitar Book
Everything® Guitar Chords Book with CD, $19.95
Everything® Home Recording Book
Everything® Music Theory Book with CD, $19.95
Everything® Reading Music Book with CD, $19.95
Everything® Rock & Blues Guitar Book (with CD), $19.95
Everything® Songwriting Book

NEW AGE

Everything® Astrology Book, 2nd Ed.
Everything® Birthday Personology Book
Everything® Dreams Book, 2nd Ed.
Everything® Love Signs Book, $9.95
Everything® Numerology Book
Everything® Paganism Book
Everything® Palmistry Book
Everything® Psychic Book
Everything® Reiki Book
Everything® Sex Signs Book, $9.95
Everything® Tarot Book, 2nd Ed.
Everything® Wicca and Witchcraft Book

PARENTING

Everything® Baby Names Book, 2nd Ed.
Everything® Baby Shower Book
Everything® Baby's First Food Book
Everything® Baby's First Year Book
Everything® Birthing Book
Everything® Breastfeeding Book
Everything® Father-to-Be Book
Everything® Father's First Year Book
Everything® Get Ready for Baby Book
Everything® Get Your Baby to Sleep Book, $9.95
Everything® Getting Pregnant Book
Everything® Guide to Raising a One-Year-Old
Everything® Guide to Raising a Two-Year-Old
Everything® Homeschooling Book
Everything® Mother's First Year Book
Everything® Parent's Guide to Children and Divorce
Everything® Parent's Guide to Children with ADD/ADHD
Everything® Parent's Guide to Children with Asperger's Syndrome
Everything® Parent's Guide to Children with Autism
Everything® Parent's Guide to Children with Bipolar Disorder
Everything® Parent's Guide to Children with Dyslexia
Everything® Parent's Guide to Positive Discipline
Everything® Parent's Guide to Raising a Successful Child
Everything® Parent's Guide to Raising Boys
Everything® Parent's Guide to Raising Siblings
Everything® Parent's Guide to Sensory Integration Disorder
Everything® Parent's Guide to Tantrums
Everything® Parent's Guide to the Overweight Child
Everything® Parent's Guide to the Strong-Willed Child
Everything® Parenting a Teenager Book
Everything® Potty Training Book, $9.95
Everything® Pregnancy Book, 2nd Ed.
Everything® Pregnancy Fitness Book
Everything® Pregnancy Nutrition Book
Everything® Pregnancy Organizer, 2nd Ed., $16.95
Everything® Toddler Activities Book
Everything® Toddler Book
Everything® Tween Book
Everything® Twins, Triplets, and More Book

PETS

Everything® Aquarium Book
Everything® Boxer Book
Everything® Cat Book, 2nd Ed.
Everything® Chihuahua Book
Everything® Dachshund Book
Everything® Dog Book
Everything® Dog Health Book
**Everything® Dog Owner's Organizer,
$16.95**
Everything® Dog Training and Tricks Book
Everything® German Shepherd Book
Everything® Golden Retriever Book
Everything® Horse Book
Everything® Horse Care Book
Everything® Horseback Riding Book
Everything® Labrador Retriever Book
Everything® Poodle Book
Everything® Pug Book
Everything® Puppy Book
Everything® Rottweiler Book
Everything® Small Dogs Book
Everything® Tropical Fish Book
Everything® Yorkshire Terrier Book

REFERENCE

Everything® Blogging Book
Everything® Build Your Vocabulary Book
Everything® Car Care Book
Everything® Classical Mythology Book
Everything® Da Vinci Book
Everything® Divorce Book
Everything® Einstein Book
Everything® Etiquette Book, 2nd Ed.
Everything® Inventions and Patents Book
Everything® Mafia Book
Everything® Philosophy Book
Everything® Psychology Book
Everything® Shakespeare Book

RELIGION

Everything® Angels Book
Everything® Bible Book
Everything® Buddhism Book
Everything® Catholicism Book
Everything® Christianity Book
Everything® History of the Bible Book
Everything® Jesus Book
Everything® Jewish History & Heritage Book
Everything® Judaism Book
Everything® Kabbalah Book
Everything® Koran Book
Everything® Mary Book

Everything® Mary Magdalene Book
Everything® Prayer Book
Everything® Saints Book
Everything® Torah Book
Everything® Understanding Islam Book
Everything® World's Religions Book
Everything® Zen Book

SCHOOL & CAREERS

Everything® Alternative Careers Book
Everything® Career Tests Book
Everything® College Major Test Book
Everything® College Survival Book, 2nd Ed.
Everything® Cover Letter Book, 2nd Ed.
Everything® Filmmaking Book
Everything® Get-a-Job Book
Everything® Guide to Being a Paralegal
Everything® Guide to Being a Real Estate
Agent
Everything® Guide to Being a Sales Rep
**Everything® Guide to Careers in Health
Care**
**Everything® Guide to Careers in Law
Enforcement**
Everything® Guide to Government Jobs
Everything® Guide to Starting and Running
a Restaurant
Everything® Job Interview Book
Everything® New Nurse Book
Everything® New Teacher Book
Everything® Paying for College Book
Everything® Practice Interview Book
Everything® Resume Book, 2nd Ed.
Everything® Study Book

SELF-HELP

Everything® Dating Book, 2nd Ed.
Everything® Great Sex Book
Everything® Kama Sutra Book
Everything® Self-Esteem Book

SPORTS & FITNESS

Everything® Easy Fitness Book
Everything® Fishing Book
Everything® Golf Instruction Book
Everything® Pilates Book
Everything® Running Book
Everything® Weight Training Book
Everything® Yoga Book

TRAVEL

Everything® Family Guide to Cruise Vacations
Everything® Family Guide to Hawaii

Everything® Family Guide to Las Vegas,
2nd Ed.
Everything® Family Guide to Mexico
Everything® Family Guide to New York City,
2nd Ed.
Everything® Family Guide to RV Travel &
Campgrounds
Everything® Family Guide to the Caribbean
Everything® Family Guide to the Walt Disney
World Resort®, Universal Studios®,
and Greater Orlando, 4th Ed.
Everything® Family Guide to Timeshares
Everything® Family Guide to Washington
D.C., 2nd Ed.
Everything® Guide to New England

WEDDINGS

Everything® Bachelorette Party Book, $9.95
Everything® Bridesmaid Book, $9.95
Everything® Destination Wedding Book
Everything® Elopement Book, $9.95
Everything® Father of the Bride Book, $9.95
Everything® Groom Book, $9.95
Everything® Mother of the Bride Book, $9.95
Everything® Outdoor Wedding Book
Everything® Wedding Book, 3rd Ed.
Everything® Wedding Checklist, $9.95
Everything® Wedding Etiquette Book, $9.95
**Everything® Wedding Organizer, 2nd Ed.,
$16.95**
Everything® Wedding Shower Book, $9.95
Everything® Wedding Vows Book, $9.95
Everything® Wedding Workout Book
Everything® Weddings on a Budget Book,
$9.95

WRITING

Everything® Creative Writing Book
Everything® Get Published Book, 2nd Ed.
Everything® Grammar and Style Book
Everything® Guide to Writing a Book
Proposal
Everything® Guide to Writing a Novel
Everything® Guide to Writing Children's
Books
Everything® Guide to Writing Research
Papers
Everything® Screenwriting Book
Everything® Writing Poetry Book
Everything® Writing Well Book
